Islamic Business and Performance Management

This unique book discovers a new dimension in the study of strategic and performance management in Islamic Business studies. It addresses the missing link of spirituality from modern-day organizational structure in the presence of high-tech pressure in all areas of human endeavours.

The authors propose an integrated study of Islamic business approach to strategic and performance management systems to achieve sustainable organizational performance. The book explores employees' wellbeing and organizations' perceiving work environment as a spiritual pathway to cultivate values in Islamic business ecosystem to sustain humanity. It is all about care, empathy, and sustenance of others, about truthfulness and management being truthful to themselves and others and endeavouring to live their values more effusively while performing their work. The book stresses the impact of spirituality in performance management, concluding that for any organization to run efficiently, spirituality is the core component to attain happiness, contentment, and success.

The book will be of interest to a variety of management scholars, including those researching and studying performance management, talent management, strategic management, and business ethics.

Achmad Firdaus is an Associate professor of Islamic Economics and Dean of the Faculty of Islamic Economics and Business at Institut Agama Islam (IAI) Tazkia, Indonesia. He earned his PhD in Islamic economics from Syarif Hidayatullah State Islamic University (UIN), Jakarta (2013), Master of Science in Management from the Graduate School of Faculty of Economics and Business – Universitas Indonesia (2004), and Bachelor of Physics from Faculty of Mathematics and Sciences – Universitas Indonesia (1993). He joined IAI Tazkia since 2012 and has held academic positions such as Head of the Master's Program and Director of Postgraduate. He has worked at PT. SANYO Jaya Components Indonesia (1993–2003) (manufacture), PT. Asuransi Takaful Keluarga (2005–2009) (insurance) and also a consultant in management (2004–2015). His primary research interests are but not limited to Islamic wealth management, Islamic performance management, Islamic strategic management, Islamic marketing, and Islamic finance/banking/insurance.

Khaliq Ahmad is currently Professor at International Institute of Islamic Thought and Civilization (ISTAC) who previously served International Islamic University (IIUM) for 27 years and joined as Research Professor at Putra Business School after serving as a full Professor at Qassim University, Saudi Arabia. Dr Ahmad, who graduated from AMU Aligarh by obtaining his doctorate, MPhil, and master's degrees, worked in the private sector for five years. He was the Dean, Kulliyah (Faculty) Economics and Management Sciences (KENMS) during the years 2008–2013. As founding President – ICIFE (www.icife.net) and former Dean, Institute of Islamic Banking and Finance (2015–2016), he steered IIUM to be ranked world No. 1 in 2015 and 2016 by QS Ranking in Islamic Finance research and publication citation index. His academic interest is but not limited to Corporate Governance, Leadership, Strategic & Islamic Management, Islamic Social Finance, and Islamic Marketing.

Islamic Business and Management

With the rapid development of Islamic countries, there is an increasing need for a comprehensive body of thought on Islamic business and management. This new series offers a collection of cutting-edge monographs from across the globe, exploring all aspects of business and management from Islamic perspectives with a special emphasis on spirituality and ethics.

1 **Islamic Business and Performance Management**
The Maslahah-Based Performance Management System
Achmad Firdaus and Khaliq Ahmad

Islamic Business and Performance Management

The Maslahah-Based Performance Management System

Achmad Firdaus and Khaliq Ahmad

Routledge
Taylor & Francis Group
LONDON AND NEW YORK

First published 2023
by Routledge
4 Park Square, Milton Park, Abingdon, Oxon OX14 4RN

and by Routledge
605 Third Avenue, New York, NY 10158

Routledge is an imprint of the Taylor & Francis Group, an informa business

British Library Cataloguing-in-Publication Data
A catalogue record for this book is available from the British Library

ISBN: 978-1-032-48822-6 (hbk)
ISBN: 978-1-032-48823-3 (pbk)
ISBN: 978-1-003-39094-7 (ebk)

DOI: 10.4324/9781003390947

Typeset in Bembo
by KnowledgeWorks Global Ltd.

Contents

Foreword

Spirituality is a missing link from modern-day organization. Earlier on, the importance of IQ was over emphasized, whereas currently, emotional intelligence (EQ) is said to be a better predictor of organizational performance, thus its sustainability. Sustainable growth and development, as agreed upon for ensuring the future of millennials, will hardly be possible without inculcating values as inscribed by major organized faiths globally. Therefore, spirituality and its pursuit by adherents of faiths will be crucial to strive for a sustainable environment, respect for the scarce and naturally bestowed resources, avoiding wastage, and respecting the right of others to achieve not only gross national product (GNP) as an index of growth but also gross national happiness index (GNH) that will matter the most for our next generation. It is unbecoming for corporate organizations to ignore the importance of spirituality as a corporate imperative required of today's CEOs, Presidents, Directors, and Board Members as well as the community per se.

As we live in the changeover period, shifting from the ancient meaning of work as subsistence to the new meaning of work as a livelihood, novel management methods, and new organizational systems are necessary to keep up with this emergent context. Spirituality in the workplace expects human beings to seek nourishment for both the extents, i.e., their vertical relationship with God and horizontal with fellow human beings, as well as the ecosystem. This encompasses the scope and extent of their spirituality at work. It is about people and organizations perceiving work as a spiritual sojourn, a chance to cultivate and do something with compassion for the entire humanity. It is all about care, empathy, and sustenance of others, about truthfulness and being truthful to oneself and others, endeavouring to live their values more effusively while performing their work more effectively. The present book entitled "Islamic Business and Performance Management – The Maslahah-Based Performance Management System" stresses the impact of spirituality in addressing the issues of performance management in a sustainable way. The study concludes that for any organization to run effectively and efficiently, spirituality is the core to attain happiness, contentment, and success at the same time.

This book is written from an Islamic spirituality perspective and is an effort in the right direction. Congratulations to both authors, Dr Achmad Firdaus of Tazkia University and Prof Khaliq Ahmad of ISTAC at IIUM, for this timely publication. I wish them grand success in their academic endeavour in realizing a better and more a better world and more equitable as mercy to all. I hope academics and students, including management practitioners, will find the book published by Routledge (Taylor & Francis) very useful and a helpful companion in bringing back the soul to performance management.

Dzulkifli Abdul Razak
Professor Emeritus Tan Sri Dato'
Rector, International Islamic University Malaysia

Preface

This is Almighty Allah (*s.w.t.*), the sole creator of all the worldly and heavenly creations on the earth, in the skies and underneath. Allah (*s.w.t.*) created human beings as well but as special creation. He called them as His vicegerent on the earth. Hence this is Him knows every one of us. Our relationship with Him is especially as Lord and His servant. But we tend to forget this dimensionality of spiritual relationships in managing organizational affairs.

Other researchers who conducted studies so far in the area of management and organizational theories are usually preoccupied with organizational efficiency and effectiveness alone. These theories highlighted the fact that the bird flies with two wings but forgets the bird's head and the direction. These two elements have given us tremendous management knowledge concerning of output and productivity as the management churned resources efficiently and were preoccupied with the wellbeing of the workers. Nevertheless, present management literature has been ignored altogether until very recently; the third element of spirituality, since human is also a spiritual being, was a lesson covered in religious teaching in ancient literatures.

اَللّٰهُ خَالِقُ كُلِّ شَيۡءٍ‌ۖ وَّهُوَ عَلٰى كُلِّ شَيۡءٍ وَّكِيۡلٌ

Allah is the Creator of all things, and He is,
over all things, Disposer of affairs.
(Az-Zumar 39: 62, Aayat No 62)

It implies that nothing happens by chance. Illness, injury, marriage, divorce or love, lost moments, loss of wealth, etc. Everything happens through His will. All occur to test the limits of your soul. Without these small tests, if they were events, illnesses, or relationships, life would be like a smoothly paved, straight, flat road to nowhere. These twists and turns take place to guide you towards the right path. They carve you in a way that you turn back to Allah (*s.w.t.*) and ask guidance from Him alone. Always have *Tawakkal* in Allah (*s.w.t.*). Everything that has ever happened to you is by the will of your *Rabb* (Lord). He's brought you to it, and He alone will bring you through it.

This book is an attempt in this direction to indicating a need for spirituality in managing contemporary organizations. This publication is a likely contribution to the existing knowledge of the management and organizational studies written from the point of view of Islamic spirituality. Once this academic endeavor is succeeded and translated into actual practice, the world will see the emergence of spirited executives and spirited CEOs and, henceforth, a new organizational life free from corruption, nepotism, cronyism, and all organizational ills of today's white-collar crimes.

Praise to Allah (*s.w.t.*), God of the universe. The One Who Has Knowledge, the Most Merciful, the Giver of *Maṣlaḥah*. To Allah (*s.w.t.*) where our gratitude is always offered and all hope is rested. *Salawat* and greetings may always be devoted to the last Prophet Muhammad (*s.a.w.*), *qudwah ḥasanah* to all of us, and rewards in the hereafter is our sole motive of writing this book.

> And We have enjoined upon man, to his parents, good treatment. His mother carried him with hardship and gave birth to him with hardship, and his gestation and weaning [period] is thirty months. [He grows] until, when he reaches maturity and reaches [the age of] forty years, he says, "My Lord, enable me to be grateful for Your favor which You have bestowed upon me and upon my parents and to work righteousness of which You will approve and make righteous for me my offspring. Indeed, I have repented to You, and indeed, I am of the Muslims."
>
> Al Qur'an, al-Ahqaf 46: 15

In this book, we have divided the manuscript as a whole into four parts. Part I deals with the question of why an organization requires a *Maslahah*; this whole part has four chapters explaining details in special reference to the Malay Muslims and Ummah and the largest Muslim populated nation – Indonesia. Part II discusses *Maslahah* for the understanding of its application in an organizational performance system; this whole part has three chapters elaborating the need of *Maslahah* in an organizational setting. Part III suggests the use of managing a *Maslahah* based organizational performance system; this whole part is encompassing five chapters dealing with the implementation of PDCA for effective planning and control purpose. Finally, Part IV has three chapters. The focus is on the implementation plan and included a case study followed by the conclusion.

March, 2023
Author(s)
Achmad Firdaus and Khaliq Ahmad

Acknowledgements

There are many who deserve our sincere acknowledgement and we feel obliged for their contributions in writing the present book.

Firstly, we would like to express our special thanks of gratitude to the Ministry of Religion of the Republic of Indonesia for Research Assistance, Scientific Publications, and Community Development for Fiscal Year 2021.

Secondly, We would also like to thank Anita Priantina for proofreading and editing this draft.

We will be failing in our duty not to acknowledge the contributions and help and would place our highest level of gratitude to our colleagues, family members, and members of staff of Tazkia University and ISTAC (IIUM). They deserve our mention due to their encouragement and inspiration. Many friends who facilitated us in the completion process of this book which may not have seen the light of day without their *doa* (prayers) and sincere help, we also pray for them. Oh, **Allah** – please accept all our good intentions for writing this book as good deeds that are due to unbroken help, as you have promised to your weak people. Our special thank goes to our parents who are still alive and have contributed by giving their blessings. Finally, we acknowledge Routledge, the publisher and its team members of this book, for its timely support. May God bless all of you.

O Allah, please give the blessings to this work as a charity in reward to the people who may not have found any mention in this book, but they directly or indirectly have contributed to the enlightenment of knowledge to both of us, so that we could complete this book. *Amin Ya Rabbal Alamiin.*

Part I

Organization Requires done *Maslahah*

Introduction

It is up to me! This is my organization; Why should I think about others?

Life is just once, why should I think about death

Don't be too picky, it's hard to get what's *Haram*, let alone what's *Halal*

Organizations, if established without the foundation of religion, may cause oppression by one to another. An oppressed party may eventually pray for bad things to happen to the organizations. Organizations will then get worse and eventually disbanded. Without mentioning details from all cases one by one, there are real examples where organizations end up experiencing damages and become bankrupt.

On the other hand, organizations whose foundations are based on religion will bring *Maslahah* for many people. People who get those *Maslahah* might always pray for good things to happen to the organizations. Organizations will then gain merit and may continuously grow and progress. Finally, the organizations will become long-lasting.

Islam emphasizes that organizations are created to realize a human role as Allah's *Khalifah* on the earth. Therefore, the organization must also provide *Maslahah* for many people. This is the alignment of the organizations' goals and the objective of *Shari'ah* (*Maqasid al-shari'ah*). The principle is generally different from the views of those organizational experts who argue that organizations are created to improve the welfare of shareholders. This view is initiated by the capitalist notion that the welfare of shareholders is the main goal of the organization because they are the capital owners.

The awareness of the organizational actors towards the true purpose of the organization continuously grows and develops. This can be seen from the rapid growth of *Shari'ah*-based industries, especially in Indonesia. However, this speedy progress of *Shari'ah*-based industries has not been able to give an idea about how much the *Maslahah* of business is received by the stakeholders. This is due to the absence of an appropriate methodology to measure the performance of organizational *Maslahah*, in the form of contributions to

DOI: 10.4324/9781003390947-1

economic improvement and equity of the society. One of the reasons is the limited number of research about the measurement of organizational *Maslahah* performance.

On the other hand, there is a huge number of research on the measurement of conventional organization performance. Devinney *et al.* (2009)[1] found that since 2005 until 2007, there were 722 journal articles on organizational performance measurement. There are 188 articles under the *Academy of Management Journal*, 49 articles under the *Administrative Science Quarterly*, 157 under the *Journal of International Business Studies*, 120 in the *Journal of Management*, and 208 in the *Strategic Management Journal*. The data shows that research on the measurement of organizational performance is a favoured topic for researchers.

Among the research on the *Maslahah* of organizations that have been conducted was a study by Mohammed and Abdu Razak (2008)[2] and Shaukat (2009),[3] who measured Islamic bank performance. They assessed three aspects of *Maslahah* implementation, which consisted of education – justice enforcement – welfare, and financial performance ratio.

Ismail and Arshad (2010)[4] conducted the measurement of microfinance institution performance in Amanah Ikhtiar Malaysia (AIM). They observed the process of obtaining assets, the process of equitable asset distribution, and financial performance, which are not only seen from financial ratio but also from the capabilities of the Malaysian Financial Institution (MFI) in distributing equitable income.

Sani (2012)[5] argued that the method of performance measurement ordinarily used to measure the performance of conventional banks such as Data Envelopment Analysis (DEA), Econometric Frontier Analysis (EFA), and Stochastic Frontier Approach (SFA) cannot be employed to measure Islamic bank performance. There are differences in operational principles between Islamic banks and conventional banks.

Bedoui (2012)[6] pointed out that performance measurement of *Maqasid al-shari'ah* from Muslim scholars still highlights the aspect of assets or finance. He stated that the application of the *Maqasid al-shari'ah* concept is supposed to be based on the balance among the five basic needs. The concept of balanced measurement is completed in two ways, which are graphical method and numerical method. Graphical explanation presented by Bedoui is in the form of a cobweb which represents five aspects of *Maslahah* (Figure 1.1).

While the performance measurement by numerical method is presented by this formula:

$$\text{Maqosid Performance} = \frac{\sin\left(2\pi/5\right)}{2}\left(p1p2 + p2p3 + p3p4 + p4p5 + p5p1\right)^{7}$$

- *p*1 religious performance measure (*al-Din*)
- *p*2 life performance measure (*al-Nafs*)
- *p*3 intellectual performance measure (*al-'Aql*)
- *p*4 descendant performance measure (*al-Nasl*)
- *p*5 wealth performance measure (*al-Mal*)

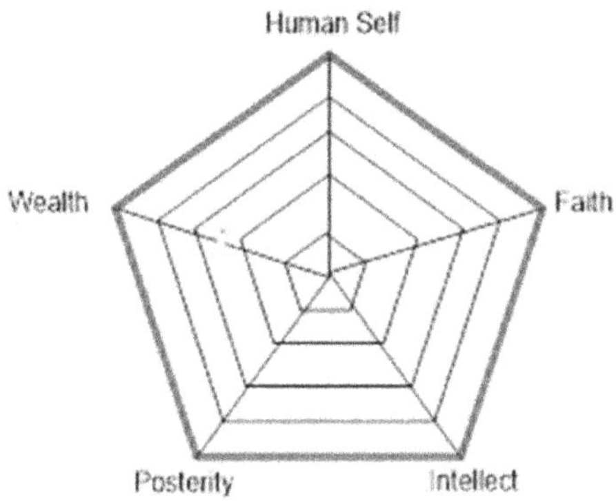

Figure 1.1 Equilibrium of Fulfilling Basic Needs.

Source: Bedoui (2012: 5)

The score of $p1$, $p2$, $p3$, $p4$, and $p5$ has the lowest score of 1, which indicates unsatisfactory performance, far below expectations. The highest score is 5 which shows that the performance is highly satisfying, far above expectation. If all aspects have a performance that is far above the expectation, then the performance of *Maqasid* becomes $\left(\frac{125}{2}\right)\sin(2\pi/5) \approx 59.44$.

The strength of this research is the balance of measurements from all aspects of *Maslahah*, which are religion (*al-Din*), life (*al-Nafs*), descendant (*al-Nasl*), intellect (*al-'Aql*), and wealth (*al-Mal*). However, this research only elaborates on the performance measurement without explaining the process of achieving each performance.

Firdaus (2012a)[8] explained that in the business context, achieving the *Maslahah* highly depends on fulfilling six aspects of business *Maslahah* orientation. The first is the worship orientation to explain the protection and preservation of religion (*al-Din*) in business.[9] The second is internal process orientation to explain the protection and preservation of business life (*al-nafs*). The third is talent orientation to explain the protection and preservation of descendant (*al-nasl*). The fourth is learning orientation to explain the protection and preservation of intellect (*al-'aql*). The fifth is customer orientation to explain the protection and preservation of relationships with customers.[10] The sixth is wealth orientation to explain the protection and preservation of wealth (*al-mal*).

The organizational *Maslahah* means that the business creates value for Allah (*s.w.t.*), stakeholders, and the environment in a sustainable way.[11] The *Maslahah* of organizations is not limited by the age of the organization or the age of the manager. The *Maslahah* of the organization will continuously exist even when the organization or manager has passed away. Therefore, the sustainability of the *Maslahah* of organizations is the goal which must be protected and preserved.

Maslahah is a qualitative concept. Therefore, an appropriate methodology is required to measure the *Maslahah* application in organizations. In this case, there is a need for score quantification on the performance management in fulfilling the basic organizational needs. This is the reason why *Maslahah*-based organizational performance management system or is also called *Maslahah* Performa or MaP is essential. This is aligned with Kaplan and Norton (1996b),[12] who said that "if you can't measure an organization, then you will not be able to manage the organization."

Why Organization Require *Maslahah*? False Measure, if *Mafsadah* Are Considered *Maslahah*, What Happens?

Do ones still remember the news about liquor poisoning in Indramayu, West Java, Indonesia, on *Ramadhan* 1429 H? It went around on television, newspapers, magazines, and radio, as well as online media, and dozens of people were killed in binge drinking. The start of the news was the fall of victims of poisonous alcoholic drinks at the beginning of *Ramadhan* 1429 H in Losarang, Indramayu District – West Java, Indonesia. The alcoholic party made dozens of people dead, and dozens were treated in all hospitals in the Indramayu area. Another tragic news occurred in the Indramayu Eretan area. It was an irony since the number of casualties that happened was on the eve of *Takbiran* ahead of *Idul Fitri* 1429 H.

Like a fiction, the next news came from Tugu Sliyeg Village, Indramayu – West Java, Indonesia. As reported on Radar Cirebon on Sunday, 5 October 2008, a number of residents of Sliyeg suffered blindness after drinking liquor during *Halal bil halal*. The event *Halal bil halal* is filled with single-organ entertainment. During the event, several people took the initiative to hold a liquor party. Suddenly the perpetrators suffered blindness shortly after drinking alcohol. Tragic, their fate was tragic. As a person born in Indramayu, it was sad to hear the news. Map of distribution and consumption of liquor includes almost all of the Indramayu region. What is with the Indramayu community, my birthplace?

On the sidelines of contemplation, it had crossed the intellect of the writer. An extraordinary event that shocked the Indonesian people evens the world some time before. Exactly a year before the event, the victim of alcoholic drinks, a very large tectonic earthquake (7.3 on the Richter scale) occurred on Thursday, 9 August 2007. The epicentre was 286 km below Indramayu.

The great earthquake was beyond the logic of the world's geophysicists and geologists. How could the northern region of Java be a tectonic earthquake source? Geophysicists and geologists have understood that Indramayu, which is located at 107°51′–108°36′ BT and 6°15′–6°40′ LS is in the northern region of Java which is not an active tectonic zone. Why is Indramayu the source of the earthquake?

Geophysicists and world geologists then proposed various theories. One of the theories put forward is that far below the surface of Indramayu, there is a tectonic fault plate. The other end of the tectonic plate is under Sukabumi City. That means a tectonic plate crosses the northern part of Java and ends in the southern part of Java. That is why even though the epicentre was below the surface of Indramayu, the worst damage occurred in Sukabumi. This earthquake occurred as the Indo-Australian plate was moving down and pressing the Euro-Asia plate. The wave of earthquake propagates through tectonic plates from the earthquake source under Indramayu to the surface under Sukabumi.

Why did the author think of connecting the tectonic earthquake events in the category beneath the surface of Indramayu with the death and fall of victims in the Losarang, Eretan, and Sliyeg areas in October 2008? As an alumnus of the University of Indonesia's Geophysics Study Program, the author believes that there is no connection at all between the two events. Because besides the two events are distinguished by long distances, both events are scientifically uncorrelated. However, as someone who believes that blessing and punishment always come from Allah (*s.w.t.*), and blessings and doom always come in the way, so the authors believe that the two events are correlated with each other.

With these two events, the author believes that something is happening in Indramayu, so Allah (*s.w.t.*) must give a warning to the people of Indramayu. The earthquake in the category that occurred in 2007 could be a sign from Allah (*s.w.t.*) of a bad deed committed by some people of Indramayu.

Nevertheless, unfortunately, the sign of Allah (*s.w.t.*) in the form of an earthquake has not been able to awaken the people of Indramayu. Therefore, Allah (*s.w.t.*) subsequently imposes a punishment in the form of intoxicating liquor for an Indramayu community. Then what bad deeds have caused the punishment of Allah (*s.w.t.*) towards some of Indramayu's people? Let us look at the quote that was published in Republika Online on Tuesday, 7 October 2008, at 8:41 p.m.

Fishermen Regard Alcohol as Herbal Medicine

Republika Newspaper on Tuesday, 7 October 2008 at 8:41 p.m. reported the following case.

CIREBON – Several anglers in Indramayu Regency have believed that drinking alcohol to be a rheumatic pain after a week of working hard to find fish in the middle of the sea so that the habit is difficult to remove.

This was the result of an interview between *Antara* and several anglers who were poisoned by alcoholic drinks and treated at the MA Sentot Patrol Hospital, Indramayu Regency on Tuesday.

According to Tanto (23), anglers from Eretan Kulon Village, he has routinely done the habit of drinking alcohol for five years after searching for fish in the ocean between seven and ten days.

"It has been five years since I became a crew of a large ship, and when I landed then at night, I drank alcohol which is usually mixed with wine. If I don't drink the aches in the body will not disappear and I may not go to sea for one week," he said.

He said after drinking, the crew usually immediately fell asleep and the next day could be refreshed, after which they returned to work to prepare to go to the sea the next day.

A similar thing was also revealed by Taryono (29), a village angler who had also drunk alcohol for almost ten years after loading fish caught in the sea. "The habit is difficult to lose, drinking alcohol is tantamount to drinking stiff herbal medicine because it can eliminate aches for a week in the middle of the sea," he said, still lying limp with Nursanto, his younger brother who was also a victim.

Seven anglers who were still lying in MA Sentot Hospital on Tuesday were a small part of hundreds of anglers who experienced symptoms of alcohol poisoning or intoxication after having an alcoholic feast on the recent *Eid al-Fitri* day. Even though they consume alcohol with a different brand, the effect is the same, so it is assumed that the alcoholic raw material is almost the same even though it is packaged in different brands.

Tanto recounted the afternoon in *Eid al-Fitri*, he bought three bottles of Manson alcoholic drinks for Rp 45,000 per bottle and mixed them with three bottles of Rajawali brand Kolesom Wine for Rp 17,000 per bottle.

"The three of us then drank together, but two of my friends, Conjol and Idin, went straight to sea one day and until now there has been no news," he said.

While Taryono claimed after the Eid prayer, they drank with six friends by drinking a mixture of Nusantara brand Kolesom Wine with black beer and white beer, the last two brands of Bir Bintang.

"Before I bought a few bottles of the W & N brand, but the person said it was poisonous, so I replaced it with the Nusantara brand wine. In fact, the mixture also made me feel exhausted, weak, and short of breath," he said.

However, there are also other anglers; Sobur (47), an angler from Eretan Kulon Village who claimed to drink only Nusantara Wine, without any other mixture, but his fate was the same and received treatment at the MA Sentot Patrol Hospital.

Until now, due to drinking alcohol suspected of being poisoned on *Lebaran* yesterday, 12 people died, 8 of whom were fishermen from Eretan Wetan Village, Herman (30), Sapeng (60), Beni (23), Warnadi (36), Heryanto (25), Rusdi (22), Surjana (27), and Wasmin (25). Other dead victims were Abdul Gofur (41), a resident of Babakan Jaya Village, Gabus Wetan Subdistrict, Turya Alias Subur (50) residents of Merkarjati Village, Sulaeman Haurgeulis Villagers, and Kasman Bin Rustayim (22) Bunder Block Patrol Village.

In addition to the death toll, it was recorded that 99 people had received treatment at MA Sentot Hospital, 65 people at Bhayangkara Losarang Hospital, and 26 people at Indramayu Hospital.

Notes

1 Richard, P. J., Devinney, T. M., Yip, G. S. and Johnson, G. (2009). Measuring Organizational Performance: Towards Methodological Best Practice. *Journal of Management* Vol. 35, No. 3. 721–722.

2 Mohammed, M. O. and Razak, D. A. (2008). *The Performance Measures of Islamic Banking Based on the Maqasid Framework*. Paper presented at The IIUM International Accounting Conference (INTAC IV), Putra Jaya.

3 Shaukat, Mughees. (2009). *The Recent Financial Growth of Islamic Banks and Their Fulfillments of Maqāsid Al-Sharī'ah, Gap Analysis.* INCEIF, Kuala Lumpur, Malaysia.

4 Ismail, A. G. and Arshad, N. C. (8–9 December 2010). *Financial Ratio and Maqasid Shari'ah in Evaluating the Performance of Microfinance Institutions.* Paper presented at The 2nd International Workshop in Islamic Economics Theory: Islamic Micro-Finance Towards Global Poverty Alleviation and Sustainable Development, Bangi, Selangor, Malaysia.

5 Sani. (5 August 2012). *A Conceptual Model of Measuring Performance Efficiency of Islamic Banks: Objectives of Islamic Law (Maqasid al- shari'ah) Approach.* http://ssrn.com/abstract=2070397 (Accessed on 5 August 2012).

6 Bedoui, M. H. E. (January 2012). *Shari'ah*-Based Ethical Performance Measurement Framework. *Chair for Ethics and Financial Norms, Working Paper in Islamic Economics and Finance* No. 1020.

7 $\text{Sin}\left(2\pi/5\right)$ means Sinus ($360^{o}/5$) or Sinus (72°) = 0.951.

8 Firdaus, A. (21–22 November 2012). *Pengukuran Kinerja PT. Asuransi Takaful Keluarga dengan Menggunakan Sistem Pengukuran Kinerja Maslahah Scorecard (MaSC).* Paper presented at the 1st Islamic Economics and Finance Research Forum (ISEFRF), New Era of Indonesian Islamic Economics and Finance. The Indonesian Association of Islamic Economist, Bank Indonesia and Universitas Islam Negeri Sultan Syarif Kasim, Pekanbaru.

9 The word "worship," which is meant in the orientation of worship is worship in a very broad sense, all efforts, and activities carried out by the business in the context of worshiping the Supreme Giver of *Rizq* (life sustenance).

10 Customers are very important and very influential for businesses. Customer is an intermediary or media for the *Rizq* given by Allah to the business. Without customers, it will be impossible to create a function of the *maslahat* for business; therefore, in order to realize *maslahat*, customer orientation is required.

11 From Abu Hurairah r.a., he narrated: "Rasulullah (*s.a.w.*) said: 'When a man dies, his deeds come to an end except for three things: Sadaqah Jariyah (ceaseless charity); a knowledge which is beneficial, or a virtuous descendant who prays for him (for the deceased)'" (Narrated by Muslim).

12 Kaplan, R. S. and Norton, D. P. (January–February 1992). The Balanced Scorecard – Measures that Drive Performance. *Harvard Business Review.* Vol. 70, No. 1: 71–9.

1 Islamic Economic System

Maslahah in a Muslim State Economy

Introduction

In general, economy is understood as the concept related to human activities which always calculates costs and expects rewards, economic person is considered as someone who blindly do anything to get what they want (Ariff, 2007).[1] This principle is the main guideline for capitalists. Capitalism is the concept which places capital as the main goal in economic development. This thought develops the assumption that human needs are unlimited, economic resources are relatively limited, and pursuit of fulfilling individual needs or utility maximation of self-interest) is relatively unlimited (Swasono, 2003).[2]

The assumptions above have a background understanding that everyone has a personal interest (self-interest) that must be prioritized to be fulfilled. This is the principle of individualism which requires the existence of unlimited freedom (liberalism). Both principles are supported by the *laissez-faire* principle.[3] All of them form an understanding that people always compete with each other or compete freely among themselves through a free market mechanism. Free market as a representation of the interests of people who have capital by himself regulates economic interests. Therefore, in the capitalistic system, the role of capital and capital owners is very central compared to the role of marginalized people. This view is known as neoclassical mainstream economics (Swasono, 2004).[4]

The assumption above contradicts the fact that there are good people. Therefore, economics should also be based on kindness. Swasono[5] stated that economic science is a moral science. Economics should also recognize justice, care about equality and fairness, humanity, and respect for religious values.

Neoclassical mainstream economics gets opposition from structuralists. In Indonesia, structuralists appreciate economic democracy. Economic democracy places humans as the main goal in economic development. The basis of economic democracy is the understanding that economic democracy prioritizes the interests of the people (mutual interest) not the interests of individual(s). Society consisting of individuals is social being (homo socius). They are created as social creatures (given). Society forms social consensus among members. Individuals in society live collectively in harmony, share,

DOI: 10.4324/9781003390947-2

and cooperate with each other. Shared interests always regulate the market. The market must be subject to mutual interests (Swasono, 2010).[6] Therefore, the state, as the highest institution, designs and organizes the economy in order to realize the common interest of welfare and social justice for the entire community.

Indonesia Economic System

Various assumptions developed by the capitalism are very contradictory, both with the Indonesian economic system and with the Islamic economic system. The Indonesian economic system is neither in the middle of neoclassical economics and the socialist economic system nor a combination of both. Indonesia's economic system is a straight path, the third path that places economics as a moral science. Indonesia's economic system leads to a new form of economic system, namely the Pancasila economic system (Swasono, 2012).[7]

Pancasila economic system is synonymous with economic democracy. Economic democracy implies that the highest power is in the hands of the people. It applies not only for the political field but also for the economy. The main sources of production are also in the control of the people. In fact, the people of a country that adheres to the sovereignty of the people have the full right to natural resources for the greatest well-being of their own prosperity (Swasono, 1988).[8]

Pancasila economic system is an economic system inspired by Pancasila ideology, namely the economic system, which is a joint effort based on family and national unity (Mubyarto, 1987: 32).[9] Pancasila economic system, according to Swasono (1987),[10] has the characteristics of togetherness (mutualism) and kinship, moral non-discrimination and non-exploitatory, anti-monopoly, structuralist, cooperation based, religious value based, institutional value based, non-usurious, and social well-being based.

Mubyarto (in Swasono, 2008)[11] stated that the Pancasila economy has these characteristics: (1) Wheels of the economy are driven by economic, social, and moral stimuli. (2) The strong will of the whole community towards a state of social equality (egalitarianism) in accordance with the principle of humanity. (3) The priority of economic policy is the creation of a resilient national economy, meaning nationalism inspires every economic policy. (4) Cooperatives are the pillars of the economy and are the most concrete form of joint ventures. (5) There is a clear and firm balance between planning at the national level and decentralization of economic activities to ensure economic and social justice.

The legal foundation of the Pancasila economic system (Swasono, 2008:16) is article 33[12] of the 1945 Constitution, the background of the Preamble of the 1945 Constitution, supported and supplemented by Articles: 18,[13] 23,[14] 27 verse (2),[15] and 34.[16]

Article 33 of the 1945 Constitution regulates the national economy and social welfare.[17] This article has two transformational values, namely economic transformation and social transformation (Swasono, 2003).[18] The transformation of the economy implies upholding economic democracy, carrying out joint efforts, implementing the principle of kinship, rejecting the principle of individuals, and adjusting the colonial KUHD to Article 33 of the 1945 Constitution. Social transformation implies forming economic relations, forming partnerships, and implementing three cos': co-ownership, co-determination, and co-responsibility.

Section (1) Article 33 of the 1945 Constitution has four keywords of the Indonesian economic system, namely: economy, organized, common endeavour, joint business, and principles of the family system (Swasono, 2010).[19] Swasono said that what is meant by "economy" in this section is the triple-co: co-ownership, co-determination, and co-responsibility.

The word "organized" in Section (1) Article 33 of the 1945 Constitution is interpreted as a system that is not self-regulated. The state develops and designs the economic system. The words "joint venture" and "principles of the family system" have the meaning that the form of the economic system is in the form of a joint endeavour based on mutual interests. The form of joint venture is managed based on the principle of brotherhood and cooperation.

Section (2) Article 33 of the 1945 Constitution (Swasono, 2010) is intended by the founding fathers as an effort to save the country's economic sovereignty and to prioritize the interests of the people. The term "under the power of the State in the verse" means that the state controls and has branches of production. Control without being accompanied by ownership results in the ineffectiveness of the state's branches of production.

Section (3) Article 33 of the 1945 Constitution (Swasono, 2010) reinforces the meaning of economic democracy that the economy is held for the sake of social welfare for all people. The main interest is that of the people, not the interests of individuals. This verse also affirms that Indonesian democracy is based on the principle of togetherness (mutualism), not the principle of individuals or liberalism. This understanding certainly is different from western thought, which tends to mean "democratization" with "privatization."

Indonesia Economic System in the Perspective of Islamic Economic System

Chapra (2007a)[20] stated that the purpose of an economic system was essentially determined by the worldview. Islam as an economic system has a worldview which is based on three fundamental concepts such as *tawhid, Khilafah,* and justice.

Tawhid is the most important basis of two other concepts because the other concepts are the logical consequences of *tawhid. Tawhid* is an understanding of the oneness of Allah (*s.w.t.*), understanding that the universe was designed and created by the Supreme Creator[21] with a specific purpose. All things are created by Him, not by accident. That purpose also accompanies the creation of the universe including humans. Humans as creatures must pursue these goals, which is referred to as a form of human worship to Allah (*s.w.t.*).

As a *Khalifah*,[22] humans are commanded by Allah (*s.w.t.*) to guard and manage the earth.[23] Therefore, all economic activities are part of carrying out the duties and functions of the human caliphate on earth (Amin, 2007).[24] The consequence is that economic activities carried out must always refer to the instructions or guidelines given by Allah (*s.w.t.*). The instructions contain beliefs, values, and laws about behaviour, as explained in the al-Qur'an, and the hadith of the Prophet.

The *Khilafah* basically stands with the principle of unity and brotherhood of mankind.[25] Brotherhood/kinship will become a meaningless concept if it is not imbued with justice. Islam places justice as a virtue that must be fought for because upholding justice is a form of devotion to Allah (*s.w.t.*). This is implemented by utilizing the knowledge, gifts, and abilities that have been given by Allah (*s.w.t.*) to humans (Qardhawi, 2004).[26] Therefore, Islamic economics places great emphasis on humanity in all of its activities. Humanity, such as independence, glory, justice, brotherhood, mutual love, and mutual help, is an obligation that must be upheld, whereas the characteristics that are in conflicts to humanity, such as hostility, envy, mutual hatred, cheating, oppression, and injustice, are forbidden.

Kahf (2007)[27] stated that Islamic economic systems have three main principles. First, the principle of absolute ownership which belongs to Allah (*s.w.t.*). The earth[28] and everything inside, even the universe is created by Allah (*s.w.t.*) and belongs to Allah (*s.w.t.*).[29] The implication of this concept is that human's ownership of various resources is limited and not absolute. The use of various resources by humans will be accountable to Allah (*s.w.t.*) in the hereafter. Second, the principle of balance or non-partisanship. Although some natural resources are owned by one group and some other resources are owned by another group, but the use of resources still considers the social interests. Third, the principle of justice,[30] where fair means using personal rights without ignoring the rights of others.

Pancasila economy is in line and in harmony with the Islamic economy. Both economic systems are compatible even though they are not fully substitutable (Swasono, 2006).[31] The concept of human as caliphate on earth could be interpreted from the statement of Bung Hatta (Swasono, 1992: 143)[32] is "This world belongs solely to Allah (*s.w.t.*), provided for temporary human habitation on his journey to the immortal world. The obligation of man is not to own the world – for it belongs to Allah (*s.w.t.*) – but to preserve it as well as possible and leaves it to the next generation in a better condition than what he received from the previous generation."

Swasono (2004)[33] explains the function of the human caliphate on earth. All forms of ownership by humans on earth are on the mandate of Allah (*s.w.t.*). Allah (*s.w.t.*) then obligates humans with responsibility. The ownership could be obtained through efforts to collect *Rizq* which certainly has certain limits. Some of these obligations and boundaries are manifested in the prohibition on the monopoly of ownership and the obligation to pay *Zakat* and *Infaq*. Those who practice monopolies, like Qorun and Abu Lahab, are condemned. This is what Swasono meant by economic justice and economic democracy, where the principle of kinship and togetherness (mutualism) serve as the foundation.

The first paragraph of the Preamble of the 1945 Constitution states that

> Whereas independence is the inalienable right of all nations, therefore, all colonialism must be abolished in this world as it is not in conformity with humanity and justice.

The statement above shows the principle of *Maslahah* recognized by the Pancasila economy.

Al-Ghazali (1982)[34] explains that *Maslahah* means something that brings benefits and keeps away from *Mudarat* or harm. Preventing any deviance or damaging actions is an activity to achieve *Maslahah*. The occupation of a nation over another nation is an oppressive activity that results in inequality. Deviations from justice to oppression, from prosperity to poverty, from brotherhood to hostility, from compassion to violence, and from happiness to misery are activities that bring harm or damage (Swasono, 2004).[35]

The second paragraph of the Preamble of the 1945 Constitution mentions that

> and the moment of rejoicing has arrived in the struggle of the Indonesian independence movement to guide the people safely and well to the gate of the independence of the state of Indonesia which shall be independent, united, sovereign, just and prosperous.

The statement above contains concept like *Falah* principles in Islamic economics.

Raghib al-As fahani in Khan (1994)[36] mentions that the concept of *Falah* in world life could be illustrated by three things, namely: survival/continuity in goodness, freedom of desire/wealth and strength, glory, and honour. Khan stated that *Falah* has a multi-dimensional concept that has implications for individual behaviour (micro level) and collective behaviour (macro level).

Happiness, safety, security, independence, unity, sovereignty, justice, and prosperity are conditions and behaviours at the micro (individual) and macro (collective) level, which are contained in terms of survival/continuity in goodness, freedom of desire/wealth and strength, glory, and honour, as those meaning are contained in the concept of *Falah*.

Section (1) of Article 33 of the 1945 Constitution, which underlies Pancasila economic system, namely the foundation of togetherness (*mutualism*) and the principle of kinship, is aligned and in line with the concept of *Khilafah* which is based on the principle of unity and brotherhood of mankind as explained by Chapra. Article 33 of paragraph (2) and paragraph (3) of the 1945 Constitution, which explains the role of the state in creating people's prosperity, is also in line with Islamic policies in maintaining market balance, economic unity to maintain justice and improve people's prosperity.

Fatah (2012)[37] stated that in the Abbasid era, a permanent and independent economic institution called *Hisbah* had an active role in maintaining economic balance and justice. In his time, too, many *Caliphs* appointed economic supervisory officers (*Muhtasib*) who were tasked with overseeing economic activity. The existence of *Hisbah* institution shows the active role of the government in structuring economic activities.

Article 33 of the 1945 Constitution, which forms the basis of the Pancasila economic system, has the value of social transformation, namely the value of a non-usurious system (Swasono, 2003).[38] Swasono (2008)[39] stated that usury is an ideological mindset that is imbued in an economic system, the foundation is self-interest, greed, and hegemonic rip-off originates from liberalism. This is in line with the concept of prohibiting usury in the Islamic economic system. The moral values of Pancasila economy that are non-discriminatory, non-exploitative, anti-monopoly, anti-concentration of mastering productive assets, divine ethics, and cooperation (the principle of togetherness and kinship) basically have noble values which are also contained in the Islamic economic system. All of the above explanations imply a very close relationship between the Indonesian economic system and the Islamic economic system.

Tawhid, Foundation of Economic Spirituality

Spirituality means the process of searching the meaning of life. It is the self-understanding that there is an enormous amount of power affecting oneself. It is something non-material (Sheep, 2003).[40] Janfeshan *et al.* (2011)[41] mentioned that spirituality is reflected through trust in God, love to each other, perseverance, movement, endurance, piety, humility, maturity, service, kindness, hope in the future, sincerity in acceptance, optimism, virtue, satisfaction, gratitude, honesty, economy, independence, sacrifice as well as loyalty.

The spiritual element in human beings makes them always wonder why they do something, and it makes them look for better ways to do it (Zohar and Marshal, 2004).[42] Spiritual elements make people hope that the life and efforts they make are meaningful. Spirituality can create a social ethos (Rahardjo, 1999).[43] The ethos is believed, appreciated, and practiced consistently so that it inflicts certain social impacts associated with a person and some community groups.[44]

Spirituality is an esoteric dimension or the spirit of religion. In the modern day, spirituality includes the quality of faith, quality of life, mental quality, quality of emotional intelligence, and the quality of spiritual intelligence derived from religious belief.[45] The founders of Indonesia also realized the importance of spirituality in national life. Therefore, it is necessary to present spiritual side in the national life as stated in the Preamble of the 1945 Constitution of the Republic of Indonesia, which is

> By the grace of God Almighty and motivated by the noble desire to live a free national life, the people of Indonesian hereby declare their independence.

There is a very fundamental difference about the spiritual understanding between Western scholars and Eastern scholars (Islam). The difference lies in whether spirituality is related to religious teachings or not. Weber (1958),[46] Chaleff (1998),[47] Guillory (1997),[48] and Friedman and Friedman (2008)[49] mentioned that spirituality is different from religion. Spirituality and religion were two distinct things despite having related phenomena. Spirituality came from inner consciousness, apart from the faith system, whether these systems were taught or studied in religion. While in Islam, spirituality is a part of a religious system that is believed, appreciated, and practiced. Islam teaches that spirituality is the form of worship of a creature to the Creator. The worship should be done to carry out the functions of the human *Caliph* on earth.

The manifestation of a human's role as a *Caliph* on earth is to guide people to have a vision of achieving happiness in the hereafter without ignoring the success of life in the world. The success of life in the world is an intermediary target or a milestone. It is a short-term goal, and it is not everything. The goal is happiness in the hereafter, the long-term, and the eternal life. It is an achievement that must be fully fought for, the final goal of all life activities.

The tendency of a Muslim towards the afterlife does not mean that he relies on and surrenders to fate. His dependence on various circumstances and opportunities, as well as the feeling of being unable to strive forward and work, is an expression of feeling as the *Caliph* of Allah (*s.w.t.*) on earth (Ash-Shadr, 2008).[50]

For a Muslim, the salvation in the hereafter and the success in the world are ideals that must be fought for and understood as:

i That success is not only from the perception between humans but also from the perception between humans and Allah (*s.w.t.*), the Creator.
ii That happiness is that which is not only visible physically but also spiritually.
iii That success is not only seen from physical material but also non-physical and non-material.
iv That success is not only from the perception of self-understanding but also from the judgement of others.
v That if human beings are safe, then that safety should not only be enjoyed by themselves but also by others.
vi That success is not only having a lot of wealth but also feeling happiness when others can enjoy the wealth as well.
vii That success and salvation are when the things mentioned above are carried out with the motivation to worship the Creator not for others.

Ash-Shadr stated if all activities in the world are presented in the framework of the hereafter and working with others is given the quality of "obligation" and interpreted as worship, surely the contemplation of a Muslim towards the unseen will transform into a driving force for the creation of the greatest participation to boost the economy (Ash-Shadr, 2008).

Life in the World Is a Process, the Afterlife Is a Result

Al-Ghazali (Ghazanfar, 1997)[51] explained that the afterlife was the final place for human settlement for everything they had done during their life in the world. The settlement could be either reward or punishment. That means living in the world is not only temporary but also the place for struggling and preparing for the Judgment Day. It can be said that the world life is only an intermediary objective or a short-term goal while the afterlife is the final goal or long-term goal. For this reason, the effort made in the world is not only to pursue worldly interests but also to dedicate oneself to obtain merit in the afterlife.

Regarding the efforts made to obtain salvation in the hereafter, Al-Ghazali (Zidan, 1997)[52] divided people into three groups: The first, those who ignored the afterlife by indulging themselves on everything worldly; thus, they would be destroyed. The second, people whose life in the world is dedicated to pursuing the afterlife. They will get success. The third, people who follow the middle ground, that is, people who, in all activities of world life, always follow the *Shari'ah*, including in economic activities. They will get salvation.

Related to the worldly life, it is certainly easy to notice, observe, analyze, and take a decision on one thing that is discussed. It is different with the afterlife. Afterlife cannot be observed because of the limitations that humans have.[53] However, life in the hereafter is a result of everything done in the world; therefore, the performance in the afterlife can still be predicted from the achievement of performance in the world. In the simple math term, it can be proxied that the life in the world is an independent variable while the afterlife is a dependent variable.

Participation and Cooperation

In carrying out economic activities, there is competition among economic actors. However, it does not mean that the competition must ignore the relationships or unity. Cooperation in collaboration with the concept of working together and mutual assistance is the main economic strength. Cooperation and helping each other are links to a competition which does not disregard brotherhood.[54]

Competition and cooperation are the twin strengths of one another that cannot be separated in moving world economy in real terms (Swasono, 2003).[55] Competition and cooperation in populist economy are accomplished in harmony with the foundation of togetherness or mutualism and brotherhood (Swasono, 2004).[56] The principle of family has the meaning of companionship, mutual help, and working together. This is in line with the Prophet's hadith:

> Allah (*s.w.t.*) always helps people if they always help their family (a Muslim).
> (Narrated by Ahmad)

Competition manifested in a free market becomes the basis for the capitalists to mutually sway each other, not mutually harmonious and even overpower each other. This is different from the principle of cooperative, which maintains the existence of each economic power (Swasono, 2010).[57] Competition becomes the main generator of the capitalist economic system, although they also realized that competition had a negative impact, as evidenced by the occurrence of World War I and World War II. After both wars, there was a vacuum. Collaboration made the world enthusiastic by the development of the League of Nations after World War I and the United Nations after World War II.

Collaboration or mutual help in economic activities is among the characteristics of the Islamic economic system.[58] Akram (1994)[59] stated that Islamic economy is a study that aims to create *Falah,* achieved by managing natural resources on earth, based on cooperation and participation.

Collaboration creates the harmonic system. Learning is derived from the harmony of the universe. Harmony is seen in the regular rotation of the earth against its axis, also in the circulation of the earth to the sun,[60] circulation to the moon, stars, and sun,[61] the rain cycle,[62] the cycle of human growth in the womb,[63] the life cycle, death, and resurrection from the graves.[64]

Choudhury (1986)[65] stated that equality and cooperation in Islamic economy are a manifestation of *Tawhid* principle and brotherhood. The principle teaches that, in truth, a human is originally one or alone. Then, Allah (*s.w.t.*) created his partner, then from the couple, Allah (*s.w.t.*) bred humans.[66] As for why Allah (*s.w.t.*) created inequality in humans in physical differences, knowledge, wealth, and strength, it is not intended as disharmony but has a purpose so that among humans can complement each other,[67] ask each other,[68] and become brothers.[69]

The spirit of participation is the behaviour taught by Rasulullah (*s.w.a.*). He taught the prohibition of fighting non-Muslims, as long as they participate in paying taxes; sharing food with all people; sharing goods by prioritizing the interests of others without any strings attached;[70] sharing war spoils fairly;[71] and distributing *Zakat* for those who deserve to receive it.[72]

> Hadith by Abdurrahman bin Abu Bakar ra, he said: We were 130 people with the Prophet. Then the Prophet (*s.a.w.*). asked: "Do any of you have food?" There was someone who had about one sha' of wheat and then made a mixture.
>
> Then a tall polytheist who tangled his hair came while herding goats. The Prophet (*s.a.w.*). asked: "Is this sold or given or rewarded?". The person replied: "For sale!" Rasulullah (*s.a.w.*). bought a goat from him. After being slaughtered, Rasulullah (*s.a.w.*). instructed to take the goat's heart for grilled. Abdurrahman bin Abu Bakar said: "For Allah's sake!" We were one hundred and thirty people (and everybody) got a piece of goat's heart from Rasulullah. If a person was present, then Rasulullah gave it

> away and if someone was absent, then Prophet Muhammad kept it. The food was divided into two trays. We all ate from both of the trays and were full. I left the rest of the two trails on the camel.
>
> (Shahih Muslim No. 3832)

Islam always reminds us of the importance of cooperation and participation. There is a legal provision that from every asset obtained; basically, there are rights for other people.[73] There are provisions which prohibits the creation of business contracts that involve one type of contract exclusively without dividing risk (Vogel, 1998).[74] There are provisions that prohibit making business contracts that tend to make disputes between parties involved[75] or the prohibition on taking usury.[76]

Regarding the prohibition of usury, jurisprudence experts agree that usury is prohibited as it has an element of dominating and tyrannizing each party. The creditor's right to receive interest is guaranteed regardless of whether the asset increases the value or not for the debtors. Usury makes one party eat the other party's wealth without effort and risk. Usury is obtained not from employee well-beings or services; it also ignores the human aspect to obtain wealth.

Togetherness and mutual participation are also values embraced by Pancasila economic system. This economic system is also known as people's economy. People's economy is the understanding and original concept of the Indonesian people. The people's economy is a unity of words and not just a series of words, "economy" and "people." The word people in people's economy are related to togetherness, mutual support, participation, etc. (Mubyarto, 1997).[77]

The people's economy means that economic development is centred on people. The people's economic system considers people as both the goal of economic development as well as means and actors of development. This is aligned with the Islamic economic system, which places humanity as the goal of all economic activities besides a means and economic actor.

People's economic development is carried out by increasing people's productivity and making utilization of available resources effectively. This is what referred to as grass root-based and resources-based strategies. People's economic development is also carried out with a bottom-up participatory and emancipatory approach. The whole is conducted to accelerate economic transformation and social transformation (Swasono, 2002).[78]

People's participation in economic development guarantees the economic added value that is produced and can be directly received by people (Swasono, 2003).[79] The equity is achieved along with the economic growth. People become human development asset. This encourages the growth of the middle class. The growth of the middle class will increase people's purchasing power, so people are able to develop themselves. This condition increases bargaining position collectively. People become more active and productive, and the economic added value is increasing. People's economic development is adaptive to resources and is people centred. In the end, economic development absorbs more labours.

Brotherhood and Fair Distribution

The founders of Indonesia Nation have stated that social justice is the goal of the establishment of the Republic of Indonesia, as stated in the Preamble of the 1945 Constitution.

> Subsequent thereto, to form a government of the state of Indonesia which shall protect all the people of Indonesia and all the independence and the land that has been struggled for, and to improve public welfare, to educate the life of the people and to participate toward the establishment of a world order based on freedom, perpetual peace and social justice, therefore the independence of Indonesia shall be formulated into a constitution of the Republic of Indonesia which shall be built into a sovereign state based on a belief in the One and Only God, just and civilised humanity, the unity of Indonesia, and democratic life led by wisdom of thoughts in deliberation amongst representatives of the people, and achieving social justice for all the people of Indonesia.

Asshiddiqie (2012)[80] explained that social justice in the fourth paragraph of the Preamble of the 1945 Constitution was formulated as "something" that is concrete in nature, not just abstract-philosophical political jargon without meaning. Social justice is not only a state basic subject that is final and static but is something that must be realized dynamically in the form of social justice for all Indonesian people.

However, Swasono (2011: 5–6)[81] mentioned that social justice meant in the Preamble of the 1945 Constitution is as explained in Article 27 paragraph (2) as well as Article 33 of the 1945 Constitution, namely prioritizing people's interests for the sake of the people's sovereignty rather than the market sovereignty. By implementing the principle of family system and togetherness, as mentioned by Article 33 of the 1945 Constitution, Indonesia can create justice as desired. This happened as the family principle gave birth to the *homo ethicus* character that prioritized justice. While the adherents of individualism and liberalism interpret justice as power. An assessment of the sense of justice depends on the decisions of the large capital owners. The notion of individualism produces *homo economicus'* morals with the behaviour of *homo homini lupus* (Swasono, 2004).[82]

Rawls (1999)[83] criticizes the concept of justice understood by capitalists. Rawls said that justice could not be realized through a free market. Rawls developed the theory of justice. Justice, according to Rawls, is that everyone has the same rights from their reasonable positions. In order for justice to be achieved, the constitutional, political, and economic structure and rules regarding rights to wealth must apply equally for all. Everyone must put aside the attributes that differentiate people (veil of ignorance). The attributes in question are ability, wealth, social position, religious and philosophical views, and conception of values. Rawls emphasized the concept of justice in possession of the main social goods per person. Inequality is a problem caused by community members who do not have social goods evenly. The community members are entitled to compensation. Institutions are needed to manage the above inequalities.

Rawls's concept of justice received criticism from Dworkin. Dworkin (2000)[84] stated that individuals in society do not see inequalities that arise between citizens from the ownership of goods. Inequality is caused by choices made by individuals to use their social goods. Dworkin emphasized the responsibility that individuals have in choosing to use social goods.

Sen agreed with Rawls and Dworkin about the emphasis on intellectuality as the search engine for justice. However, Sen gave sharp criticism to both Rawls' and Dworkin's theories. Sen (2008)[85] mentioned that the concept of justice relates to four things, namely: focus on life and freedom, connecting responsibility for effective power, comparative, not transcendental, assessment, and globally unrestricted coverage.

In Sen's view, the institutionalism promoted by Rawls produces the Kew Garden principle,[86] a view that regards institutions as moral agents or moral guards. Sen argues that the so-called "second generation human rights" concerns both perfect obligations (i.e., asserting that the state is an institution of guarding justice) and imperfect obligation (i.e., not explicitly calling who is a moral agent) and also concerns the suffering of others from other countries.

Sen believes that equality must be seen from the efforts of the community in achieving what is planned and what is desired in their lives. Sen sees that welfare is not seen from social goods that must be owned by individuals or society but to the extent to which individuals or communities can realize freedom. The extent to which individuals can convert the resources they have to get something they want. Thus, freedom can be seen from the ability to achieve goals.

The concept of brotherhood in Islamic economic systems arises from spiritual renewal and not from social dissection (Mannan, 1970),[87] as implemented in the communistic economic system. The communistic economic system implements the brotherhood principle to guarantee social security. Islam has the view that Allah (*s.w.t.*) created humans with various tribes and nations meant for them to know each other.[88] Brotherhood is a favour given by Allah (*s.w.t.*) to Muslims where during the time of ignorance they were hostile to each other.[89] The pleasure of brotherhood was also given by God to the Muhajirin and the Ansar as well as those before them.[90] Some of the Prophet's hadith also explain the privilege of brotherhood: connecting brotherhood is a practice that can draw oneself closer to heaven and keep one away from hell.[91] Brotherhood is more important than personal interests.[92]

Swasono (2010)[93] used kinship to refer to brotherhood as the principle of the application of Pancasila economic system. The principle of kinship means that the relationship between fellow citizens is like a big family, a relationship with *Ukhuwah*, which for a pluralistic Indonesia, means having *Ukhuwah wathoniah*. Thus, the principle of kinship is not a nepotistic principle.

Brotherhood is carried out to uphold justice. The teachings of Islam emphasize *Tawhid*-based brotherhood (Choudhury, 1986).[94] The principle of *Tawhid* teaches people about relationships and interactions with others. The interaction and relationship are as he relates to Allah (*s.w.t.*) the Creator. Therefore, all economic activities such as market exchange, allocation of resources, maximization of utilities, and profits always have a basis for trustworthiness.

Justice is not something scientific and tangible, which can be measured or observed or subject to experimental testing, but it is an estimation and moral judgment. Justice in Islamic economic systems is an integral part of Islamic teachings. The Islamic economic system upholds the ideology of justice. This is different from other economic systems, which contains a theory of justice explaining the reality of economic life but separated from ideology or ideals of justice (Ash-Shadr, 2008).[95]

The doctrine of justice that must be upheld is as instructed by Allah (*s.w.t.*).[96] This verse shows that upholding justice is closely related to human devotion to its Creator.[97] Naqwi (1985)[98] explained that the implication of the verse is that there is a guarantee of independence for individuals in the face of abuse of power, economically, socially, or physically by the people who have it.

Social justice applies to all social structures, both rich and poor in all aspects of human life.[99] Social justice must be explained in everyday life and must be upheld even against hated people.[100] Doing justice means not cheating by manipulating scales or measures so as not to harm the other party.[101]

In the Islamic economic system, justice is enforced on the principle that:

i Everything in the universe belongs to Allah (*s.w.t.*).[102]
ii Humans can have assets but as the gift from Allah (*s.w.t.*)[103] and are bound to the provisions governing its use.
iii Allah (*s.w.t.*) makes the inequality of marginal income to stimulate individual initiative.[104]

Islam does not heed all anti-social economic activities that do not encourage shared prosperity. This is the basis for the prohibition of monopoly and speculative activities in Islam because these activities are not useful, and it takes advantage from the suffering of others (Mannan, 1970).[105] Therefore, realizing social justice should be rooted in human faith in Allah (*s.w.t.*).[106]

Social Welfare as an Economic Objective

Mubyarto (1997)[107] mentioned that economic systems that are not intended for the welfare of the people, sooner or later, will meet a dead end if not destroyed. Any economic system will only run smoothly if supported by people who can participate while taking advantage of his participation.

Rahardjo (1999)[108] stated that the indications explained by Mubyarto were predicted by Roepke (1899–1966), who predicted the destruction of collective economy of the Soviet Union and socialist countries in Eastern European in his book, *The Moral Foundations of Civil Society*. Roepke explained that the collective economy developed by the Soviet Union and socialist countries in Eastern European was applied by force. A socialist economy was built to go against Western capitalists, not to prosper and flourish the people.

The concept of welfare in the Indonesian economic system is as stated in the fourth paragraph of the Preamble of the 1945 Constitution.

The application of social welfare is as stated by the Article 33 of the 1945 Constitution. Bung Hatta in Swasono (1992)[109] explained that social welfare intended in the article is the fulfilment of various life necessities of Indonesian people. The above foundation becomes the basis for the State of Indonesia to become a welfare state. This concept is a political economy choice taken by the founders of the Indonesian nation at that time.

Sen (1998)[110] described the choice of the founding fathers with a figure of speech. The choice, which was decided through political compromise at the time, could be described as a camel that is considered as a horse. On the other hand, camels could be seen as half horse or half other shaped.[111] Sen explained the meaning of the parable that the results of the public choice could be something great but can also be just confusing.

The choice as a welfare state cannot yet be realized. This happened since, in the Dutch colonial era, the Indonesian nation carried out export activities to fulfil the various needs of the people. While after 1945 independence until now, the Indonesian State carried out economic activities to fulfil various needs of foreign countries, not to fulfil the welfare of its people (Mubyarto, 2011).[112]. This situation despite getting Independence from colonial master did not make the nation and the Indonesian people enjoy the welfare, as enshrined in Article 33 of the 1945 Constitution:

> An economic development is said to be successful if, in the adequate development process followed and the economy produces added value for the both physical and spiritual humans' welfare either tangible or intangible part of the life. The well-being should be encompassing an increase in material value, increased employment opportunities, increased productivity, and increased efficiency.
>
> (Habibie, 1997).[113]

Social welfare, according to Swasono (1992),[114] includes clothing, food, place to live, labour wage above minimum level, health, intellect, education, patience, confidence, etc. All the above requirements, according to Swasono, can be fulfilled by building a spirit of cooperation and helping each other. If Pareto priority is made, it is certain that fulfilling the welfare of the community is more noteworthy compared to the welfare of individual.

Meanwhile, according to Mannan (1970),[115] welfare includes two criteria, namely, objective and subjective. Objective criteria are welfare that can be measured by financial factors and subjective criteria are welfare measured in terms of ethics based on the commands of Allah (*s.w.t.*) in the Al-Qur'an and Hadith. Included in the objective criteria are the increase of workers' income, the increasing number of workers involved in the production process, and the amount and quality of useful goods and services, while the subjective criteria are not producing liquor, avoiding the usury system, etc. Mannan explained that if the production of goods and services only meets the criteria objectively, the goods and services produced would not guarantee the welfare of the people to the fullest.

Siddiqi (1996)[116] stated that there are several needs that must be fulfilled, first, the very basic needs of food, clothing, and a place to stay. Basic needs are needs that must be fulfilled, whatever the conditions the people and the country are in. There are needs that depend on climate and weather such as water for drinking, fuel, and electricity. There are needs that depend on location such as medical care, eradication of illiteracy, transportation needs for the community living in a big city, financial support for marriage, and financial support to pay off debt.

The second type of need is the need for religious teaching. This is often exemplified by Rasulullah (*s.a.w.*) and his companions. Rasulullah (*s.a.w.*) sent Sa'id bin al-As to teach the people of Medina to write and read. Umar bin Abdul Aziz recruited teachers to teach people in the countryside. Umar bin Abdul Aziz also gave gifts for married people.

Third, the need that is related to the public. This need must be referring to a country's average standard of living. For poor countries or those which do not have a high surplus then the standard of living is defined as more than living conditions with reasonable efficiency or minimum living standards. Whereas for rich countries, or those with surplus of *Zakat* and *Fay*,[117] then the fulfilment of needs is at the average level of citizens' life.

Various opinions on welfare above are in line with Sen's opinion (1992)[118] that the socio-economic conditions of one individual can be compared with other individuals through focal variables, namely variables used to assess justice, or it can also be said that focal variables are differentiator variables. Included in focal variables are income, health, rights, freedom, opportunity, education, etc.

Sen stated that the assessment of the distribution of justice in equality becomes irrelevant if what is meant as an equality is ownership on an economic commodity or goods. This is due to the differences in luck and misfortune for each individual. Luck and misfortunes are caused by environmental conditions, social conditions, and physical of an individual. Since birth, an individual has a difference to other individuals in terms of gender, social conditions, physical character, descendant, environment, etc. Therefore, an equality assessment between one individual to other individuals is not proper if the equality is only seen in terms of income or ownership of an economic commodity. Focal variable becomes the basis for Sen to assess the equality of individuals in a society group.

Sen argued that an individual in achieving their goals (well-being) is influenced by freedom and capability. Freedom is liberty owned by individuals in achieving their goals. Capability is the ability of individuals to use the freedom they have to achieve their goals.

Zarqa (2007)[119] mentioned that various activities carried out for increasing social welfare[120] is called *Maslahah* or utility. Al-Ghazali and al-Shatibi in Zarqa divided social utility into three levels, namely necessities, conveniences, and refinements.[121]

Necessities consist of all activities and everything that is important for maintaining five basic needs of individuals and social life, namely religion, life, intellect, lineage, and wealth. Conveniences consist of all activities and everything that is not fatal for the maintenance of individual basic needs or social life but is needed to eliminate obstacles or difficulties in life. Included in the category of convenience is having a vehicle for transportation, a comfortable bed, etc. When many people need the vehicle or the bed, the vehicle manufacturing industry and beds are included in the category of refinements.

Social welfare can be achieved through *Ihsan*'s attitude (Choudhury, 1986),[122] that is, the attitude of giving up the best wholeheartedly to others, which is dedicated to the Creator.[123] Choudhury said that the main key of the creation of *Ihsan*'s attitude is *Taqwa* and hereafter orientation. *Taqwa* means virtues inspired by fear of Allah (*s.w.t.*). Hereafter is the belief in the existence of the reward in other life for all actions that have been carried out in the world.

Economic Independence and Self-Esteem of People

The statement of independence of the nation is stated in the second paragraph of the Preamble of the 1945 Constitution:

> And the moment of rejoicing has arrived in the struggle of the Indonesian independence movement to guide the people safely and well to the gate of the independence of the state of Indonesia which shall be independent, united, sovereign, just and prosperous.

The statements "Independent and sovereign" are written in a sequence of the sentence. This shows that sovereignty and independence are a series condition. It is not possible to create independence without sovereignty.

Independence has become a political demand for an independent Indonesia. Independence is an integral part of the meaning of independence itself. There is no true freedom without independence. The meaning of independence for an independent nation is where independence is the dignity of the nation.

The freedom, independence, and dignity of the nation are essentially the meaning of *Rahmatan lil 'alamin* for the nation (Swasono, 2003).[124]

Independence of the nation and state is created when economic development is carried out in favour of the people, namely economic development that places the people's economic sector as a pillar of the national economy. This is a strategic action so that the national economy grows and roots in the country so that it will build the domestic economic fundamentals (Swasono, 2002).[125]

Alignment to the people is done by setting various regulations in the economic field that is more dedicated to the low-income earners such as farmers, fishermen, small businesses, etc., rather than conglomerates (Sulistyono, 2007).[126] However, the effort to do this, according to Sulistyono, is not easy, as for hundreds of years, we have consumed the economic legal system, which is of liberal quality or serves the interests of capitalist countries. It takes effort and hard work to make this happen.

The independence of the people means that the people should have various abilities, expertise, and infrastructures that enable the fulfilment of needs both material and spiritual. Independence of the people sought with the enactment of *Fardu kifayah* in studying science, charity, industry, and other ability (Qardhawi, 2004).[127] Enforcement is intended so that the people can implement it religiously and do the world affairs properly. Independence of the people causes the people not to depend on other people so that other people do not control them.

Independence of the people will enforce *Izz*[128] or the self-esteem of Muslims that Allah (*s.w.t.*) has given them.[129] Independence of the people creates the realization of the chosen society and role models for other people.[130] Independence of the people means freedom, free from persecution and oppression. Independence must be placed as the main target in national development. Other targets, such as economic growth, should be placed as supporting roles (Swasono, 2003).[131]

Summary

Beside the introduction, this chapter deals with the Indonesian economic system based upon the Maslahah and Tawhid, which is basically a Foundation of Economic Spirituality, Participation, and Cooperation for achieving humanity through brother and sisterhoods. This is intended for the welfare of the people and fair distribution of wealth and economic independence and self-esteem of people at large.

Notes

1 Ariff, M. (2007). *Economics and Ethics. Reading in the Concept and Methodology of Islamic Economics.* Kualalumpur, Malaysia: Cert Publication.

2 Swasono, S-E. (2003). *Ekspose Ekonomika, Mewaspadai Globalisme dan Pasar Bebas.* Yogyakarta: Pusat Studi Ekonomi Pancasila (Pustep) UGM.

3 *Laissez-faire* is translated into letting something go as desired, let someone do as he wants, the problem is handled self-regulated without the rules of the country.

4 Swasono, S-E. (2004). *Kebersamaan dan Asas Kekeluargaan, Mutualism & Brotherhood, Kerkayatan, Nasionalisme, dan Kemandirian.* Jakarta: UNJ Press.
5 In Chapter III, page 138, Sri-Edi Swasono explained that as a moral science, economic science has a moral measure: first, moral sentiments (homo economicus vs. homo ethicus); second, ideology: mutualism/brotherhood vs. individualism/liberalism; third is the principles of justice, fairness, equity, goodness, goodwill, and altruism; fourth is the principles of equality, humanity, brotherhood, solidarity, and religious values; fifth is competition, cooperation, coo petition (increasing competitiveness); sixth is the principle of liberty and pursuit of happiness vs. social welfare and social justice. Seventh is nationalism.
6 Swasono, S-E. (2010). *Kembali ke Pasal 33 UUD 1945 Menolak Neoliberalisme.* Jakarta: Penerbit Yayasan Hatta.
7 Swasono, S-E. (5 Juli 2012). *Demokrasi Volkssouvereiniteit/Kedaulatan Rakyat.* Paper presented at Deklarasi Gerakan Pemantapan Pancasila, Surabaya, Indonesia.
8 Swasono, S-E. (1988). *Demokrasi Ekonomi: Komitmen dan Pembangunan Indonesia.* Paper presented at Pengukuhan Guru Besar Fakultas Ekonomi Universitas Indonesia, Jakarta.
9 Mubyarto. (1987). *Ekonomi Pancasila: Gagasan dan Kemungkinan.* Jakarta: LP3ES.
10 Swasono, S-E. (14 Maret 1987). *Pandangan Islam dalam Sistem Ekonomi Indonesia.* Paper presented at pidato ilmiah wisuda sarjana negara ke-tiga, Universitas Muhammadiyah, Medan.
11 Swasono, S-E. (1–3 Agustus 2008). *Ekonomi Islam dalam Pancasila.* Paper presented at International Seminar on Implementation of Islamic Economics. Annual Meeting of Indonesian Economics Experts Association. Universitas Airlangga, Surabaya.
12 Article 33 of the 1945 Constitution consists of three verses. Article 33 consists of five sections after the fourth amendment was carried out. Sections (1), (2), and (3) remain the same and are added with two additional sections: Sections (4) and (5).
13 Chapter VI on Regional Government, Article 18 of the 1945 Constitution consists of one section, which states: Dividing areas of large and small regions, with the form of the structure of the government are stipulated by law by considering the basis of consultation in the State Government discussion and the rights of origin in special areas. After the amendment, it changes to Chapter VI on Regional Government, Article 18 (consisting of seven sections), Article 18A (consisting of two sections), and Article 18B (consisting of two sections).
14 Article 23 of the 1945 Constitution before the amendment is stated in Chapter VIII of financial matters, consisting of six sections, but after the second amendment, Article 23 has three sections, plus Article 23A, 23B, 23C, 23D, and Chapter VIIIA on Supreme Audit Agency Article 23E, 23F, 23G.
15 Article 27 of the 1945 Constitution consists of two sections: (1) All citizens shall be equal before the law and the government and shall be required to respect the law and the government, with no exceptions. (2) Every citizen shall have the right to work and to earn a humane livelihood. Article 27 changes into three verses after the amendment. No changes for Section (1) and (2), with addition to section states: (3) Each citizen shall have the right and duty to participate in the effort of defending the state.
16 Article 34 of the 1945 Constitution consists of one section states: Impoverished persons and abandoned children shall be taken care of by the State. After the fourth amendment, it now has four sections.
17 Sri-Edi Swasono, in a testimony submitted to the Constitutional Court regarding Request for Judicial Review of Law No. 30 of 2009 by the SP-PLN DPP concerning Electricity relating to Article 33 section (2) of the 1945 Constitution, states that with the amendment to the title of Chapter XIV of the 1945 Constitution became "National Economy and Social Welfare," then through the amendment, it must be interpreted that all national economic activities must eventually end in achieving joint social welfare of all societies in the context of societal welfare or societal well-being.

18 Swasono, S-E. (2003). *Ekspose Ekonomika, Mewaspadai Globalisme dan Pasar Bebas.* Yogyakarta: Pusat Studi Ekonomi Pancasila (Pustep) UGM.
19 Swasono, S-E. (2010). Testimoni Sri Edi Swasono. *Permohonan Judicial Review UU No. 30 Tahun 2009 oleh DPP SP-PLN Tentang Ketenagalistrikan berkaitan dengan Pasal 33 ayat (2) UUD 1945.*
20 Chapra, M. U. (2007). *Islam and Economic Development.* New Delhi: Adam Publishers & Distributors.
21 QS Ali-'Imrān 3: 191; QS Ṣad 38: 27. Constitutional Court, Jakarta, 29 April 2010.
22 QS al-Baqarah 2: 29–30; QS al-An'ām 6: 165; QS al-Faṭir 35: 39; QS Ṣad 38: 28.
23 In Surah al-Nūr 24: 33, it is explained that "... and give them from the wealth of Allah which He has given you ..."
24 Amin, A. R. (2007). *The Celestial Management.* Jakarta: Senayan Abadi Publishing.
25 The term brotherhood is used in the Indonesian economic system with kinship.
26 Qardhawi, Y. (2004). *Darul Qiyam Wa al-Akhlak Fil Iqtishadil Islami, Terjemahan Bahasa Indonesia.* Jakarta: Robbani Press.
27 Kahf, M. (2007). *Islamic Economics System – A Review. Reading in the Concept and Methodology of Islamic Economics.* Kualalumpur. Malaysia: Cert Publication.
28 QS al-A'rāf 7: 128.
29 QS al-Ḥadīd 57: 5.
30 Kahf mentioned that the word "justice" and "descendants" are the third most mentioned words in the Qur'an. The most mentioned word is "Allah" and "knowledge."
31 Swasono, S-E. (2008). Ekonomi Islam dalam Pancasila. Paper presented at The International Seminar on Implementation of Islamic Economics, *Annual Meeting of Indonesian Economics Experts Association,* Unibersitas Airlangga, Surabya.
32 Swasono, S-E and Fauzie, R. (1992). *Mohammad Hatta, Demokrasi Kita, Bebas Aktif, Ekonomi Masa Depan.* Jakarta: UI Press, 143.
33 Swasono, S-E. (2004). *Kebersamaan dan Asas Kekeluargaan, Mutualism & Brotherhood, Kerkayatan, Nasionalisme, dan Kemandirian.* Jakarta: UNJ Press.
34 Al-Ghazali, A. H. (1982). *Al-Arba'in fi Usul al-Din.* Bayrut: Dar al-Afaq al-Jadidah.
35 Swasono, S-E. (2004). *Kebersamaan dan Asas Kekeluargaan, Mutualism & Brotherhood, Kerkayatan, Nasionalisme, dan Kemandirian.* Jakarta: UNJ Press.
36 Khan, M. A. (1994). *Introduction to Islamic Economics.* Islamabad, Pakistan: International Institute of Islamic Thought and Institute of Policy Studies.
37 Fatah, D. A. (2012). *Pasar & Keadilan dalam Perspektif Ekonomi Islam.* Jakarta: Gaung Persada Press.
38 Swasono, S-E. (2003). *Ekspose Ekonomika, Mewaspadai Globalisme dan Pasar Bebas.* Yogyakarta: Pusat Studi Ekonomi Pancasila (Pustep) UGM.
39 Swasono, S-E. (1–3 Agustus 2008). *Ekonomi Islam dalam Pancasila.* Paper presented at International Seminar on Implementation of Islamic Economics. Annual Meeting of Indonesian Economics Experts Association. Universitas Airlangga, Surabaya.
40 Sheep, M. L. (2003). Nurturing the Whole Person: A Model of Spirituality at Work and Performance. *Journal of Business Ethics.* 66: 357–375. https://doi.org/10.1007/s10551-006-0014-5.
41 Kamran J., Belal P., Seid, M. V. and Farideh, K. (2001). *Spirituality in the Workplace and Its Impact on the Efficiency of Management.* Paper presented at 2nd International Conference on Business and Economic Research (2nd ICBER 2011). 14th to 15th March 2011. Langkawi, Kedah, Malaysia.
42 Zohar, D. and Ian, M. (2004). *Spiritual Capital, Wealth We Can Live by.* Berrett-Koehler Publishers. San Francisco.
43 Rahardjo, D. (1999). *Intelektual, Intelegensia dan Perilaku Politik Bangsa, Risalah Cendekiawan Muslim.* Bandung: Penerbit Mizan.
44 Rahardjo mentioned that social ethos is the basic attitude of a person or group of people which characterizes a particular society.

45 Lajnah Pentashihan Mushaf al-Qur'an Badan Litbang dan Diklat Kementrian Agama RI. (2010b). *Tafsir al-Quran Tematik, Kitab Spiritualitas dan Akhlak.* Jakarta. It is stated that spirituality is things that concern the psyche. In the Al-Qur'an itself, there is no basis for the word "spirit," but there is a meaning closer to it, namely the word "ruh" or related words to it, such as *rūhani* and *rūhaniyyah* which is then translated into bahasa Indonesia (*Kamus Besar Bahasa Indonesia*) into the spirit, spiritual and spiritual with the meaning: (1) Something that lives, that does not have physical body, mindedness and feeling and (2) life, the subtle body.

46 Weber, M. (1958). *The Protestant Ethic and the Spirit of Capitalism.* New York: Charles Scribner's Sons.

47 Chaleff, I. (1998). Spiritual Leadership. *Executive Excellence* 15. Vol. 15, No. 5: 9.

48 Guillory, W. A. (1997). *The Living Organization Spirituality in the Workplace.* Salt Lake City, UT: Innovations International.

49 Friedman, H. H. and Friedman, W. (2008). Can "Homo Spiritualis" Replace Homo Economicus in the Business Curriculum? *e-Journal of Business Education & Scholarship of Teaching.* Vol. 2. No. 2: 1–11.

50 Ash-Shadr, and Bqir, M. (2008). *Buku Induk Ekonomi Islam Iqtishaduna.* Jakarta: Zahra Publishing House.

51 Ghazanfar, M. S. and Islahi A. A. (1997). *Economic Thought of Al-Ghazali (450–505 A.H./1058–1111 A.D.).* Islamic Economics Research Series, King Abdulaziz University. Jeddah, Saudi Arabia.

52 Zidan, Ahmad. (1997). *Al-Ghazali's Ihya' Ulum al-Din, Revitalization of The Sciences of Religion.* Cairo, Egypt: Islamic Inc. for Publishing and Distribution.

53 QS al-Naml 27: 66 Rather, their knowledge is arrested concerning the hereafter. Rather, they are in doubt about it. Rather, they are, concerning it, blind.

54 QS al-Māidah 5: 2.

55 Swasono, S-E. (2003). *Ekspose Ekonomika, Mewaspadai Globalisme dan Pasar Bebas.* Yogyakarta: Pusat Studi Ekonomi Pancasila (Pustep) UGM.

56 Swasono, S-E. (2004). *Kebersamaan dan Asas Kekeluargaan, Mutualism & Brotherhood, Kerkayatan, Nasionalisme, dan Kemandirian.* Jakarta: UNJ Press.

57 Swasono, S-E. (2010). *Testimoni Sri Edi Swasono, Permohonan Judicial Review UU No. 30 Tahun 2009 oleh DPP SP-PLN Tentang Ketenagalistrikan berkaitan dengan Pasal 33 ayat (2) UUD 1945.*

58 QS al-Tawbah 9: 71.

59 Khan, M. A. (1994). *Introduction to Islamic Economics.* Islamabad, Pakistan: International Institute of Islamic Thought and Institute of Policy Studies.

60 QS al-A'Rāf 7: 54.

61 QS al-Ra'ad 13: 2; QS Ibrāhīm 14: 33; QS al-Anbiyā 21: 33; QS Yāsīn 36: 40.

62 QS al-Baqarah 2: 22.

63 QS al-Haj 22: 5.

64 QS al-Mu'minūn 23: 12–16.

65 Choudhury, M. A. (1986). *Contributions to Islamic Economic Theory, a Study in Social Economics.* New York: St. Martin's Press.

66 QS al-Nisā 4: 1.

67 QS al-Zukhruf 43: 32.

68 QS al-Nisā 4: 1.

69 QS al-Ḥujurāt 49: 10.

70 QS al-Ḥasyr 59: 9.

71 QS al-Ḥasyr 59: 7.

72 QS al-Tawbah 9: 60.

73 QS al-Nisā 4: 32; QS al-Dhāriyāt 51: 19.

74 Vogel, F. E. and Samuel, L. H. (1998). *III, Islamic Law and Finance, Religion, Risk, and Return.* The Hague, the Netherlands: Kluwer Law International.

75 Akram mentioned that such contracts are prohibited in Islam since they have an exploitation tendency of one party to another.
76 QS al-Baqarah 2: 275, 276, 278, QS Ali-'Imrān 3: 130; QS al-Nisā 4: 161.
77 Mubyarto. (1997). Paradigma Pembangunan yang Bertumpu pada Kekuatan Ekonomi Rakyat. *Wawasan dan Visi Pembangunan Abad 21*, Editor M. Dawam Rahardjo. Jakarta: PT. Intermasa.
78 Swasono, S-E. (02 Agustus 2012). *Prospek dan Perkembangan Perekonomian Rakyat: Antara Kedaulatan Rakyat dan Kedaulatan Pasar. Kedaulatan Rakyat Daily*, Friday, August 2.
79 Swasono, S-E. (2003). *Ekspose Ekonomika, Mewaspadai Globalisme dan Pasar Bebas*. Yogyakarta: Pusat Studi Ekonomi Pancasila (Pustep) UGM.
80 Asshiddiqie, J. (n.d). *Pesan Konstitusional Keadilan Sosial*.
81 Swasono, S-E. (2011). Jangan Menjual Indonesiaku. *Swara 33 eBulletin Mubins*. Edisi 001 Mei: 5–6.
82 Swasono, S-E. (2004). *Kebersamaan dan Asas Kekeluargaan, Mutualism & Brotherhood, Kerkayatan, Nasionalisme, dan Kemandirian*. Jakarta: UNJ Press.
83 Rawls, J. (1999). *A Theory of Justice*. Cambridge, Massachusetts: Harvard University Press.
84 Dworkin, R. (2000). *Sovereign Virtue, the Theory and Practice of Equality*. Cambridge, Massachusetts: Harvard University Press.
85 Sen, A. (2008). The Idea of Justice. *Journal of Human Development*. Vol. 9, No. 3: 331–342.
86 Sen made an example of a girl being attacked at Kew Gardens in New York at night. The girl shouted for help, but no one who lived around helped her, even just to call the police to ask for help. This is because they assumed that the party acts as a moral agency (the party who is obliged) to help its institution/police. Finally, the girl was killed without anyone helping her.
87 Mannan, M. A. (1970). *Islamic Economic: Theory and Practice*. Islamabad: Houder and Stoughton.
88 QS al-Ḥujurat 49: 13.
89 QS Ali-'Imrān 3: 103.
90 QS al-Ḥasyr 59: 10.
91 Abu Ayyub Al-Ansari R.A. Hadith:

> That a Badui offered to Rasulullah (*s.a.w.*) to hold his camel bridle on a trip. Then the person said: O Rasulullah or Ya Muhammad, tell me what can bring me closer to heaven and keep me from hell. Rasulullah (*s.a.w.*). Did not answer immediately. He looked at the friends, while saying: He really got a guidance. Then he asked the person: "What did you ask?" The person then repeated his words. Then Rasulullah (*s.a.w.*). Said: You worship Allah (*s.w.t.*), do not associate Him with anything, establish prayer, fulfill *Zakat* and connecting brotherhood. Now, leave the camel.
>
> (Shahih Muslim No. 14).

92 Ibnu Abbas r.a. said, "Rasulullah (*s.a.w.*) in his sickness, in which he died from, came out by tying his head with pieces of cloth. He sat in the pulpit then he praised Allah (*s.w.t.*), then he said, 'There is no one who is more generous to me in his life and wealth than Abu Bakar ibn Abu Quhafah. If I wish to take a lover from human, surely, I will take Abu Bakar as a lover. However, Islamic friendship is more important'" (In other narration: "However, he is my brother and my best friend" 4/19]. In another narration from Ibnu Abbas, "As for the saying of the Prophet Muhammad, 'If I wish I had taken a lover from this people surely, I take Abu Bakar, but the Islamic brotherhood is more important or better,' 'he said this because he placed Abu Bakar as a father (in-laws)' 8/7) 'Close every door in this mosque from me except the door of Abu Bakar.'"

93 Swasono, S-E. (2010). *Testimoni Sri Edi Swasono, Permohonan Judicial Review UU No. 30 Tahun 2009 oleh DPP SP-PLN Tentang Ketenagalistrikan berkaitan dengan Pasal 33 ayat (2) UUD 1945.*
94 Choudhury, M. A. (1986). *Contributions to Islamic Economic Theory, a Study in Social Economics*. New York: St. Martin's Press.
95 Ash-Shadr, M. B. (2008). *Buku Induk Ekonomi Islam Iqtishaduna*. Jakarta: Zahra Publishing House.
96 QS al-Māidah 5: 8.
97 QS al-A'Rāf 7: 29.
98 Naqwi, S. N. H. (1985). *Ethics and Economics: An Islamic Synthesis*, Terjemahan Bahasa Indonesia. Bandung: Penerbit Mizan.
99 QS al-Nisā 4: 135.
100 QS al-Māidah 5: 8.
101 QS Hūd 11: 85.
102 QS Ali-'Imrān 3: 180.
103 QS al Qasas 28: 82.
104 QS al-An'ām 6: 165.
105 Mannan, M. A. (1970). *Islamic Economic: Theory and Practice*. Islamabad: Houder and Stoughton.
106 QS al-An'ām 6: 82.
107 Mubyarto. (1997). Paradigma Pembangunan yang Bertumpu pada Kekuatan Ekonomi Rakyat, *Wawasan dan Visi Pembangunan Abad 21*, Editor M. Dawam Rahardjo. Jakarta: PT. Intermasa.
108 Rahardjo, M. D. (1999). *Intelektual, Intelegensia dan Perilaku Politik Bangsa, Risalah Cendekiawan. Muslim*. Bandung: Penerbit Mizan.
109 Bung Hatta stated that the economy of a country is determined by three things, namely land, the position towards other countries in the international environment, and the nature and skills of the people towards his ideals. Special for Indonesians, according to Bung Hatta, one thing must be added, that is the history of the Indonesian nation as a colony.
110 Sen, A. K. (June 1999). The Possibility of Social Choice. *American Economic Review*. Vol. 89, No. 3:. 349–378.
111 The figure above, according to Sen, was to put meaning on a social public choice. Public choice can show the majesty of the goal but can also be confusing because it is too accommodating in many different interests.
112 Mubyarto. (Mei 2011). Ekonomi Indonesia Terjajah Kembali. *Swara 33 eBulletin Mubins*. 001: 9–13. Mubyarto explained that many regions whose natural resources had been exploited by the central government or by foreign investors. This can be seen from the degree of absorption by comparing the value of the Gross Regional Domestic Product (GRDP) per capita with the consumption expenditure value per capita. If the value of GDP per capita is much higher than the consumption expenditure value per capita of the population, it means that locals do not enjoy most of its production. It means that part of the local production is indeed "sent" back to the owner or investor from outside the region. Mubyarto found that in 1996 "the degree of exploitation" of the most resource-rich provinces, namely NAD, Riau, East Kalimantan, and Papua (Irian Jaya), was very high, 81%, 84%, 89%, and 82%. This means that from every 100%-production value, the portion enjoyed by local residents is only 19% (NAD), 16% (Riau), 11% (East Kalimantan), and 18% (Papua), and the rest is enjoyed by outside investors. DKI Jakarta Province, which is the center of Indonesia's money circulation, has also been "sucked" by foreign investors, amounting to 78%, or only 22% enjoyed by DKI Jakarta residents.
113 Habibie, Bacharuddin Jusuf. (1997). "Pembangunan Sumber Daya Manusia Berorientasi Nilai Tambah," *Wawasan dan Visi Pembangunan Abad 21*, Editor M. Dawam Rahardjo. Jakarta: PT. Intermasa.

114 Swasono, S-E and Ridjal, F. (1992). *Mohammad Hatta, Demokrasi Kita, Bebas Aktif, Ekonomi Masa Depan*. Jakarta: UI Press: 143.

115 Mannan, M. A. (1970). *Islamic Economic: Theory and Practice*. Islamabad: Houder and Stoughton.

116 Siddiqi, M. N. (1996). *Role of the State in the Economy, an Islamic Perspective*. Leicester, UK: The Islamic Foundation.

117 Management of spoils of wars.

118 Sen, A. K. (1992). *Inequality Reexamined*. New York, Cambridge, MA: Russell Sage Foundation, Harvard University Press.

119 Zarqa, A. (2007). Islamic Economics: An Approach to Human Welfare. *Reading in the Concept and Methodology of Islamic Economics*. Kualalumpur, Malaysia: Cert Publication.

120 Amartya Kumar Sen used the language *freedom to achieve*.

121 The three levels referred to by Zarqa are *daruriyah* (primary/necessities), *hajiyah* (secondary/conveniences), and *tahsiniyah* (tertiary/refinements).

122 Choudhury, M. A. (1986). *Contributions to Islamic Economic Theory, a Study in Social Economics*. New York: St. Martin's Press.

123 In the Hadith, Arbain An-Nawawi explained that *ihsan* is making things become well. *Ihsan*'s nature varies according to the context of the conversation. In the context of worship, the essence of *ihsan* is as explained in the second hadith of the Hadith Arbain, which says: "Worship Allah as if you saw Him. However, if you cannot (worship as if you) saw Him, in fact He saw you" (Narrated by Muslim).

In the context of human relations (*muamalah*), the essence of *ihsan* is to fulfill the rights of each other and do not violate them. As the 17th hadith of the Hadith Arbain: From Abu Ya'la Syaddad bin Aus rodhiallohu 'anhu, Rasululloh sholallahu 'alaihi wa sallam once said, "Indeed Allah requires (you) to do good for everything, then if you want to kill people (in war or others), kill in a proper way, and if you slaughter (animals), then slaughter in a proper way, sharpen your knives and treat animals to gently slaughter" (Muslim).

124 Swasono, S-E. (2003). *Ekspose Ekonomika, Mewaspadai Globalisme dan Pasar Bebas*. Yogyakarta: Pusat Studi Ekonomi Pancasila (Pustep) UGM.

125 Swasono, S-E. (2002). Prospek dan Perkembangan Perekonomian Rakyat: Antara Kedaulatan Rakyat dan Kedaulatan Pasar. *Kedaulatan Rakyat Post*. Friday, August 2, 2002.

126 Sulistyono, A. (17 Nopember 2007). Pembangunan Hukum Ekonomi Untuk Mendukung Pencapaian Visi Indonesia 2030. *Pidato Pengukuhan Guru Besar Hukum Ekonomi Pada Fakultas Hukum Universitas Sebelas Maret Surakarta*. Surakarta: UNS.

127 Qardhawi, Y. (2004). *Darul Qiyam Wa al-Akhlak Fil Iqtishadil Islami*. Terjemahan Bahasa Indonesia. Jakarta: Robbani Press.

128 Akram mentioned that *'izz* has the meaning of strength, glory, and honor in world life. In the afterlife, *Izz* has the meaning of eternal glory without humiliation.

129 QS al-Munāfiqūn 63: 8.

130 QS ali-'Imrān 3: 110.

131 Swasono, S-E. (2003). *Ekspose Ekonomika, Mewaspadai Globalisme dan Pasar Bebas*. Yogyakarta: Pusat Studi Ekonomi Pancasila (Pustep) UGM.

2 *Falah* as Organizational Goal

Some youngsters drove Honda Jazz. When they entered the residential area, they had to pass a road full of speed bump. When looking at those obstacles, did they feel annoyed? On the other hand, did they spin the direction to avoid it?

"No!" They even decided. The atmosphere was cheerful. Audio in the car was playing. Fresh and cheerful music was heard. Their faces were sparkling! Just relax! Enjoy it! Then, when the car passed over the speed bump so that the car was shaken, their bodies also were jolted. The rhythm of the audio was in harmony with the shaken car. They could make the annoying atmosphere into a fresh atmosphere, a happy ambience. Why was that? Because they enjoyed the trip!

Falah vis a vis an Organizational Goal

To be happy is a dream for many. However, not everyone can feel happiness. Some people have food, drink, home, and clothing materials that have been fulfilled but are still not satisfied. This happens because the non-material needs in the form of peace of mind and recognition of social status are still not fulfilled.

Happiness experienced by materialistic and hedonistic people always refers to physical appearance, namely material wealth.[1] Therefore, happiness is full of lies and deceit. Lifestyle is built based on lies and not in accordance with human nature. Therefore, the happiness felt is a superficial happiness. It is a happiness which only appears from the outside. Of course, we often hear stress numbers, memory loss, and even mental illness in these societies.

Thus, how can we define that someone has happiness? The Tabi'in once asked Ibnu Abbas r.a., one of the companions of Rasulullah (*s.a.w.*) regarding the happiness of the world. Ibnu Abbas explained about seven indicators of worldly happiness, namely: a heart which is always grateful, a good life partner, a pious child, a conducive environment to maintain faith, halal wealth, a passion for understanding religion, and a blessed life.

Happiness that is *Kaffah* will never be felt by anyone preserving the pattern of life and culture of tyranny, as well as the pattern of life which is full of sin both personal and social life.[2] Happiness that is *Kaffah* is happiness built on these principles: a steady faith, personal communication with Allah (*s.w.t.*) through *solat khushu*, an efficient and effective lifestyle by keeping oneself

DOI: 10.4324/9781003390947-3

away from useless work and words, care and social responsibility by paying zakat and giving infaq and alms to the poor, maintaining a sexual relationship only with couple who is tied by legal marriage.

The real happiness, as explained in Qur'an, is good fortune[3] or success both material and non-material, and both dimensions of current life and the afterlife are called *Falah* (Chapra, 2007b).[4] The happiness concept included in the term *Falah* includes the physical, intellectual, emotional, spiritual, social, birth, inner, world, and hereafter dimensions. The peak of happiness can only be obtained through consistent struggles throughout life in the framework of the salvation of life (*Tazkiyatun-nafs*) from heathenism, polytheism, hypocrisy, ruthlessness, vile deeds, and great sins.[5]

> And it will be said to those who feared Allah (*s.w.t.*), "What did your Lord send down?" They will say, "[That which is] good." For those who do good in this world is good; and the home of the Hereafter is better. And how excellent is the home of the righteous.
>
> (QS an-Nahl 16: 30)

The Holy Qur'an does not directly mention the word *Falah*, but with various derivative words, namely *Muflihun*, *Tuflihun*, and *Falah*. The meaning contained in it is long-term fortune in the world and the hereafter.[6] *Falah* (Khan, 1994)[7] in Arabic comes from the word *falah*. The form of the verb is *Aflah, Yuflihu*, which means to flourish, to develop, to be happy, to have luck or success, to be successful. Meanwhile, according to Ibnu Manzūr,[8] epistemologically, *Falah* means *Al-fawzu wannajatu wal baqaw finna'imi wal khayri* or luck, salvation, and continuity in pleasure and kindness.

Rāghib al-Aṣfahānī[9] stated *Falah* as the concept of two worlds, namely the world and hereafter. In the life of the world, *Falah* describes by three things:

a *Baqa* (survival and continuity in goodness),
b *Ghana* (freedom in desire and wealth), and
c *'Izz* (strength, glory, and honour).

For the life in the hereafter, *Falah* includes four perceptions:

a *Baqa bila fana* (eternal survival or eternity without destruction),
b *Ghana bila faqr* (wealth without fidelity or eternal welfare),
c *'Izz bila dhul* (eternal glory without humiliation), and
d *'Ilm bila jahl* (eternal knowledge or free from all ignorance).

According to Khan, *Falah* has the meaning of developing, being happy, getting luck or success, and being full of success. *Falah* also has a multi-dimensional concept that will have implications for individual behaviour (micro level) and collective behaviour (macro level). The above statement explains that the purpose of human life is not only materialistic (worldly) but also spiritualistic (hereafter).

Table 2.1 Falah Elements of Individual Behaviour (Micro Level) and Collective Behaviour (Macro Level)

Falah *Elements*	*Micro Level*	*Macro Level*
Life sustainability	Biological survival: physical health, free from disease	Ecological balance, healthy environment, medical equipment availability for everyone
	Economic survival: ownership of production factors	Management of natural resources to generate employment opportunities for all residents
	Social survival: brotherhood and harmonious interpersonal relationships	Good social life, lack of conflict between different groups
	Political survival: freedom and participation in political relations	Independence and identity as a group
Freedom of desire	Reducing poverty	Provision of resources for the entire residents
	Independence of life: to work is better than being lazy like a parasite	Provision of resources for future generations
Strength and self-esteem	Pride	Economic strength and freedom from debt
	Freedom, protection towards honour and life	Military power

Source: Khan, M. A. (1994).

Falah Elements in Individual Behaviour and Collective Behaviour

The word *Falah* is very comprehensive. When one uses the term from Quranic perspective, it encompasses success in both the world – in this mundane life – and the hereafter life. The complete meaning of *Falah* as is meant by Khan is described in Table 2.1.

Al-Ghazali in Zidan (1997)[10] explained that the main purpose of all activities is happiness and success in the hereafter life. Therefore, all activities, including economic activities, should not only pursue something that is worldly but also consider reward in the hereafter. Al-Ghazali further warned businessmen and traders that in developing their businesses, they should not ignore the main objectives above. He stressed the importance of the factor "precision" in carrying out economic activities. If the intention is in line with *shari'ah*, then the activities of businessmen and traders will be equivalent to worship activity.

In fact, according to Al-Ghazali, there are three types of people related to economic activities:

a People who ignore the afterlife by indulging themselves on everything that is worldly, thus they will be destroyed.
b People who are in the worldly life always pursue the afterlife; thus, they will get success.
c People who follow the middle way, people who are in all activities of world life always follow the rules of *shari'ah*. They will be safe.

In line with the opinion of Al-Ghazali, Amin believes that organizational activities are management activities like human life. Humans have the characteristics of growing and developing. Starting with being born, humans grow into children, teens, and adults until they die. Like organizations' life cycle, organizations have a cycle of birth, growing to reach the maturity and harvest phase. Then the organization finally meets the end.

Organizations are not machines. They are living organisms. Organizations have the same characteristics and cycles like humans. Hence, organizations should be treated similar to human beings. This is what underlies the main purpose of the creation of an organization like the goal of human creation. Whereas the mission of creating organizations is the same as the mission of creating humans; therefore, the purpose of creating an organization is to reach the *Falah*. The mission of creating organization is to manifest the function of the *Caliphs* of Allah (*s.w.t.*) on earth, not others!

To be able to realize organizational goals, namely *Falah*, the organization must be able to meet needs in a balanced manner. A condition resulted from the fulfilment of needs called *Maslahah*. The referred balance is the balance of both material and non-material, short-term (world) as well as long-term goals (afterlife) which can increase human position as the noblest creation. So, it can be agreed that *Falah* is the goal of the organization and *Maslahah*[11] is an intermediary objective to develop the real purpose of human life.

There are four actions as elaborated below which need to be taken to reach *Falah*.[12]

- i Loving Allah (*s.w.t.*), which is an act to not only believe that Allah (*s.w.t.*) exists but also accompanied by the expression of *uluhiyah* – *rububiyah* and commitment. Attributes of Allah (*s.w.t.*) should be applied in organizational life. There is nothing in the organizational activity that does not refer to the attributes of Allah (*s.w.t.*).
- ii Having faith in Allah (*s.w.t.*) in all aspects of organizational activities. Starting from the process of planning, implementing, and monitoring until the level of actions. Starting from the marketing process, purchasing, production processes, and sales processes to the after-sales process.
- iii Worshiping Allah (*s.w.t.*). All activities are intended to worship Allah (*s.w.t.*), namely, to get closer to Allah (*s.w.t.*). Interactions with suppliers, partners, customers, employees, shareholders, and the environment should be in order to worship Allah (*s.w.t.*) as the Giver of *Rizq*.
- iv *Jihad* in the way of Allah (*s.w.t.*) in accordance with the provisions and rules of Allah (*s.w.t.*). Organizations are created, fostered, raised, nurtured, and developed as a medium for struggling in the way of Allah (*jihad*).

Summary

Falah is organizational goal. Therefore, organizational goals are not only related to materialistic (worldly) but also spiritualistic (hereafter), short-term (world) as well as long-term goals (life hereafter). This is a part of Islamic *Aqidah* and part of *Iman* for adherents' faith to be subscribed.

Notes

1 QS al-Wāqi'ah 56: 41–47.
2 QS al-An'ām 6: 21, 135; QS Yūsuf 12: 23; QS Yūnus 10: 17; QS al-Qaṣaṣ 28: 37.
3 QS Alī-'imrān 3: 104, 130; QS al-A'rāf 7: 8, 157; QS al-Tawbah 9: 88; QS al-Mu'minūn 23: 1, 102; QS al-Nūr 24: 51; QS al-Ḥashr 59: 9; QS al-Taghābun 64: 16; QS al-A'lā 87: 14; QS al-Shams 91: 9.
4 Chapra, M. Umer. (September 2007a). *The Islamic Vision of Development in the Light of Maqāsid Al-Sharī'ah*. Jeddah: Islamic Research and Training Institute Islamic Development Bank.
5 QS al-A'lā 87: 14–19.
6 QS al-'Imrān 3: 104, 130; QS al-A'rāf 7: 8, 157; QS al-Tawbah 9: 88; QS al-Mu'minūn 23: 1, 102; QS al-Nūr 24: 51; QS al-Ḥashr 59: 9; QS at-Taghābun 64: 16; QS al-A'lā 87: 14; QS al-Shams 91: 9.
7 Khan, M. A. (1994). *Introduction to Islamic Economics*. Islamabad, Pakistan: International Institute of Islamic Thought and Institute of Policy Studies.
8 As quoted by thematic interpretations of Jamāluddīn Abī al-Faḍl Muhammad bin Makram Ibnu Manzūr al-AnṣarīnṣarIfriqī al-MiṣrīiṣLisānul 'Arab, Beirut: Dārul Kutub al-'Ilmiyyah, 2003M/1424 H.
9 As quoted by Muhammad Akram Khan from Rāghib al-Isfahāni, al-Mufradāt fī Gharīb al-Quran, Karachi Noor Mohammad, Kārkhanah-i Tijārat-I Kutub.
10 Zidan, A. (1997). *Al-Ghazali's Ihya' Ulum al-Din, Revitalization of the Sciences of Religion*. Cairo, Egypt: Islamic Inc. for Publishing and Distribution.
11 In al-Quran, *Maslahah* is mentioned with many terms, *ẓalama* (doing *zalim*) QS 5: 39, *fasada* (damaging) as stated in QS al-Sha 'arā 26: 123; QS al-Naml 27: 142; QS al-Baqarah 2: 220; QS al-An'ām 6: 76; QS Ibrahīm 14: 5; QS al-Isrā 17: 28; QS al-Kahfi 18: 21; QS al-Naml 27: 55; QS al-Baqarah 2: 269; QS al-Nūr 24: 41; QS al-Dhāriyāt 51: 56; QS Hūd 11: 61.
12 Lajnah Pentashihan Mushaf al-Quran Badan Litbang dan Diklat Kementrian Agama RI. (2010b). *Tafsir al-Quran Tematik, Kitab Spiritualitas dan Akhlak*. Jakarta, Indonesia: Kemenag RI.

3 *Maslahah* as the Intermediary Organizational Objective

A complex of school buildings stands majestically in an area, magnificent and neatly arranged. The school building is equipped with various facilities like five star hotels. Large and sturdy walls cover the entire school area. The teachers are the best graduates in their field. Understandably, the owner of the school is a successful businessperson in various fields. This contrasts with the surrounding environment.

Nearby, many school buildings are almost collapsed. Supporting educational facilities available are lacking. There are dropout rates and high number of illiterate people. Under these conditions, is it appropriate that the first mentioned school is said to have provided *Maslahah* to the surrounding community?

The same thing happens in a mining area. Tons of mines have been extracted from the bottom of the earth. Mining companies exploit the area twenty-four hours nonstop. The holes and large caves of former excavation are visible throughout the mining area. The land around becomes barren. There is no more clean water available to residents around. The workers work passionately. When they are saturated and tired, they treat it with worldly entertainment. Liquor become a friend; prostitution mushroomed around the area. Social diseases also hit the surrounding community. The poverty and ignorance that befell the community is in stark contrast to the lives of the connoisseurs of mining products. What a contrasting phenomenon, where poverty and ignorance occur in area with abundant natural resources. Why is the *Maslahah* so difficult to realize?

Three Levels of *Maslahah*

Al-Shāṭibi divided *Maslahah* into three levels, namely *Daruriyah* (necessities), *Hajiyah* (needs), and *Tahsiniyah* (complementary/wants).[1]

Daruriyah

Daruriyah is a basic or primary requirement. The basic elements in human life that must absolutely be fulfilled to realize happiness in both the current life in this world and in the after life. *Maslahah daruriyah* includes the maintenance

DOI: 10.4324/9781003390947-4

of five things: religion (*al-Din*), life (*al-nafs*), intellect (*al-'aql*), descent (*al-nasl*), and wealth (*al-mal*).

If one of the primary needs is not fulfilled, imbalance will happen. This situation can lead to destruction in the worldly life, which results in the loss of salvation and mercy in the afterlife. Fulfilment of *Maslahah daruriyah* can be conducted by two approaches. The first is implementation from *al-Wujūd* point of view, which means strengthening existence or being positive. The second is *al-'adam* approach or guarding against things that can damage or frustrate. *Al-'adam* is preventive. Activities included in the *al-wujūd* group is like ritual worship, customs (traditions, habits), and *muamalat* (commerce) while the activities included in the *al-'adam* group are implementing criminal laws (*Jinayat*).

In management language, the al wujūd approach is corrective action and al'adam is preventive action.

The example of the fulfilment of basic *Maslahah* or *Maslahah daruriyah* through *al-wujūd* approach is the maintenance of religion by performing *Solat*, *Zakat*, fasting, and hajj. Meeting the needs of life is by fulfilling basic needs such as clothing, food, and shelter. Fulfilling the needs for offspring protection is done through the fulfilment of good education for our children so that they can become pious. Protecting wealth is by working to obtain property properly and lawfully. Fulfilment of the intellectual protection is through pursuing knowledge gained from training and education.

As for the example of fulfilling basic *Maslahah* or *Maslahah daruriyah* with the *al-'adam* approach is to imply the law of *Jinayat*.[2] Al-Shāṭibi defined *Jinayat* as anything that concerns five components of basic *Maslahah*, which is done preventively. In this case, *Jinayat* is intended to avoid or prevent criminal acts not solely to carry out punishments through hand cutting or caning, etc.

Maslahah daruriyah is intermediary values that have the purpose of maintaining a good life for humans, both as individual beings and as part of the community. The good life can only be achieved if the five basic things (*Daruriyah*) can be fulfilled.

Hajiyah

Hajiyah is a secondary need whose existence is needed to eliminate difficulties or to better achieve the fulfilment of the five primary needs. This is needed to ease human life. If this does not exist, it will only result in difficulties in living life but does not result in destruction as well as the absence of *Daruriyah*. *Hajiyah* applies to worship, customs, or traditions, *Mu'amalah* and *Jinayat*.

Some examples of *Hajiyah* related to worship activity is like the implementation of performing *Solat* and fasting for people who are sick or on a journey or *Musafir*. If there is no dispensation for people who are sick or traveling, then it will certainly cause difficulties in performing *Solat* and fasting. As for the example of *Hajiyah* in terms of customs, it is permissible to hunt or have fun through entertainment if these activities are carried out within the limits of halal. As for the example of *Hajiyah* in *Muamalah* context, it is like to have vehicles, land, buildings, and others. Another example of *Hajiyah* in muamalah activity is *Qiraḍ*[3] transaction, Al-Shāṭibi stated that all types of *Mu'amalah* that do not include in *Daruriyah* can be grouped in *Hajiyah*.

Tahsiniyah

Tahsiniyah is a tertiary need that should exist due to the demands of courtesy and customs. The existence of *Tahsiniyah* is intended so that humans can do their best towards improvement in the context of maintaining the five basic needs. The absence of *Tahsiniyah* will have an impact on decency or impropriety. However, the absence of *Tahsiniyah* will not cause damage to *Daruriyah*. An example of *Tahsiniyah* is covering the nakedness in worship and staying away from unclean food and drinks.

Every level of *Tahsiniyah* must fulfil the requirement in which they cannot cancel the original law. This is because, as a complement, *Tahsiniyah* will be cancelled in the absence of the original law. On this basis, there are two provisions:

i If the original law is aborted, then the law of *Tahsiniyah* is invalid. This condition can occur as *Tahsiniyah* is like a trait attached to something. If something does not exist, then the attributes are missing as well.
ii If there is a conflict between *Maslahah daruriyah* and *Maslahah tahsiniyah*, then even though *Maslahah tahsiniyah* can be realized with the absence of *Maslahah daruriyah*, but *Maslahah daruriyah* still takes precedence. In other situations, *Maslahah tahsiniyah* can take precedence as long as *Maslahah daruriyah* is valid. For instance, the origin law of sale and purchase is *Daruriyah*, while the prohibition of *Gharar* (obscurity) in buying and selling is *Maslahah tahsiniyah*.

If we are faced with two choices, then choosing *Daruriyah* is prioritized, for example, when we worship in a congregation position. At that time, when we know that the imam is a *Fajir* (often involved in sin), we should continue to pray in congregation because the existence of a righteous imam for prayer is complementary (*Maslahah tahsiniyah*). We should not leave the congregation prayer because the imam is *Fajir*. Doing congregation is part of the Islamic religion, which is highly recommended. Here the provisions apply that the origin *Maslahah* will not be cancelled due to the absence of a complementary *Maslahah*.

Al-Shāṭibi explained that the three levels of *Maslahah* namely *Daruriyah*, *Hajiyah*, and *Tahsiniyah* apply in sequence. It means that if there is a case of contrasting *Daruriyah* and *Hajiyah* or *Tahsiniyah*, then *Daruriyah* is prioritized. Other example is in the implementation of prayer, if we cannot close the *Aurat*, then the prayer must still be conducted and may not be aborted just because we cannot close the *Aurat*.

But under normal conditions, *Maslahah* level is complementary, *Tahsiniyah* completes *Hajiyah*, then completes *Daruriyah*. Al-Shātibi also explained that

Daruriyah is the basis for *Hajiyah* and *Tahsiniyah*. When *Daruriyah* is absent, the others are cancelled, but this does not apply in the opposite direction. However, sometimes the absence of *Hajiyah* and *Tahsiniyah* can absolutely affect the quality of *Daruriyah*. Hence, *Hajiyah* and *Tahsiniyah* need to be maintained to protect *Daruriyah*.

In short, the relationship between the three *Maslahah* is explained as below:

- i *Maslahah daruriyah* is the origin or basis of all *Maslahah* level.
- ii The absence of *Maslahah daruriyah* has an impact on the absence of *Maslahah hajiyah* and *Tahsiniyah* completely.
- iii The absence of *Maslahah hajiyah* and *Tahsiniyah* does not necessarily have an impact on the absence of *Maslahah daruriyah*.
- iv However, sometimes the absence of *Maslahah hajiyah* and *Tahsiniyah* has an impact on the absence of *Maslahah daruriyah*.
- v Maintaining *Maslahah hajiyah* and *Tahsiniyah* is necessary for preserving *Maslahah daruriyah*.

The discussion about *Maslahah* finally gives an explanation that *Maslahah* has two meanings. *Maslahah* etymologically refers to the purpose of fulfilling human needs, whereas *Maslahah* in the sense of *Shari'ah* is something that becomes the starting point of reference or the purpose of creating *Shari'ah (Maqasid al-shari'ah)*. The purpose of establishing a *Shari'ah* is to preserve or to protect religion, life, intellect, descendent, and wealth.

It can be said that *Maslahah* is something considered as good or in line with *Shari'ah* because it brings goodness and avoids evil or damage for both the worldly life and the afterlife, both physical and spiritual, tangible (life, descendants, and wealth) or intangible (religion, intellect), for all humanity both as individuals and as members of society and carried out in order to protect or maintain religion, life, intellect, descendent and wealth.

For instance, it is forbidden to control the wealth of others by *Baṭil* means such as stealing or corruption. The prohibition, according to common sense, contains the goodness of protecting damage to the mental or life, intellect, and descendants. This prohibition is in line with the purpose of *Shari'ah*, which is protecting the rights of others in the form of maintaining their wealth. Even this prohibition is issued because the act of seizing other person's wealth illegally will be harmful not only to the wealth owner but also to the perpetrator, his family, and his descendants and will even have an impact on society.

The Character and Level of *Maslahah Daruriyah*

Al-Ghāzali in Nyazee (2003)[4] divided the aim of *Shari'ah* into two interests, namely for the worldly life for the benefit of the afterlife. Between these two interests, prioritizing the purpose of life in the hereafter is the main goal of *Shari'ah*. This means that the purpose of life in the hereafter has a higher priority than the purpose of life in the world.

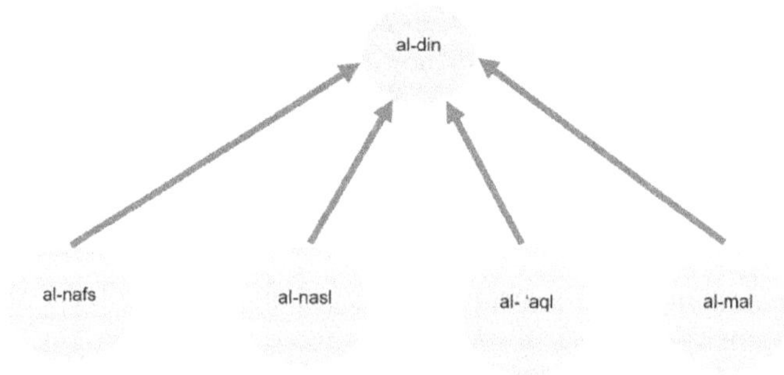

Figure 3.1 The Relation of Interests in Fulfilling Basic Needs.
Source: Nyazee (2003)

Al-Ghāzali also stated that the main goal of *Shari'ah* in the current life is to maintain and nurture *al-Din* (religion). Therefore, in fulfilling the basic needs of life (*al-nafs*), intellect (*al-'aql*), descent (*al-nasl*), and wealth (*al-mal*), humans must prioritize religious needs (*al-din*). Nyazee described the importance of relationship from fulfilling basic human needs in Figure 3.1.

Regarding the priority order for fulfilling basic needs, Nyazee stated that fulfillment towards religious needs (*al-din*) has a higher priority than life (*al-nafs*). Fulfillment towards the needs of the life (*al-nafs*) has a higher priority than the descendant (*al-nasl*). Fulfillment of the need for descendant (*al-nasl*) has a higher priority than the intellect *(al-'aql*). Fulfillment of intellectual needs *(al-'aql*) has a higher right or priority than wealth (*al-mal*). Nyazee described the level of individual rights/priorities with the description as shown in Figure 3.2.

In line with Al-Ghāzali and Nyazee, Ahmad (2008)[5] said that religious and self *Maslahah* are preferred to the wealth-related *Mafsadah*. For instance, we

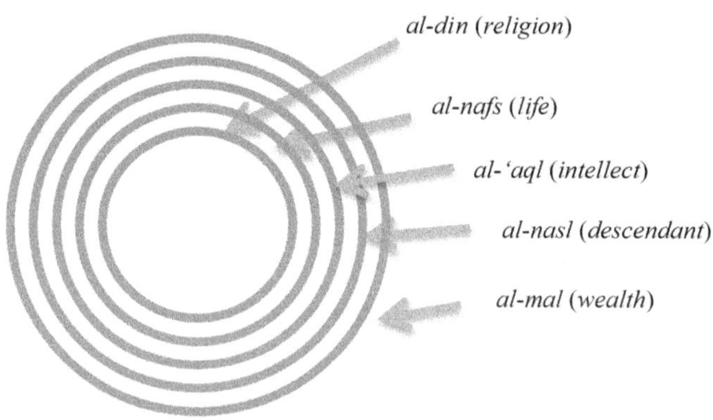

Figure 3.2 Individual Priority Levels.
Source: Nyazee (2003: 23)

are allowed to give ransom to the enemy to free the captured Muslim army if there is no other way to free them. Although giving money to the enemy will bring *Mafsadah* of losing wealth and it can also strengthen the enemy's economy, that will release the Muslim army, and it will prevent the suffering of the Muslim army from the evil treatment from the enemy and even prevent the loss of the lives of Muslim soldiers. The return of the captive Muslim army can also add to the strength of Islam.

Regarding to the order of *Maslahah* fulfilment priorities, there are differences of views by many experts who discuss *Maqasid-al-shari'ah.* Chapra (2007a),[6] said: between Al-Shāṭibi and Al-Ghāzali also have differences in sorting five basic needs. Al-Shāṭibi wrote in the same order as Al-Ghāzali on page 38 of Vol.1 (al- Muwāfaqāt fī Usūl al-Sharī'ah, Cairo: al-Maktabah al-Tijariyyah al-Kubrā. n.d.). However, on page 46-7 of Vol.3 the order of the priority fulfilment written is al-din, al-nafs, al-nasl, al-māl, and al-'aql, Even Fakhr al-din al-Rāzi (d.606/1209), hundreds of years after Al-Ghāzali, set the priority order for fulfilling basic needs by placing al-nafs in the first place.

The experts wrote the order of basic needs fulfilment according to the objectives of the discussion that is being agreed upon. Therefore, the order can be changed following the purpose of discussion at that time. Chapra sorted the order of five basic needs as: al-nafs, al-din, al-'aql, al-nasl and al-māl. Beside the sequence of the basic needs, the interrelationship between needs is still discussed by experts, whether there is causality, or each need is stand-alone.

Related to the position of descent *Maslahah* compared to the wealth *Mafsadah,* Ahmad (2008) stated that descent *Maslahah* is higher than the wealth *Mafsadah.* For instance, giving money to bad man who is about to commit adultery or rape a woman. If there is no other way, then the act of providing ransom, in this case, is not the same with paying a wage to the criminal but defending descent *Maslahah* is more important than the wealth *Mafsadah.* Loss of wealth is a *Mafsadah,* but loss of *maruah* and descent is irreplaceable.

Indeed, the levels of priorities above are human rights as individuals, whereas humans are social creatures. Of course, according to Al-Ghāzali, the level of social rights or priority is higher than the individuals. Above all, Allah's rights or priorities as the Creator are higher than the people's rights or priorities.

The three levels of *Maslahah* are sourced from al-Quran and hadith. Al-Allaf (2003) proposed the orbital model of *Maqasid,* which depict the relationship between al-Quran and hadith as the source with *Maslahah* as the orbit of *Maslahah. Maslahah daruriyah, Maslahah hajiyah,* and *Maslahah tahsiniyah* circulate around the Quran and hadith as the center of the circulation (Figure 3.3).

The Preservation of Religion (al-din)

Embracing religion is a basic right or human right, or in other terms, it can be said that embracing religion is a natural tendency and an instinct from birth. Therefore, freedom in religion or belief must be preserved and maintained.

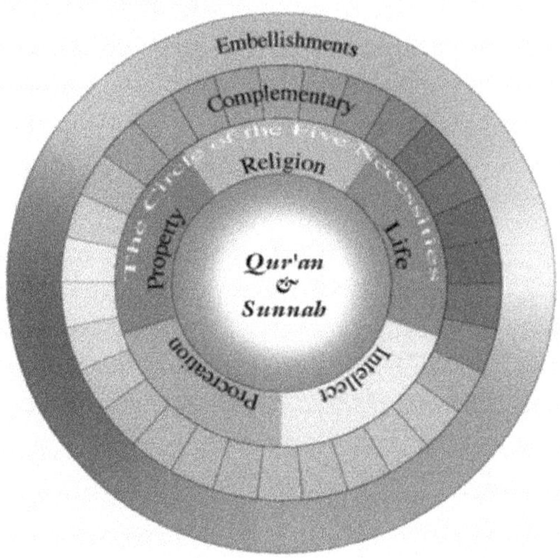

Figure 3.3 Al-Allaf *Maqasid* Model.

Source: Al-Allaf (2003: 85)

The obligation to respect human rights is reflected in the Preamble of the 1945 Constitution, which inspires the whole article in the body of Constitution, especially with regard to the equality of citizens before the law and government, the right for getting decent work and livelihood, freedom to associate and to assemble, the right to express opinion both oral and written, freedom to choose and to practice religion, as well as the right to obtain education.

Universal Declaration of Human Rights Article 18[7] states that everyone has the right to freedom of thought, conscience, and religion. This right includes freedom to change his religion or belief, and freedom, either alone or in community with others and in public or private.

Law Number 39 year 1999[8] concerning Human Rights at the General Explanation section I states that the freedom of each person is limited by the human rights of others. It means that everyone has an obligation to recognize and respect the human rights of others. Obligations also apply to every organization at any level, especially the state and government. States and governments are responsible for respecting, protecting, defending, and guaranteeing the human rights of every citizen and society without discrimination.

The Qur'an explains that there must be no coercion in embracing religion.[9] In the thematic interpretation of the Ministry of Religion,[10] it is stated that Allah (*s.w.t.*) uses the word *al-Rushd*, which means intelligence and maturity, not *al-hūda*, or *al-haq,* with the intention that although embracing religion is someone's freedom, he tends to embrace the right religion if he has a pure level of intelligence and high maturity.

Amirul mukminin Umar bin Khaṭṭab once made a treaty letter to the residents of Eliya (*al-Quds*), which contained guarantees for the protection of religious freedom as well as the freedom of their places of worship and *Syiar.* Jauhar explained that this is the protection given by the servant of Allah (*s.w.t.*), Umar Amirul Mukminin to the inhabitants of Eliya. He provided safety guarantees for their life, wealth, church, monks, and religion. Their church is not inhabited, broken down, and reduced or narrowed. They were also not forced into religious matters. The various descriptions above explain to all of us that freedom in embracing a particular religion is a basic human right that cannot be intercepted by others.

In fulfilling religious needs, Allah (*s.w.t.*) has instructed the religion protection that must be maintained by everyone.[11] The preservation of religion aims to protect and maintain human dignity as a creature of God whose dignity is higher than creatures of God. Religion is the thing that engages the conscience of a creature compared to other creatures.

Safeguarding religion does not only mean guarding religion against compulsion from people who dislike the religion we hold firm but also guarding religion against the impulses of worldly lust. Zaharah (1958)[12] uses the term *al-muḥāfizatu 'alā al-din* or guarantees of religious safety carried out by avoiding the emergence of slander and salvation in religion and anticipating the impulses of lust and actions that lead to full damage. Rasulullah (*s.a.w.*) also reminded all of us to preserve the religion we have by restraining lust in the form of competing for worldly treasures.

From 'Amr bin 'Auf al-Anshari r.a. that Rasulullah (*s.a.w.*) sent Abu 'Ubaidah al-Jarrah r.a. to the Bahrain area – an area that belonged to Iraq. His arrival there is to take taxes. After completing his assignment, he arrived with (bringing) assets from Bahrain. The Anshar heard of the arrival of Abu Ubaidah, and they then performed the Fajr *Solat* – subuh – with Rasulullah (*s.a.w.*).

After Rasulullah (*s.a.w.*) prayed, he returned, then they went to meet him. *Rasulullah* (*s.a.w.*) then smiled when he saw them. "I think you all have heard that Abu Ubaidah arrived from Bahrain with something in his possession." They replied: "Yes, Rasulullah." He then said: "Rejoice, all you and may you expect something that will please you. In God's name, it is not the paganism that I fear from you all, but I fear that the wealth of the world will be extended to you all – that you all become rich, which has been expanded to those who were before you, then you are competing with each other to look for them as they were also competing to pursue them, then the treasures of the world will destroy your religion as it has corrupted their religion" (Muttafaq 'alaih).

Al-Shāṭibi explained that the action that must be taken to protect religion is by creating conditions that facilitate worship and by carrying out the worship itself, which is through *al-wujūd* approaches such as practicing *Shahadat, Solat, Zakat*, fasting, and *Hajj*.[13] Furthermore, it also can be done with *al-'Adam* approach, that is, *Jihad* in Allah's way.[14]

The implementation of worship in a person will have an impact on moral ethics in his everyday life. Nata (2008) argues that if a person has a strong faith and performs worship with sincerity and solemnity, then that person will ideally be ethical or virtuous. A servant who has belief in the existence of Allah (*s.w.t.*) with all His perfect qualities feels the full assurance that Allah (*s.w.t.*) only approves good things. Allah (*s.w.t.*) knows everything that has or is being done or what will be done by His servants. Nothing can escape from Allah's vision and knowledge. Humans are not alone because Allah (*s.w.t.*) stay by his servants' side forever and sees what His servants are doing.

The Preservation of the Life (al-Nafs)

The soul is created by God and is incorporated into the body at birth, taken from the body when death and reassembled with the body on the day of vengeance (Mc Auliffe, 2006). "Soul" as intended, in Arabic has two words interchangeably, namely *Ruh* (meaning breath, spirit) and *Nafs,* which means self. The word *Ruh* in the Qur'an is mentioned 21 times, always in the form of a single noun. *Ruh* often refers to the spirit of revelation sent by God to His prophet.[15] *Ruh* also refers to the Angel *Jibril,* who revealed revelations to His prophet.[16] *Ruh* can mean the breath of life.[17] It is only Allah (*s.w.t.*) Who Knows the true meaning of the *Ruh* itself.[18]

The word *al-Nafs* is derived from the words air, breath, and life. The word *al-Nafs* means breathing. In the Qur'an, the word *Nafs* is also written as *Nafs*, *Anfus*, and *Nufus*, which are repeated 250 times in the Qur'an. *Al-Nafs* (self)[19] refers to humans, genie, and devil, and also God.[20] The meaning contained in the word *al-Nafs* (self) is not something that is spiritual but reflects human character or behaviour such as egoism or selfishness,[21] personal responsibility, and conscience. *Nafs* (self) also has a more general meaning, which is related to human life.[22] On the other hand, *Nafs* has the meaning of humanity itself.[23]

Jauhar (2009) used the term life to refer to the soul. In the process of someone's death, the soul will leave the human body.[24] There are fundamental differences between death and murder. Jauhar argued that death is the process of the release of life from the human body where the structure of the human body is in a healthy or perfect condition. Only Allah (*s.w.t.*) can turn it off. As for the process of murder, there were cases of destructing the structure of the human body carried out by the killer against the victim. Someone who dies has his life removed from the human body. Humans can live because they have a life and humans die when the life is removed from his body.

When talking about the protection of life, it cannot be separated from one's right to live, where the right to life is a human right. To preserve and maintain the right to life, Allah (*s.w.t.*) has given various laws such as *Qisas*[25] or balanced retribution (QS al-Baqarah 2: 178, 179). In verse 179, it is explained that in the *Qisas* law, there is a system of guarantee of survival for humankind. The existence of the *Qisas* law causes people to feel afraid to kill. It can be said that the law of *Qisas* is a system of prevention in a legal system. The end of the enforcement of this law is when we all become virtuous people.

Zaharah (1958)[26] used the term *al-Muhafizatu 'alā al-Nafs* or guarantee of salvation, namely the guarantee of safety for the right of life that is honourable and noble. Included in life safety guarantees are guaranteed safety of life, limbs and guaranteed human dignity such as freedom of choice, freedom of thought or opinion, freedom of speech, and freedom to choose a place to live.

Al-Shāṭibi mentioned that the needs of life can be guaranteed by creating conditions for survival, namely through the *al-Wujūd* approach that is carried out by fulfilling the needs of food with nutritious food, maintaining health, clothing needs, and the needs of the housing. It can also be achieved with the *al-'Adam* approach, namely by the enactment of various Islamic laws known as *Jinayat* law such as *Qisas, Diyat, Had*, and *Ta'zir.*

The Preservation of Descendants **(al-Nasl)**

Islam strongly emphasizes the preservation of descendants. QS al-Nisa 4: 9[27] states that as parents, we should feel worried about the weakness of our children after our death. This worry feeling should also be a manifestation of our responsibility that has been given a mandate by Allah (*s.w.t.*) to protect, care for and nurture our children. Therefore, we must fight for the preservation of our descendants.

Zaharah (1958)[28] used the terms *al-Muhafizatu 'ala al-nasl* or guarantee of descent or family safety, namely the guarantee of the preservation of the human population to stay alive and grow healthily and sturdy, both in character and religion. This can be done through structuring household life by providing education and affection to children to have a righteous character and an adequate level of intelligence.

Al-Shātibi stated that the needs of descendants are supported by facilitating and carrying out family life through the *al-Wujūd* approach by maintaining family mental health and through the institution of marriage with the aim of producing next generation. It can also be done with the *al-'adam* approach, namely with enforcing various laws such as marriage law,[29] stipulating whom are prohibited to get married to,[30] regulating divorce procedures,[31] prohibiting adultery,[32] and enforcing *Had* law in the form of whip law[33] or regulating the issue of adopted children in order to protect *Nasab* or descendants.

The Preservation of Intellect **(al-'Aql)**

The intellect is a gift from Allah (*s.w.t.*) to humans, which functions as a differentiator from other creatures of Allah (*s.w.t.*). This privilege also makes humans have advantages than others.[34] Intellect is a source of wisdom, lanterns in the darkness, priceless resources, the gate of *Ma'rifat*, the determinant to improving something that is not good to the better, and the media to happiness both in the world and in the hereafter.

Jauhar said that intellect is called *'Aql* as it can bind and prevent its owner from doing bad things and doing immorality. It is named so since intellect resembles the bond of a camel. A bond will prevent humans from obeying the lust that is out of control. It is like a bond that can prevent the camel from escaping.

The high value and existence of intellect are mentioned in the Qur'an. Among them, it is mentioned that intelligent people are people who always remember and pay attention to Allah's creatures. Intellect is created by Allah (*s.w.t.*) with the aim of filtering the good and then carrying out what Allah (*s.w.t.*) has commanded.[35] Intellect is used to study from history and take a lesson from that.[36] People who use their intellect as well as their functions, they are classified as believers.[37] On the other hand, the Qur'an explains that those who do not use their intellects have a low value of human dignity.[38]

Zaharah (1958)[39] used the term *al-Muhafizatu 'ala al-'aql* or intellect safety guarantee to explain the assurance of the intellect from damage that causes people to become useless in society or a source of evil. Prevention efforts carried out by *Islamic Shari'ah* are intended to enhance intellectual ability and keep it from things that can endanger it. An example is the prohibition of liquor or all intoxicating consumption to prevent damage to the intellect.

Protecting and preserving the intellect can be done by keeping the intellect itself from disasters that can weaken and damage it or cause the owner to be the criminal and scumbag in the community.

According to Al-Shāṭibi, intellect needs are guarded through intellectual growth, namely through the approach of *al-Wujūd* by demanding knowledge. Whereas the actions taken through the *al-'Adam* approach is the prohibition of drinking liquor[40] which can damage intellectuality.

Why is liquor prohibited? Jauhar said that *Sukr* or getting drunk is the unconsciousness because of consuming *Khamr* or the like. Getting drunk means to block the intellect from functioning well but not to the degree of eliminating it. In contrast, it leads to a crazy condition that eliminates reasoning. Getting drunk is a condition of loss of logical sense or ability to reason at any given time caused by the influence of the use of an intoxicating liquid or alike.

The Preservation of Wealth (al-Mal)

Essentially, the earth[41] and the contents in it, even the whole universe belong to Allah (*s.w.t.*).[42] Allah (*s.w.t.*) then delegated His authority to humans and made humans as caliphs on earth.[43] Humans are commanded by Allah (*s.w.t.*) to guard the earth and are given the right to manage it.[44] Humans are allowed to do anything except those forbidden by Allah (*s.w.t.*). The status of property rights management is solely an entrusted commodity.

The default wealth owner is Allah (*s.w.t.*). Allah (*s.w.t.*) lends it to the people He wants. Allah (*s.w.t.*) set a standard of operation on how to obtain and how to use wealth through the Qur'an and Hadith (*Shari'ah*). If the method of obtaining or using it is not in accordance with the rules given by Allah (*s.w.t.*), then Allah (*s.w.t.*) has the right to withdraw all the wealth entrusted anytime. On the other hand, if the way to get and to use wealth is in accordance with the standard of operation, then Allah (*s.w.t.*) will add the amount. If Allah (*s.w.t.*) blesses what that person does, then Allah (*s.w.t.*) will give him the bonus of using wealth. The bonus given by Allah (*s.w.t.*) is not only given when the holder of the right to use life in the world, but Allah (*s.w.t.*) multiplies the bonus in the afterlife. The bonus given could be in multiplied amount compared to the number of wealth entrusted. It can be said that Allah (*s.w.t.*) gives down payment of wealth usage to holders of utilization rights in the world, whereas Allah (*s.w.t.*) will give the total payment in the hereafter, *Subhanallah*.

The viewpoint of wealth utilization is not only for worldly purposes but also for the hereafter, as stated in QS al-Ankabut 29: 64. The authority of Allah (*s.w.t.*) to take, add and reduce wealth entrusted to humans will depend on the blessing of the wealth entrusted. The more the blessings, the bigger the amount of wealth given to humans. This means that rights to wealth management are merely trustworthy, so it must be accountable to Allah (*s.w.t.*) later.

The action that must be taken to maintain the preservation of wealth, according to Zaharah (1958)[45] is to use the term *al-Muhḥafizatu 'ala al-mal* or guarantee of wealth security by increasing wealth proportionally through halal means rather than dominating economic life in an unjust manner and cheating.

Al-Shāṭibi stated that the needs of wealth are maintained through the creation of conditions that support the growth of assets, namely through the approach of *al-Wujūd* by good and lawful ways of working to obtain wealth. While the actions taken through the *al-'Adam* approach is by enacting various laws such as the law of cutting hands for robber,[46] prohibition to eat each other's wealth in a way that is unlawful,[47] the obligation to pay *Infaq* from the wealth obtained because it contains rights of other people who cannot afford to gain wealth,[48] prohibition of usury,[49] the obligation to pay debt,[50] etc.

Summary

Three levels of *Maslahah* are *Daruriyah, Hajiyah, Tahsiniyah*. The level of *Maslahah daruriyah*: the preservation of religion (*al-Din*), the preservation of life (*al-Nafs*), the preservation of descendants (*al-Nasl*), the preservation of intellect (*al-'Aql*), and the preservation of wealth (al-Mal) are considered the higher level of objectives defined as *Maqasid Shari'ah* in Islam.

Notes

1 Al-Shāṭibi describes the concept of *Maslahah* in a book entitled *al-Muwāfaqātu fi Uṣul al-shari'ah*. This book consists of four books. Of the four books, the concept of the level of *Maslahah* is elaborated very detailed in the second book.

2 That is a law related to the form of criminal acts like murder, adultery, accusing *zina*, theft, drunkenness, and other acts of crime. Islam has *Jinayat* law like *Qisas, Diyat, Had,* and *Ta'zir*. *Qisas* is a punishment given to the criminal in which the type of sentence is the same as the type of act committed, like death sentence as a punishment for the murderer. *Diyat* (blood ransom) is a punishment in the form of compensation for the murdered family in the form of blood money (*Diyat*) that must be paid by the *Aqilah* (father's/ brother's) of the accused. In these cases, *Qisas* and *Diyat* are set to protect life. *Had* is a punishment for a criminal act whose type of sentence has been determined in the texts of the Qur'an and hadith. *Had* against the prohibition of

liquor is made to protect the intellect. *Had* for forbidding *Zina* is made to protect *Nasab* or descendants. *Ta'zir* is an educative punishment that is determined by a judge; or a sinful act whose sentence has not been determined by the Qur'an and hadith.

3 Provision of capital from someone to another person to be used as business capital and profits divided between them in accordance with the agreement. Islam allows *Qiraḍ* with a foundation for cooperation and help, as in QS al-Māidah, 5: 2, "And cooperate in righteousness and piety, but do not cooperate in sin and aggression. And fear Allah; indeed, Allah is severe in penalty."

4 Nyazee, Imran Ahsan Khan. (2003). *Islamic Jurisprudence.* Selangor, Malaysia: The Other Press 607 Mutiara Majestic.

5 Ahmad, Ridzwan. (2008). Metode Pentarjihan *Maslahah* dan *Mafsadah* Dalam Hukum Islam Semasa. *Shariah Journal.* Vol. 16, No. 1: 107–143.

6 Chapra, M. Umer. (2007b). *Islam and Economic Development.* New Delhi: Adam Publishers & Distributors.

7 The Universal Declaration of Human Rights announced by the UN General Assembly on 10 December 1948 through resolution 217 A (III) in Article 18, states that everyone has the right to freedom of intellect, conscience, and religion; in this case, including the freedom to change religion or belief, with the freedom to express religion or belief by teaching it, doing it, worshiping and obeying it, both alone and together with others, both publicly and individually.

8 Article 22 of Law Number 39 of 1999 also stated that (1) Everyone has the freedom to embrace his own religion and to worship according to his religion and belief. (2) The state guarantees the freedom of each person to embrace their respective religion and to worship according to their religion and belief.

9 QS al-Baqarah 2: 256, "There shall be no compulsion in [acceptance of] the religion. The right course has become clear from the wrong. So, whoever disbelieves in Taghut and believes in Allah has grasped the most trustworthy handhold with no break in it. And Allah is Hearing and Knowing."

10 Lajnah Pentashihan Mushaf al-Quran Badan Litbang dan Diklat Kementrian Agama. (2010a). *Tafsir Tematik, Hukum, Keadilan, dan Hak Asasi Manusia*, 5 (2010).

11 QS al-Asūrā 42: 13, "He has ordained for you of religion what He enjoined upon Noah and that which We have revealed to you, [O Muhammad], and what We enjoined upon Abraham and Moses and Jesus - to establish the religion and not be divided therein. Difficult for those who associate others with Allah is that to which you invite them. Allah chooses for Himself whom He wills and guides to Himself whoever turns back [to Him]."

12 Abu Zaharah, Muhammad. (1958). *Usul al-Fiqh.* Cairo: Dar al-Fikr al-Arabi.

13 The worship meant by al-Shātibi is worship in a special sense. Abuddin Nata in the "Thematic Study of the Holy Quran concerning *Fiqh* of Worship" mentions that worship epistemologically is all activities whose provisions have been determined by the Holy Quran and as *Sunnah.* All the worship has been perfectly arranged by the Holy Quran and hadith. The worship ritual activity cannot allow no changes, additions, or deductions. The basic principle applies in worship is that all acts of worship are forbidden and illegitimate except those that have been regulated and stipulated by *Nash.*

14 QS al-Hāj 22: 78.

15 QS al-Mu'min 40: 15, QS al-Nahl 16: 2.

16 QS al-Ma 'ārij 70: 4, QS al-Qodr 97: 4.

17 QS al-Sajadah 32: 9, QS al-Hijr 15: 29, QS Shōd 38: 72.

18 QS al-Isrō 17: 85.

19 QS Alī-imrōn 3: 61.

20 QS al-An 'ām 6: 12, 130, QS al-Kahfi 18: 51, QS al-Anbiyā 21: 43.

21 QS al-Isrā 17: 25, QS Yūnus 10: 108, QS Alī-imrān 3: 117.

22 QS al-Qasaṣ 28: 33, QS al-Anbiyā 17: 33, QS al-Kahfi 18: 74, QS al-Furqān 25: 68, QS al-Māidah 5: 45, QS al-Sāf 61: 11, QS al-Taubah 9: 20, 41, 44, 81, 88.

23 QS al-Mudaṣir 74: 38, QS al-Mu'minūn 23: 62, QS al-Infitār 82: 3.
24 The verses in the Qur'an that define life with *ruh* included in QS al-Zumar 39: 42, QS al-Mā'idah 5:45.
25 QS al-Baqarah 2: 178, 179, "O you who have believed, prescribed for you is legal retribution for those murdered - the free for the free, the slave for the slave, and the female for the female. But whoever overlooks from his brother anything, then there should be a suitable follow-up and payment to him with good conduct. This is an alleviation from your Lord and a mercy. But whoever transgresses after that will have a painful punishment" (178). "And there is for you in legal retribution [saving of] life, O you [people] of understanding, that you may become righteous" (179).
26 Abu Zahara, Muhammad. (1958). *Usul al-Fiqh*. Cairo: Dar al-Fikr al-Arabi.
27 "And God fear those who leave behind them weak children, whom they fear for. Therefore, let them fear God and let them say the right words."
28 Abu Zahara, Muhammad. (1958). *Usul al-Fiqh*. Cairo: Dar al-Fikr al-Arabi.
29 QS al-Nisā 4: 3–4.
30 QS al-Nisā 4: 22–24, QS al-Baqarah 2: 221.
31 QS ath-Thalāq 65: 1–7, QS al-Baqarah 2: 226–237, QS al-Ahzāb 33: 49.
32 QS al-Nūr 24: 30–31, QS al-Isrā 17: 32.
33 QS al-Nūr 24: 2–9.
34 QS al-Isrā 17: 70.
35 QS al-Zumar 39: 18.
36 QS Yūsuf 12: 111.
37 QS al-Thalāq 65: 10.
38 QS al-Baqarah 2: 170–171, QS al-A'rāf 7: 179.
39 Abu Zahara, Muhammad. (1958). *Usul al-Fiqh*. Cairo: Dar al-Fikr al-Arabi.
40 QS al-Mā idah 5: 90.
41 QS al-A'rāf 7: 128.
42 QS al-Hadīd 57: 5.
43 QS al-Baqarah 2: 29–30.
44 QS al-Nūr 24: 33 explains that "... give them from the wealth of Allah which He has given you. ..."
45 Abu Zahara, Muhammad. (1958). *Usul al-Fiqh*. Cairo: Dar al-Fikr al-Arabi.
46 QS al-Mā idah 5: 38.
47 QS al-Nisā 4: 29.
48 QS adh-Dhāriyāt 51: 19, QS al-Ma'ārij 70: 24–25.
49 QS al-Baqarah 2: 275–279, QS al-'Imrān 130.
50 QS al-Baqarah 2: 280–283.

4 Individual *Maslahah* Fulfilment Efforts

> We often hear in everyday life, that a person who has a high formal educational degree, like a master's or doctorate degree, with their abundant wealth, because they have no religious hold, commits acts of manipulation, abuse of authority, corruption, and money laundering. Households that initially got along well, quietly and comfortably, break down. Children are displaced and even they have to live in prison.

There are numerous highly educated people who own many businesses and great wealth but do not bring serenity and benefits to many people. This is because there are no descendants who share the same vision and mission as the founders of the business. The accumulated wealth is consumed by the conflict between them. The fight for inheritance for the interests of the third parties is inevitable. Countless costs incurred to pay for family disputes. In the end, the accumulated wealth cannot bring serenity and happiness to many.

According to a report by BBC Indonesia on 28 February 2012 – 16:05 WIB via http://www.bbc.co.uk/indonesia/dunia/2012/02/120228 _samsung-inheritance.shtml (accessed 3 June 2012), Samsung Electronic's main director, Lee Kun-hee, was sued by his younger sister Lee Sook-hee over a share inheritance. The lawsuit against Director Lee (70) included claims for assets worth 190 billion won (equivalent to IDR1.5 trillion) left by their late father. The lawsuit is in line with the lawsuit filed two weeks earlier by Director Lee's older brother, Lee Maeng-hee. The lawsuit filed by Lee's eldest son's worth 700 billion won (equivalent to IDR 5.7 trillion) in shares of the company's main business empire, Samsung Electronics, and Samsung Life Insurance.

According to court documents filed by Lee Maeng-hee, "these shares are assets that were contributed in a management body in the name of persons who are not heirs, even though they should be due to the holders of inheritance rights according to the law." Lee Kun-hee is accused of trying to control the shares for himself.

Lee Byung-chull, the father of the plaintiffs and defendants, died in 1987 after establishing Samsung in 1938 as a seller of dried fish in South Korea. Now the Samsung Group is evolving into a conglomerate with businesses

DOI: 10.4324/9781003390947-5

such as shipbuilding, telecommunications, electronics, and construction, which had a turnover of USD 220 billion (IDR 2000 trillion) in 2010.

Lee Kun-hee was appointed to the highest seat of the Samsung conglomerate as a replacement official in 1987. However, he resigned in April 2008 after being dogged by cases of alleged tax evasion and violation of investor confidence. Eventually, Lee was charged with violating tax laws but was given the president's pardon in 2009, allowing him to return to the chair of the president director of Samsung in 2010. According to the 2010 Forbes' list of the richest people, Lee is the richest person in South Korea with a personal fortune of USD 7.9 billion (IDR 72 trillion).

Worship Orientation as the Centre of All Orientations

Many successful entrepreneurs with great wealth suffer from excessive stress due to the pressure of work. The state of life is unstable, although – the body is physically healthy. Nightlife is an escape. But the mental pain makes the stress take over. Shortcuts are chosen, domestic violence, crimes, and even suicide are committed.

The WHO Constitution defines health as a state of complete physical, mental, and social well-being, not merely the absence of disease or infirmity. Research conducted by WHO in recent years shows that mental health influences each other and is inextricably linked. Mental health affects physical health and physical health affects mental health (WHO, "mhGAP, Mental Health Gap Action Programme Scaling up Care for Mental, Neurological, and substance use disorders," 2008: 1).

An inferior intellect makes it easy for people to commit crimes. The lack of wisdom causes people to ignore ethics and morals. People who lack of wisdom will easily cheat, gamble, deceive, lie, fib, or rob. People who are drunk will easily hurt, oppress, and even kill other people. The intellect is a tool to understand and know what is good or bad and right or wrong, while the brain gives the data to reason. Good or bad has to do with social provisions, while right or wrong is related to adherence or violation of religious norms (*Shari'ah*).

Lack of prosperity forces people to change religion. The lure of a change in worldly life that is better than before can easily lead people to change their *Aqidah* with new religions. Poverty can also cause people to easily lost their intellect, easily commit crimes, and easily commit various social irregularities. Poverty can lead to social insecurity in the community. Because of the importance of the problem of poverty, anyone who becomes president should consider poverty alleviation as the top priority of government programs.

Maslahah daruriyah is a basic or primary need, namely religion (*al-Din*), life (*al-Nafs*), intellect (*al-'Aql*), lineage (*al-Nasl*), and wealth (*al-Mal*), which must necessarily be fulfilled in order to realize the success of life in the world and salvation in the hereafter. If any of the five basic needs are not fulfilled, it leads to an imbalance in one's life in the world. This condition may lead to a lack of benefit, security, and success in the hereafter.

The fulfilment of the needs of *al-Din* is done through worship. The fulfilment of the protection needs of *al-Nafs* is implemented through orientation towards life. The fulfilment of *al-Nasl* protection needs is carried out through orientation towards the progeny. The fulfilment of the protection needs of *al-'Aql* is carried out through the orientation towards intellect. The fulfilment of *al-Māl's* protection needs is implemented through the orientation towards wealth.

Fulfilling the protection needs of *al-Din's* is given top priority, as explained by al-Ghazali and Nyazee. This is followed by the fulfilment of *al-Nafs, al-Nasl, al-'Aql,* and *al-Māl.* Moreover, there is causality between the fulfilment of one's needs and the fulfilment of other needs.

Worship orientation is the centre of all *Maslahah* orientations. This means that the worship orientation is the first orientation to be fought before fighting for other orientations. The high priority of fulfilling the worship orientation is because the worship orientation is the basis for establishing the order of *Maslahah.* A weakness in relation to one orientation has little impact on the other orientations. However, a weakness in the worshipful orientation will result in the collapse of the order of *Maslahah.* Therefore, to develop the order of *Maslahah*, the worshipful alignment has the highest priority.

The worship orientation is the control centre for the movements of the other four orientations. The centre of the worship orientation is the centre of the circulation of the other orientations. Just as the sun is the centre of the Milkyway. The Ka'bah is the centre of the movement of the people performing the *Thawaf.* It can be said that the worship orientation is the centre of the orbit of the other four orientations.

The absence of a body part causes a person's life to be different from the life of a person with complete limbs. However, that person's life can still go well. The life of an incomplete person can even surpass the lives of people with complete body parts.

Not so with someone who has a deficiency in the brain. Even if other limbs are complete, but if they have a deficiency in the brain, many other limbs become non-functional.

The worship orientation is the brain for the other orientations. This means that the worship orientation is a command centre for other orientations. The brain regulates other organs. Without the brain, the function of other organs does not work properly. Like the earth's core of which can move the earth's tectonic plates, the worship orientation is able to move other orientations.

Without the energy from the worship orientation, the other orientations are still able to move themselves. This is because each orientation basically has its own intrinsic value. However, for other orientations, the worship orientation becomes an external style that can accelerate each orientation. Thus, the movements generated by all orientations become greater.

According to Transparency International (January 2019), Indonesia is the 89th most corrupt country in 2018. The total number of countries studied was 180 countries. Indonesia has an index of 38. Zero is perceived as very corrupt and 100 as very clean.

Worship orientation is a driving machine. The presence of a machine is very important for a vehicle. Without a machine, the vehicle could not move. The worship orientation also acts as an accelerator gear for moving vehicles. Without gears, the vehicle cannot accelerate.

The worship orientation is a perspective for maintaining religion (*Hifzu al-din*). Islam has three aspects, namely *Aqidah*, *Shari'ah,* and *Akhlaq*. To realize the function of worship orientation as it should be, the understanding and application of the aspects become very absolute. *Akhlaq* is a manifestation of the entire Islamic religious system. Without *Akhlaq*, Islam is just a pile of concepts without application. *Akhlaq* concerns the relations between human beings and God, among human beings, and of human beings with other creatures of God such as the angels, the prophets, the divine scriptures, the Last Judgement Day, destiny, family, guests, neighbours, teachers, the environment, etc. So, the worship orientation must cover all these relationships. For this reason, the worship orientation must be able to answer the question, "How can we sustain salvation in the hereafter and success in life in the world?"

The worship orientation as a centre of energy can bring forth any of the orientations (Figure 4.1). All the orientations that receive energy from the worship orientation respond to the energy of the worship orientation. The life orientation has the least inertia compared to other orientations. Therefore, the life orientation responds faster to the worship orientation than other orientations. The worship orientation makes life become calmer, gentler, more patient, more optimistic, etc. This condition makes it easier to gain personal security so that the life orientation can be fulfilled.[1]

Life orientation is the perspective of concern for life (*Hifzu al-nafs*). The existence of life is very essential. Without life, a body has no meaning. The absence of life also renders the body helpless. It is the soul which causes a handsome face that is not always charming. Life also ensures that living beings can grow and flourish. Life encourages people to have dreams and make them come true. Due

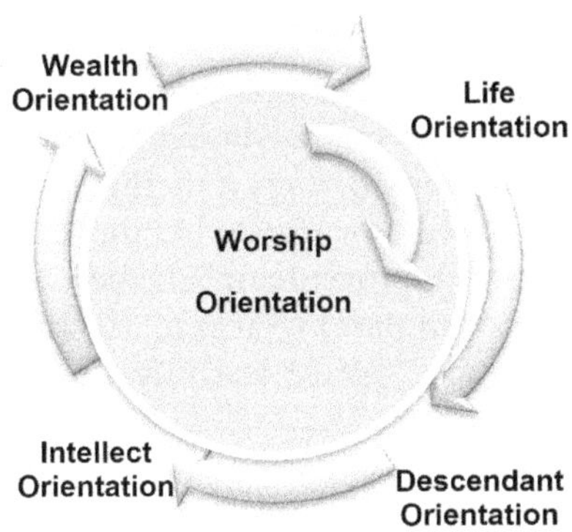

Figure 4.1 Worship Orientation as the Centre of All Orientations.

Source: Processed Data.

to the importance of life, Islam applies *Qisas* to an assassin, i.e., if a person causes the death of another, then that person's life must be revoked.[2]

Human beings are made up of two components, namely a body, which has a physical and spiritual dimension, and an intellect which has a non-physical dimension. Al-Ghazali in Kamil *et al.* (2010)[3] divides life into two different things, namely *Nafs*/spirit (when a man is alive) and *Ruh/life* (when a man dies). According to al-Ghazali, life has four different characteristics, namely: animal characteristics (lust/appetite leads to the fulfilment of desires), demonic characteristics (characteristics of evil, bad), wild characteristics (imagination), and spiritual characteristics (the nature of angels who always worship). The life orientation must be able to answer the question, "How can one shape one's life so that salvation in the hereafter and the success of one's life in this world are sustainable?"

The descendent orientation is the notion of rearing offspring (*Hifzu al-nasl*). Offspring are the inheritance of genealogy or *Nasab*. Without progeny, the genealogy will be interrupted. Descendants carry on tasks which have not yet been completed. The progeny continues the baton of the *Caliph*. The existence of descendants means to maintain the sustainability of the *Caliph*. For this reason, the descendent orientation must be able to answer the question, "What activities must be carried out for children/descendent/families so that salvation in the hereafter and success of life in the world can be sustained?"

Self-mastery is far better, and self-patience is achieved, peace of mind begins to be felt, and this will affect the family. Godly offspring are produced, the children achieve well in academics or non-academics, and the household becomes harmonious, so the descendent orientation is achieved. All this creates benefits for the family. When peace of life and family harmony are fulfilled, one and one's family will find it easier to take lessons from everything that happens. They will reflect on all the received trials, correct them, and evaluate themselves. The learning process is increasingly taking place. The tracking process certainly improves the corrective and preventive measures and also the continuous improvement process, so eventually, the intellect orientation could be achieved.

The intellectual orientation is a way of maintaining the intellect (*Hifzu al-'aql*). The function of intellect is to contemplate, think, evaluate, and do *Muhasabah*, about the tasks performed by human beings. The results of reflection will become consideration to carry out the sustained learning. If the function of intellect is not used as it should be, the learning process becomes stagnant. There is no inward improvement. Salvation in the hereafter and success in the world are abandoned. For that reason, the intellect orientation must be able to answer the question, "What learning activities should be done so that salvation in the hereafter and success of life in the world can be sustained?"

The more we do the learning process, the more we will advance the function of humanism. The serenity they acquire, the kindness they receive, and the success they acquire must be shared with others. However, to share with others requires additional fees, additional resources, and additional wealth. Therefore, other activities are needed to increase the wealth to share with others. When additional wealth has been acquired and already shared with others, then the fulfilment and realization of wealth orientation are achieved.

The wealth orientation is the perspective of preserving wealth (*Hifzu al-mal*). Salvation in the hereafter and success of life in this world should not be enjoyed alone. It is not defined as survival and success if only enjoyed alone. Survival and success must be shared with others, but to share salvation and success, extra money, treasures, and wealth are needed. For this reason, wealth orientation must be able to answer the question, "What attempt should be done to get wealth and spend it for salvation in the hereafter and success in life in the world can be sustained?"

The Synergy and Management of Five *Maslahah* Orientations

The five orientations of basic needs, namely: worship orientation, life orientation, descendent orientation, intellect orientation, and wealth orientation are consequences or responses that need to be done to balance the fulfilment of basic needs. Sinergy and control of the five orientations can be described in Figure 4.2.

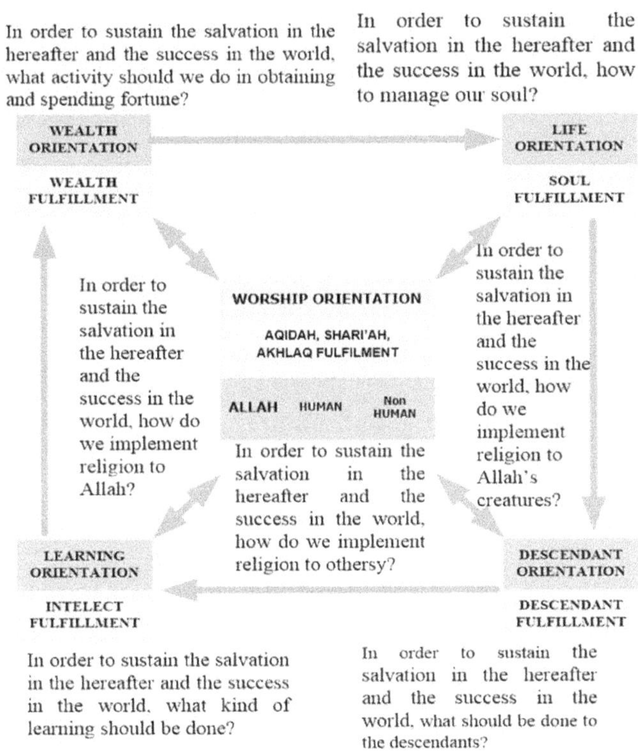

Figure 4.2 The Synergy and Management of Five *Maslahah* Orientations.

Source: Processed Data.

Summary

Worship orientation is the centre of all orientations. The worship orientation flows spiritual energy throughout the individual. Fulfilment of worship orientation is the key to gain benefit in this world and the hereafter.

Notes

1 Hawa (2004) gave the opinion about cleansing the soul through worship such as prayer, *zakah*, pilgrimage, reciting the Holy Quran and fasting. Reading the Holy Quran is a significant way to illuminate the soul, and this is a complement to prayer, *zakah*, fasting and the pilgrimage in realizing the spirituality of behaviour. In some cases, life orientation becomes the beginning of fulfilling basic needs, as explained by Chapra in "The Islamic Vision of Development in the Light of Maqasid Al-Sharī'ah, 2007." Nevertheless, M. Umer Chapra asserts that the order of fulfilment of basic needs depends on the issues discussed. This is also explained in QS al-A'la 87: 14–15.
2 The verses in the Holy Qur'an that define souls with lives or spirits include QS al-Zumar 39: 42; QS al-Maidah 5: 45.
3 Kamil, Naail Mohammed, Sulaiman, Mohamed, Osman-Gani, Aahad and Ahmad, Khaliq. (2010). Spirituality in the Workplace: The Role of Taqwa towards the Advancement of the Contemporary Organization. *Social Science Research Network*. 8th International Conference on Tawhidic Methodology Applied to Microenterprise Development, 2010. http://papers.ssrn.com/sol3/papers.cfm?abstract_id=1718946 (Accessed on 11 April 2012).

Part II

Maslahah as a Basis for the Organizational Performance System

The MaP performance system is developed considering the "radar" concept (Sokovic *et al.*, 2010).[1] Radar means results, approaches, deployment, assessment, and refinement. The MaP performance system is oriented on results. The system is integrated with the approach planning and development. The MaP performance system links current achievement to future performance. In applying the MaP performance system, the stages of socialization are carried out systematically and all employees are involved. The MaP performance system conducts not only the performance measurement process but also the review process, which is carried out through a monitoring process and analysis of the results achieved, and the results of the review then become learning materials for future improvement.

The MaP performance system complies eight criteria for a good performance measurement system, as explained by Moullin (2004).[2] Moullin described eight important criteria for a performance measurement system, namely the use of a balanced measure that describes the whole activity and domain, ensuring that what is being measured is a problem related to users and stakeholders, involving all staff in setting the measure, including the perception of the measure and the presence of performance indicators, the use of a combination of the result and the process performance, including the elements of cost-effectiveness and value delivered to customers, the presence of a clear system for translating organizational strategies into performance measures. Finally, the performance of the measurement system must be focused on sustained improvement rather than blaming something when the performance is not as expected.

The MaP performance system covers all processes in the organization. This means that the MaP performance system meets the criteria for a good performance measurement system, according to Neely (2004).[3] Neely explains that the area within the organization whose performance needs to be measured includes accounting, marketing, and operations.

MaP performance system consists of six aspects of performance measurement, with each aspect referred to as an orientation. The six orientations are worship orientation, internal process orientation, talent orientation,

DOI: 10.4324/9781003390947-6

learning orientation, customer orientation, and wealth orientation. *Maslahah* is achieved when each of the *Maslahah* orientations is equally fulfilled (Bedoui, 2012).[4]

MaP performance system uses four main variables to measure performance as used by BSC (Kaplan and Norton, 1996).[5] These are:

- i Strategic objectives, which are the answer to the question, "What should we do to succeed?"
- ii Measurement, which is the answer to the question, "What parameters will we use to determine whether we are successful?"
- iii Target, which is the answer to the question, "What quantitative value will we use to determine success?"
- iv Strategic initiative, which is the answer to the question, "What will we do to achieve the strategic objectives?"

When taking measurements, a method of measurement is required, so formula is needed as an additional variable. Formula means a pattern or method of calculating measures or the answer to the question, "How to calculate measures?" Thus, the MaP performance system uses five measurement variables. These are the strategic objectives, the measure, the formula, the target, and the strategic initiative.

Notes

1 Sokovic, M. Pavletic, D. and Kern Pipan, K. (2010). Quality Improvement Methodologies – PDCA Cycle, RADAR Matrix, DMAIC and DFSS. *Journal of Achievement in Materials and Manufacturing Engineering*. Vol. 43, No. 1: 476–477.

2 Moullin, M. (2004). Eight Essentials of Performance Measurement. *International Journal of Health Care Quality Assurance*. Vol. 17, No. 3: 110–112.

3 Andy, N. (2004). *Business Performance Measurement, Theory and Practice*. Cambridge: Cambridge University Press.

4 Bedoui, H. E. (2012). "Sharīʿah-Based Ethical Performance Measurement Framework and Relevant Data to Measure Development in Light of Maqāṣid al-Sharīʿah," Palgrave Studies in Islamic Banking, Finance and Economics, in: Salman Syed Ali (ed.), *Towards a Maqāṣid al-Sharīʿah Index of Socio-Economic Development*, Chapter 1, 55–123. Palgrave Macmillan: New York.

5 Kaplan, R. S. and Norton, D. P. (1996). *The Balanced Scorecard: Translating Strategy into Action*. Boston: Harvard Business School Press.

5 The Measures of Organizational Performance and Fulfilment Efforts

Organization Is Created to Win the Competition

BSC,[1] when freely translated, means a card which contains performance evaluation points whose measurement is balanced. The word "balanced" is intended to show that the performance of an individual, work unit, or organization is evaluated equally in the following aspects: short-term (financial) and long-term (non-financial); real/tangible (financial) and intangible (non-financial); outcome-oriented (financial) and process-oriented (non-financial); internal organization (organizational perspective) and external (customers); between the past result of business (financial) and the measurement that will drive performance in the future (non-financial); the objective outcome measurement and/or easily quantifiable (financial); and the driving factor (drivers) from various subjective/qualitative measurements (no-financial).

In the 1950s, GE undertook a project to develop performance measurement for the five business units. At that time, the development team recommended that the performance department be measured by one financial and seven non-financial measures. The eight metrics are profitability (financial), market share (customer), productivity, product leadership, public accountability, i.e., legal and ethical conduct behaviour and stakeholder responsibility (internal process), personal development and employee attitude (learning and growth), and the balance of short-term and long-term objectives.

Unfortunately, the goal of the GE project is not deeply rooted in the system management and incentive structure of the business units. This is evidenced by the pressure that business managers place on short-term profit-making. This leads managers to compromise long-term goals and their public accountability.

The BSC principle as a measurement tool for organizational performance is based on accounting management considerations. Kaplan and Norton (1992)[2] stated that the efficient use of capital for investment compared to other factors such as intellectual capital, knowledge, and customer orientation is not sustainable in improving competitive advantage. Thus, to improve the competitive advantage, organizations should not only rely on financial factors in measuring their performance but also on other factors that also strongly influence the achievement of financial performance.

DOI: 10.4324/9781003390947-7

Intellectual capital, knowledge, learning, and customer orientation factors are internal and external factors owned by the organization. These factors are very influential and can even drive the future performance of the organization. In the current performance measurement, the non-financial factors have not yet shown results, but in the future, these factors will significantly influence the financial performance.

Bramhandkar *et al.* (2007)[3] conducted research on measuring of intellectual capital performance in the pharmaceutical industry. They studied 139 drug companies. They concluded that companies with high levels of intangible assets management (intellectual capital) have better financial performance than companies with low intangible asset management. This result should be a reference for managers. Thus, if a manager expects good financial performance, he must pay attention to intangible assets.

Kaplan and Norton proposed BSC as a system to measure organizational performance from four perspectives: financial perspective, customer perspective, internal business process perspective, and learning and growth perspective.

Financial Perspective

The financial perspective is the BSC's perspective on organizational performance from the financial aspect. The financial figures or ratios in the accounting records are the starting point for evaluating organizational performance. Organizational goals are usually related to profit (profitability). An organization is considered successful if it makes a profit and conversely unsuccessful if it occurs losses.

Kaplan and Norton (1996)[4] stated that the financial goals of an organization are highly dependent on the life cycle of the organization in question. Organizational goals that are in the initial stage of growth are different from the target of the organizations that are in a sustained cycle and from the organizational goal that are in the harvest cycle (maturity – harvest) stage.

In the growth stage, organizations operate with negative cash flow and low return on investment. This happens because the organization is focused on developing and improving products and services, developing, and expanding production facilities, and making large investments in systems development, infrastructure, distribution channels, maintenance, and market development. In this situation, organizations are in dire need of high resources. Organizations that are in the growth stage have a financial target in the form of percentage growth in income and revenue in the targeted market segment.

In the sustainable stage, organizations already have an incentive to invest and reinvest in the hope of achieving a high return on investment capital. Therefore, companies are expected to maintain their market share and enter other markets. Companies invest to overcome various obstacles, increase production capacity, and improve sustainability. In this situation, the company has financial targets related to financial ratios like ROA, ROE, ROCE, operating profit, gross margin, etc.

In harvest time, the company reaps the yields made in the previous two cycles. Companies no longer need large capital expenditures; they just need enough to maintain equipment and capacity. When a new investment is made, it is expected that the investment will also be short-lived. This means that investments that are made immediately can create value for the organization. The financial targets of the organization that are in the harvesting season are characterized by smooth operating cash flow and savings in various working capital requirements.

In the performance measurement literature, some researchers use different measures to evaluate organizational performance from a financial perspective. Richard *et al.* (2009) divided financial performance measures into four broad parts, namely accounting measure (accounting), money market measure of the (financial market), mixed accounting and money market (mixed), and survive measure (survival).

Gumbus and Lyons (2002)[5] used three financial measures, namely: returns on investment (ROI) and returns on assets (ROA), as productivity measures. Profit margins are the measure of revenue and market share growth. While Ellingson and Wambsganss (2001),[6] Hoque and James (2000),[7] Maiga and Jacobs (2003),[8] and Yeniyurt (2003)[9] used operating costs and the use of material/assets as the measure of cost structure.

Customer Perspective

Kaplan and Norton mentioned that four things are important to customers, namely: time, quality, performance, and service. Therefore, they grouped the customer perspectives into three values, namely product and service attributes, customer relationships and image, and reputation. From the perspective of Total Quality Management (TQM) concept, customers evaluate companies in terms of QCDMS (Quality, Cost, Delivery, Morale, and Safety).

Regarding time, customers certainly expect delivery time to be as short as possible. As for quality, customers expect products' durability, features, customer services, beauty, flawlessness, fulfilment of production requirements, etc. In terms of services, customers expect service which is good, cheap, fast, full of smiles, understanding towards customer needs, open to suggestions, sympathy, etc.

Before the targets and performance measures can be set from the customer's point of view, the company must identify who the customer is. The process of customer identification means finding out to whom the product or service is delivered. What value is required by the customer? How should the value be delivered to the customer? Where do customers typically look for the value that they need? Kotler and Armstrong (2010)[10] stated these steps as steps to understanding and identifying the concepts of the five core customers and markets. **First**, basic needs, wants, and desires. Basic needs are physical needs that are very basic to human beings (food, clothing, warmth, safety, social needs for mutual fulfilment and influence, and the individual needs for knowledge or expression). **The second** is market supply, which is the combination of products, services, information, and experiences offered in the market to satisfy needs or wants. **The third** is value and satisfaction. Value is something that is demanded by customers. Satisfaction is the feeling customers feel when their desires can be satisfied by the value offered by the market. **The fourth** is transaction and relationship. Transaction is an action of receiving a certain object from a person who offers it. Relationship is a condition when a transaction has taken place. So, it creates a relationship between the people who need something and those who offer something. **The fifth**, the market, is a place where transactions and relationships take place.

According to Kotler and Armstrong, if companies are not able to identify customers and markets, it can lead to marketing myopia, which is a situation where the company offers goods and services, but not the goods and services that the customer really needs.

After understanding the market, the company needs to recognize the market segmentation. According to Kotler and Armstrong, market segmentation means answering the question, "What kind of market is served?"

The reason for different answers is due to the size of the market or the inhomogeneous market. The process of market segmentation is the process of dividing very large and heterogeneous markets into smaller market segments so that they can be served more efficiently with products and unique services.

The perspective goal of the customers that needs to be determined is to identify the customers and market segmentation. According to Kaplan and Norton, customer satisfaction, customer retention, new customer acquisition, customer profitability, and market share are the performance measures.

Some researchers use different metrics to evaluate performance from a customer perspective (Chen *et al.,* 2010)[11] including Ellingson and Wambsganss (2001)[12] used brand readiness measurement to measure corporate image, quality, and functionality to measure product attributes, customer response time and customer satisfaction to measure customer relationship, and image and reputation to measure organizational image. Other researchers, such as Maiga and Jacobs (2003),[13] Ellingson and Wambsganss (2001),[14] Gumbus and Lyons (2002),[15] Yeniyurt (2003),[16] Hoque and James (2000),[17] Kaplan and Norton (2004b),[18] Libby *et al.* (2004),[19] used a measure of brand reputation and willingness to measure organizational image.

Evaluation from the customer's point of view is very important. The evaluation is necessary for the success rate of the organization not to be biased. Customer evaluation is a genuine, original, and objective evaluation from outsiders.

Internal Business Process Perspective

Once you know what customers need, the next step is to improve or innovate business processes. Internal business process improvement should be continuous and consistent (continuous improvement) to adapt to customer needs.

We know that customer needs are always changing, of course. Improvement and innovation are expected to be able to make changes in a good direction to meet customer satisfaction. Companies need to be able to assess whether the technology still fits the needs of the customers.

It is fascinating how the Japanese maintain the Kaizen culture. Kaizen in Japanese means small improvements that are made continuously and consistently (Alukal and Manos, 2006).[20] Kaizen is the way of life of the Japanese in all aspects of life, including work life and social life. Due to the Kaizen culture, the Japanese have a greater competitive advantage than other peoples.

The improvement that is understood by Kaizen is small-scale improvement, but it is done continuously and consistently. The small improvement that are done continuously and consistently have a big impact and can even be said to have a dramatic effect on real life, both at home, at work, and in society.

Improvements to internal business processes can be made using the value chain analysis method. This is an analysis that looks at the organization as a sequential process from activity to value creation. Starting from the procurement of raw materials to the delivery of finished products to customers. Porter (1998), a business expert, introduced the concept of value chain analysis to explain internal business processes.

The targeted perspective of the internal business process is operations management, customer management, and innovation. The performance measures used by researchers according to Chen *et al.* (2010)[21] are: Gumbus and Lyons (2002)[22] use internal process quality as a measure of operations management. This is supported by Ellingson and Wambsganss (2001),[23] Hoque and James (2000),[24] and Maiga and Jacobs (2003).[25]

Kaplan and Norton (2004b)[26] used customer selection as a measure of customer management. Ellingson and Wambsganss (2001),[27] and Libby (2004)[28] used customer acquisition for customer management measures. Ellingson and Wambsganss (2001)[29] and Libby (2004)[30] use customer acquisition for customer management measures. Ellingson and Wambsganss (2001)[31] and Yeniyurt (2003)[32] use the customer retention target as a measure of customer management. Innovations measured by innovative opportunities by Hoque and James (2000),[33] Maiga and Jacobs (2003),[34] and Yeniyurt (2003),[35] while Hoque and James (2000),[36] Maiga and Jacobs (2003)[37] use time needed for product innovation.

Learning and Growth Perspectives

Continuous improvement of internal business processes will not change anything if there is no learning process. Therefore, companies need to develop the learning process. Learning is the key to sustainable innovation. Innovation makes it easier for the organization to adapt to environmental changes. The flexibility of the organization to environmental changes will increase the competitive advantage of the organization over its competitors. This condition makes the organization a learning organization.

Kaplan and Norton (1996)[38] stated that the goal of the learning and growth perspective is to create an infrastructure to achieve the goals of all three other perspectives. The performance of an organization from the learning and growth perspective results from three factors, namely human resources (employee capabilities), information systems (information systems capabilities), and organizational resources (motivation, empowerment, harmony). Therefore, Kaplan and Norton used three objectives for learning and growth perspective, namely human capital, information capital, and organizational capital.

The measure of human capital performance in learning and growth perspective is employee satisfaction. Measurement of employee satisfaction can be done through questionnaires. The measure of performance from the learning and growth perspective is employee retention, which is the percentage of employees who hold the primary job and leave or quit the organization. The third measure is employee productivity, a measure of the comparison between the output produced by employees and the number of employees used to produce the output.

In terms of information systems capital, Wade and Hulland (2004)[39] found that information systems resources can be an important driver for firms to achieve competitive advantage and long-term performance if they are unique and valuable and cannot be copied by competitors. Martinsons *et al.* (1999)[40] reminded that the use of information systems can increase individual productivity to achieve organizational goals. The performance of information systems is measured by the efficiency of activities related to the development and operation of information systems and the effectiveness of the contributions of information systems to increase individual productivity.

Organizational capital consists of motivation, empowerment, and harmony. Motivation is very important to workers because empowering workers and opening access to information to workers will not have much impact on the organization if worker motivation is poor. One of the methods to increase workers' motivation to work is to involve them in decision-making and other activities according to their authority and responsibility. Employees are encouraged to make suggestions or proposals to the management, which are then followed up by the management.

In quality management system, brainstorming activity is called suggestion system. The brainstorming system (Jacobson *et al.*, 2009) is important in the application of kaizen. This system is a feature of kaizen culture. The brainstorming system can empower every individual involved in problem-solving. Every suggestion gets a response, and every success in implementing the suggestion is made public so that it could be known to many people. This spurs everyone to make improvements. Therefore, the motivational performance could be measured through the number of suggestions submitted by employees and followed up by management.

Involving employees in decision-making is a good way to coach employees. One of the effects expected from employee empowerment is to increase the improvement process. Therefore, the performance of the empowerment goal is measured by the number of improvements achieved.

Another goal of organizational capital is harmony, which is the alignment between the goals of the individual, the work unit, and the organization. Harmony between individuals in organizations, work units, and organizations can be created if the relationships between individuals, relationships between supervisors and subordinates are similar, and there is coherent teamwork. For this reason, the performance of organizational capital must be measurable by measuring team performance.

Some researchers (Chen *et al.*, 2010)[41] used different measures to evaluate the performance of learning and growth perspectives, include Ellingson and Wambsganss (2001),[42] Libby (2004),[43] Ullrich and Tuttle (2004)[44] used the measure of employee skills for human capital objectives, while Kaplan and Norton (2004a)[45] used know-how. For organizational capital performance, Kaplan and Norton used two measures, employee knowledge sharing and shared vision, goals, and values. For information capital performance, Kaplan and Norton used measures of knowledge management capabilities and information accessibility. Martinsons *et al.* (1999),[46] on the other hand, used measures of business value, user orientation, internal processes, and future readiness to measure information system performance.

According to Kaplan and Norton (1992),[47] the availability of information from all four BSC perspectives serves to answer four fundamental questions in business management, namely, how do we relate to our shareholders? (financial perspective), how do customers view us? (customer perspective), what do we need to be particularly good at? (process perspective internal business), can we continue to improve and create value? (learning and growth perspective).

Organizations Are Created to Fulfil the Duty as Caliphs

Organization is created to fulfil the duty of people as Allah's vicegerent on earth. The leaders of organizations must be aware that the organization they establish is a means of worshipping Allah (*s.w.t.*) by seeking to benefit themselves and their families, their employees and their families, customers, suppliers, partners, and the environment.[48] For this reason, organizations should be established with the aim of attaining salvation in the hereafter and success of life in this world. It follows that the organization is managed not only because of personal desires, duties, regulations, and constraints but as a means of worshipping Almighty God, Almighty *Rizq*, Almighty Success and Almighty Security.

وَإِذْ قَالَ رَبُّكَ لِلْمَلَـٰٓئِكَةِ إِنِّى جَاعِلٌ فِى ٱلْأَرْضِ خَلِيفَةً ۖ قَالُوٓا۟ أَتَجْعَلُ فِيهَا مَن يُفْسِدُ
فِيهَا وَيَسْفِكُ ٱلدِّمَآءَ وَنَحْنُ نُسَبِّحُ بِحَمْدِكَ وَنُقَدِّسُ لَكَ ۖ قَالَ إِنِّىٓ أَعْلَمُ مَا لَا تَعْلَمُونَ

> And [mention, O Muḥammad], when your Lord said to the angels, "Indeed, I will make upon the earth a successive authority." 1 They said, "Will You place upon it one who causes corruption therein and sheds blood, while we exalt You with praise and declare Your perfection?" 2 He [Allāh] said, "Indeed, I know that which you do not know."
>
> (QS al-Baqarah 2: 30)

The *Maslahah* of the organization means that the organization creates value in a sustainable manner. It means that the benefits of the organization are not limited by the age of the organization or the age of the manager of the organization. The *Maslahah* of the organization will continue to flow even if the organization or the manager of the organization has passed away. Therefore, sustainability is a goal that must be protected and preserved.

> Humans were created by Allah as Allah's vicegerent on earth. Therefore, the organization established should be to carry out the function of human caliphate on earth, not for others.

The realization of *Maslahah* in the leadership of the organization depends on the fulfilment of six aspects of organizational orientation, namely worship orientation, internal process orientation, talent orientation, learning orientation, customer orientation, and wealth orientation.

The worship orientation is to explain the protection and preservation of religion within the organization. The worship orientation is to answer the question, "how can organizations apply religion in daily life towards Allah, stakeholders and the environment so that salvation in the hereafter and success of life in the world can be sustainable?"

The internal process orientation is to explain the protection and preservation of the soul of the organization. The internal process orientation is to answer the question, "How can internal processes be managed so that salvation in the hereafter and success of life in the world can be sustainable?"

Talent orientation is to explain the protection and retention of future generations of organizational managers who have a vision and mission that is consistent with the vision and mission of the founding/leading organization. Talent orientation is to answer the question, "What activities need to be carried out for the next generation of organizations (talent) so that salvation in the hereafter and success of life in the world can be sustained?"

The learning orientation is to explain the protection and maintenance of the intellect and heart of the organization. Learning orientation is to answer the question, "What learning activities need to be done so that salvation in the hereafter and success of life in the world can be sustained?"

Customer orientation is the explanation for protecting and maintaining relationships with clients. Customer orientation is the answer to the question, "What activities should be carried out for customers so that salvation in the hereafter and success of life in the world can be maintained?"

The wealth orientation is to explain the protection and preservation of wealth. The wealth orientation is to answer the question, "What efforts should be made to acquire wealth and spend wealth in order to maintain salvation in the hereafter and the success of life in the world?" the adaptation of the concept of *Maslahah* for organization is explained in Figure 5.1.

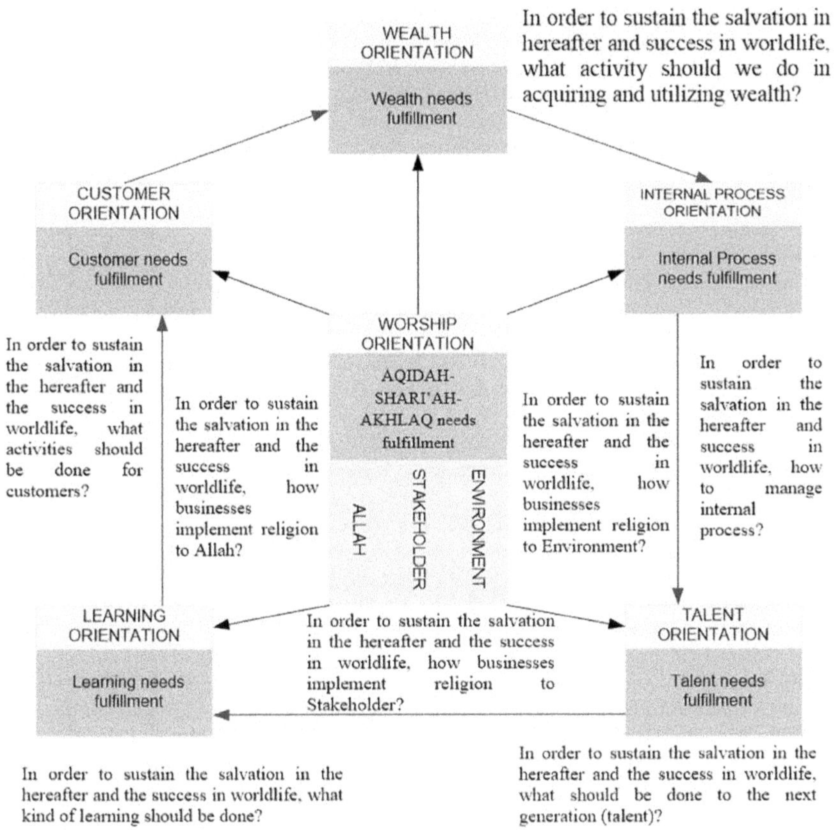

Figure 5.1 Six Orientations of *Maslahah* for Organizations.

Source: Processed data

Summary

Organizations are created to fulfil the duty as caliphs. Maslahah is a basis for organizational performance system. The worship orientation is to explain the protection and preservation of religion within the organization. The worship orientation is the key to answer the organizational performance.

Notes

1 Kaplan, R. S. and Norton, D. P. (1996). *Balanced Scorecard, Translating Strategy into Action*. Boston: Harvard Business School Press. In Page 22, Kaplan mentioned that *Balanced scorecard is a strategic performance management system that enables organization to translate its vision, mission, and strategy into a set of measurable actions.*

2 Kaplan, R. S. and Norton. D. P. (1992). The Balanced Scorecard – Measures that Drive Performance. *Harvard Business Review*. Vol. 70, No. 1: 71–79.

3 Bramhandkar, A. Erickson, S. and Applebee, I. (2007). Intellectual Capital and Organizational Performance: An Empirical Study of the Pharmaceutical Industry. *Electronic Journal of Knowledge Management.* Vol. 5: 357–359.
4 Kaplan, R. S. and Norton. D. P. (1996). *The Balanced Scorecard: Translating Vision into Action.* Boston: Harvard Business School Press.
5 Gumbus, A. and Lyons, B. (November 2002). The Balanced Scorecard at Philips Electronics. *Strategic Finance.* Vol. 84, No. 5: 4.
6 Ellingson, D. A. and Wambsganss, J. R. (2001). Modifying the Approach to Planning and Evaluation in Governmental Entities: A Balanced Scorecard Approach. *Journal of Public Budgeting, Accounting and Financial Management.* Vol. 13, No. 1: 103–120.
7 Hoque, Z. and James, W. (2000). Linking Balanced Scorecard Measures to Size and Market Factors: Impact on Organizational Performance. *Journal of Management Accounting Research.* Vol. 12: 1–17.
8 Maiga, A. S. and Jacobs, F. A. (Fall 2003). Balanced Scorecard, Activity Based Costing and Company Performance: An Empirical Analysis. *Journal of Managerial Issues.* Vol. 15, No. 3: 283–301.
9 Yeniyurt, S. (2003). A Literature Review and Integrative Performance Measurement Framework for Multinational Companies. *Marketing Intelligence and Planning.* Vol. 21, No. 3: 134–135.
10 Kotler, P. and Amstrong, G. (2010). *Principles of Marketing.* New Jersey: Pearson Education, Inc.
11 Chen, C. Y., Yang, Y-F., Chen, C-W., Chen, L-T. and Chen, T-H. (4 August 2010). Linking the Balanced Scorecard (BSC) to Business Management Performance: A Preliminary Concept of Fit Theory for Navigation Science and Management. *International Journal of the Physical Sciences.* Vol. 5, No. 8: 1296–1298.
12 Ellingson, D. A. and Wambsganss, J. R. (2001). Modifying the Approach to Planning and Evaluation in Governmental Entities: A Balanced Scorecard Approach. *Journal of Public Budgeting, Accounting and Financial Management.* Vol. 13, No. 1: 134–142.
13 Maiga, A. S. and Jacobs, F. A. (Fall 2003). Balanced Scorecard, Activity Based Costing and Company Performance: An Empirical Analysis. *Journal of Managerial Issues.* Vol 15, No. 3: 283–301.
14 Ellingson, D. A. and Wambsganss, J. R. (2001). Modifying the Approach to Planning and Evaluation in Governmental Entities: A Balanced Scorecard Approach. *Journal of Public Budgeting, Accounting and Financial Management.* Vol. 13, No. 1: 103–120.
15 Gumbus, A. and Lyons, B. (November 2002). The Balanced Scorecard at Philips Electronics. *Strategic Finance.* Vol. 84, No. 5: 4.
16 Yeniyurt, S. (2003). A Literature Review and Integrative Performance Measurement Framework for Multinational Companies. *Marketing Intelligence and Planning.* Vol. 21, No. 3: 134–142.
17 Hoque, Z. and James, W. (2000). Linking Balanced Scorecard Measures to Size and Market Factors: Impact on Organizational Performance. *Journal of Management Accounting Research.* Vol. 12: 1–17.
18 Kaplan, R. S and Norton, D. P. (2004). *Measuring the Strategic Readiness of Intangible Assets.* Boston: Harvard Business School Press.
19 Libby, T, Salterio, S. E. and Webb, A. (2004). The Balanced Scorecard: The Effects of Assurance and Process Accountability on Managerial Judgment. *Accounting Review.* Vol. 79, No. 4: 1075–1094.
20 Alukal, G. and Manos, A. (2006). *Lean Kaizen: A Simplified Approach to Process Improvements.* Milwaukee: American Society for Quality, Quality Press.
21 Chen, C. Y., Yang, Y-F. Chen, C-W, Chen, L-T. and Chen, T-H. (4 August 2010). Linking the Balanced Scorecard (BSC) to Business Management Performance: A Preliminary Concept of Fit Theory for Navigation Science and Management. *International Journal of the Physical Sciences.* Vol. 5, No. 8: 1296–1305.
22 Gumbus, A. and Lyons, B. (November 2002). The Balanced Scorecard at Philips Electronics. *Strategic Finance.* Vol. 84, No. 5: 4.

23 Ellingson, D. A. and Wambsganss, J. R. (2001). Modifying the Approach to Planning and Evaluation in Governmental Entities: A Balanced Scorecard Approach. *Journal of Public Budgeting, Accounting and Financial Management.* Vol. 13, No. 1: 103–120.
24 Hoque, Z. and James, W. (2000). Linking Balanced Scorecard Measures to Size and Market Factors: Impact on Organizational Performance. *Journal of Management Accounting Research.* Vol. 12: 1–17.
25 Maiga, A. S. and Jacobs, F. A. (Fall 2003). Balanced Scorecard, Activity Based Costing and Company Performance: An Empirical Analysis. *Journal of Managerial Issues.* Vol 15, No. 3: 283–301.
26 Kaplan, R. S. and Norton. D. P. (2004). *Measuring the Strategic Readiness of Intangible Assets.* Boston: Harvard Business School Press.
27 Ellingson, D. A. and Wambsganss, J. R. (2001). Modifying the Approach to Planning and Evaluation in Governmental Entities: A Balanced Scorecard Approach. *Journal of Public Budgeting, Accounting and Financial Management.* Vol. 13, No. 1: 103–120.
28 Libby, T. Salterio, S. E. and Webb, A. (2004). The Balanced Scorecard: The Effects of Assurance and Process Accountability on Managerial Judgment. *Accounting Review.* Vol. 79, No. 4: 1075–1094.
29 Ellingson, D. A. and Wambsganss, J. R. (2001). Modifying the Approach to Planning and Evaluation in Governmental Entities: A Balanced Scorecard Approach. *Journal of Public Budgeting, Accounting and Financial Management.* Vol. 13. No. 1: 103–120.
30 Libby, T, Salterio, S. E. and Webb, A. (2004). The Balanced Scorecard: The Effects of Assurance and Process Accountability on Managerial Judgment. *Accounting Review.* Vol. 79, No. 4: 1075–1094.
31 Ellingson, D. A. and Wambsganss, J. R. (2001). Modifying the Approach to Planning and Evaluation in Governmental Entities: A Balanced Scorecard Approach. *Journal of Public Budgeting, Accounting and Financial Management.* Vol. 13, No. 1: 103–120.
32 Yeniyurt, S. (2003). A Literature Review and Integrative Performance Measurement Framework for Multinational Companies. *Marketing Intelligence and Planning.* Vol. 21, No. 3.
33 Hoque, Z. and James, W. (2000). Linking Balanced Scorecard Measures to Size and Market Factors: Impact on Organizational Performance. *Journal of Management Accounting Research.* Vol. 12: 1–17.
34 Maiga, A. S. and Jacobs, F. A. (Fall 2003). Balanced Scorecard, Activity Based Costing and Company Performance: An Empirical Analysis. *Journal of Managerial Issues.* Vol. 15, No. 3: 283–301.
35 Yeniyurt, S. (2003). A Literature Review and Integrative Performance Measurement Framework for Multinational Companies. *Marketing Intelligence and Planning.* Vol. 21, No. 3.
36 Hoque, Z. and James, W. (2000). Linking Balanced Scorecard Measures to Size and Market Factors: Impact on Organizational Performance. *Journal of Management Accounting Research.* Vol. 12: 1–17.
37 Maiga, A. S. and Jacobs, F. A (Fall 2003). Balanced Scorecard, Activity Based Costing and Company Performance: An Empirical Analysis. *Journal of Managerial Issues.* Vol. 15, No. 3: 283–301.
38 Kaplan, R. S. and Norton. D.P. (1996). *The Balanced Scorecard: Translating Vision into Action.* Boston: Harvard Business School Press.
39 Wade, M. and Hulland, J. (2004). Review: The Resource-Based View and Information System Research: Review, Extension, and Suggestions for Future Research. *MIS Quarterly.* Vol. 28, No. 1: 107–112.
40 Martinsons, M. Davison, R. and Tse, D. (1999). The Balanced Scorecard: A Foundation for the Strategic Management of Information Systems. *Decision Support Systems.* 71–88
41 Chen, C. Y., Yang, Y-F., Chen, C-W., Chen, L-T. and Chen, T-H. (2010). Linking the Balanced Scorecard (BSC) to Business Management Performance: A Preliminary Concept of Fit Theory for Navigation Science and Management. *International Journal of the Physical Sciences.* Vol. 5, No. 8: 1296–1305.

42 Ellingson, D. A. and Wambsganss, J. R. (2001). Modifying the Approach to Planning and Evaluation in Governmental Entities: A Balanced Scorecard Approach. *Journal of Public Budgeting, Accounting and Financial Management.* Vol. 13, No. 1: 103–120.
43 Libby, T. Salterio, S. E. and Webb, A. (2004). The Balanced Scorecard: The Effects of Assurance and Process Accountability on Managerial Judgment. *Accounting Review.* Vol. 79, No. 4: 1075–1094.
44 Ullrich, M. J. and Tuttle, B. M. (2004). The Effects of Comprehensive Information Reporting Systems and Economic Incentives on Managers Time Planning Decisions. *Behav. Res. Acc.* Vol. 16: 89–105.
45 Kaplan, R. S. and Norton. D.P. (2004). *Measuring the Strategic Readiness of Intangible Assets.* Boston: Harvard Business School Press.
46 Martinsons, M. Davison, R. and Tse, D. (1999). The Balanced Scorecard: A Foundation for The Strategic Management of Information Systems. *Decision Support Systems.* Vol. 25.
47 Kaplan, R. S. and Norton. D. P. (January–February 1992). The Balanced Scorecard – Measures that Drive Performance. *Harvard Business Review.* Vol. 70, No. 1: 71–79.
48 Kaplan, R. S. and Norton, D. P. (1996). *The Balanced Scorecard: Translating Strategy into Action.* Boston: Harvard Business School Press. Kaplan did not regard the environment as a competitive business advantage. 75–85.

6 *Maslahah* and Orientations

(*Al-Din*) – Worship Orientation: The View of the Protection and Preservation of the Religion

The word "worship," which is meant in the worship orientation, is worship in a very broad sense. Not worship in the sense of a ritual of worship of a man to his Lord. Worship in the sense of ritual worship, performed by someone at a particular time, such as prayer, fasting, pilgrimage, charity, *Qurban*, even in special places such as mosques. Worship orientation has meaning, the presence of Allah (*s.w.t.*) for someone in any activity. Someone does something knowing that Allah (*s.w.t.*) sees and hears what they do.

Whatever is done is basically a worship of beings before the Almighty, who gives the trust to the caliphate. Someone is kind to another not because he loves that person. Speak well, be polite, courteous, and smile, not because you want to be appreciated by others. But because the provisions laid down by the Creator are so. Everything is done simply out of love for the Creator. This means that all the activities one performs are essentially interactions between oneself and Allah (*s.w.t.*) (Figure 6.1).

If someone loves another because of something that belongs directly to that person, so if something is less or not as good as expected, then it is certain that love for that party will decrease or be lost. However, if the love of the other is due to Allah (*s.w.t.*), then the lack or absence of something belonging to the other will not decrease or eliminate love for him. For example, service to the customer is done because of Allah (*s.w.t.*). So, if, at the time of service, the customer does not respect the service rendered, then the person will still try to give the best response. He does this because he loves Allah (*s.w.t.*) and not just because he wants the customer to be satisfied.

The presence of Allah (*s.w.t.*) in all activities has an influence on people to always do something according to Allah's wishes. Islam teaches that the one who leads an organization with honesty and does so because he is carrying out Allah's commands will receive a reward from Allah (*s.w.t.*) in the form of reward or kindness in the Hereafter (Ahmad, 1991).[1]

To apply the above principle, organizations need guidance on values, both in the form of commands and prohibitions. Both are contained in the religion.

DOI: 10.4324/9781003390947-8

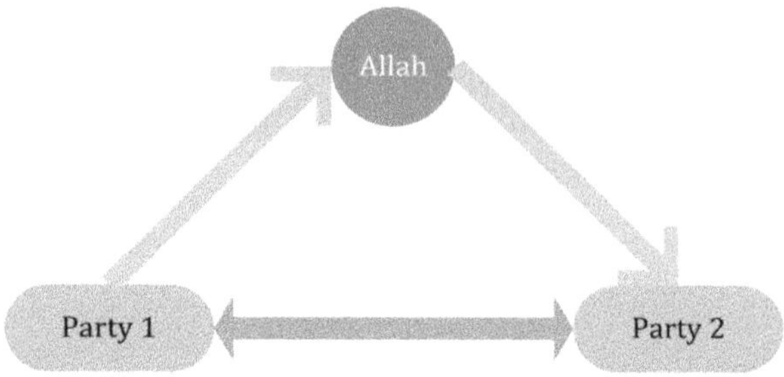

Figure 6.1 The Flow of Human Relations.

Source: Processed data

Islam is a universal religion, a religion whose existence transcends the boundaries of space and time. Islam has existed since the first man was created on earth. Islam also exists until the end of time. Islam encompasses all spaces or places. It is not limited to the land, the continent, the earth, and even the entire universe. Islam is a comprehensive religion whose teachings cover all sides of life. It is not just about ideology, politics, economics, social, and culture. Therefore, it is very important to adhere to the teachings of Islam.

Consistent implementation of religion in the organization must be given priority. This is an attempt to preserve and nurture the religion in the organization. The process of preserving and maintaining the religion must be done proactively. This means that the maintenance and preservation of religion must be done through the holistic application of all the principles of Islam within the organization.

Islam has three aspects, namely: *Aqidah, Shari'ah,* and *Akhlaq*. Each aspect has its own role (Nata, 2008).[2] *Aqidah* is a true and strong faith in the heart of every believer. *Aqidah* means believing in Allah (*s.w.t.*), the angels, the holy books, the apostles, the Hereafter, and destiny (qadar) good/bad (Al Imran, 2009).[3] Belief in Allah (*s.w.t.*) comprises of three things, namely belief in the *Rububiyah* of Allah (*s.w.t.*), belief in the *Uluhiyah* of Allah (*s.w.t.*), and belief in the names of Allah (*Asmaul husna*) and their attributes.

Belief in the *Rububiyah* of Allah has the meaning of acknowledging the deeds of Allah, the Almighty and the One Who arrange the universe. Belief in the *Rububiyah* of Allah is a manifestation of a servant's acknowledgement that only Allah is the Almighty, the All-Glorious, the All-Governing and the Ordering, the Giving, and the Preserving, the Exalted and the Exalted, the Glorifying and the Detestable, the Eternal, and the Deadly.[4]

Belief in the *Uluhiyah* of Allah has the meaning of acknowledging of his statement *Lā ilāha illa Allāh*. There is no other sacrifice entitled to be worshipped than Allah (*s.w.t.*).[5] There is no priority other than the business of Allah (*s.w.t.*). There is nothing to fear except Allah's wrath.

Belief in the names of Allah and His character are consequences of the *Rububiyah* of Allah (*s.w.t.*), belief in the absolute perfection of Allah (*s.w.t.*).

It is described in the names of *Asmaul husna*[6] and the characters. It means that Allah (*s.w.t.*) has a beautiful name and perfect qualities.

Believing in angels[7] means believing in their existence and the tasks they perform. Some of them were responsible for delivering revelations to the apostles and prophets. Some are responsible for rain and vegetation. They blow the trumpet when the Last Day dawns. Bring back the soul of the deceased person. Take care of the mountains. Take care of hell. Take care of the foetus in the womb. Nurture children. Record everyone's charity, each accompanied by two angels.[8] One angel records good deeds, and one angel records bad deeds. Two angels asked the dead when they were buried. One angel asked about good deeds, and another asked about bad deeds. There is also an angel in charge of heaven.

Believing in the Holy Book means believing in the Divine Holy Books that Allah (*s.w.t.*) sent down to His apostles and prophets.[9] The Torah was revealed to Prophet Musa (*a.s*) for the Children of Israel. The Bible was revealed by God to Prophet Isa as a justification and perfection of the Torah. The Book of Zabur was revealed by Allah (*s.w.t.*) to Prophet David (*a.s*). The book of *Suhuf* was revealed by Allah (*s.w.t.*) to Prophet Ibrahim. The Quran was revealed to Prophet Muhammad (*s.a.w.*).

Belief in the prophets means that Allah (*s.w.t.*) sent messengers and prophets to His servants as bearers of good news and as warners.[10] Belief in the Last Day is belief in the end of the day that has no day after that. Also, the belief that a resurrection day will come, where all the people who die will be resurrected.[11] After that, the time has come when a person's deeds while alive will be considered.[12] People who have done more good deeds than bad ones will receive a reward in the form of Paradise.[13] Those who have done more bad deeds than good deeds will be punished in Hell.[14]

Zeno bin Jamil (1996)[15] mentioned that believing in fate (*Qadar*),[16] in good and evil, means believing in all the provisions of Allah (*s.w.t.*) that apply to all His creatures[17] because whatever happens has been determined by God. Nevertheless, God opens opportunities for His servants to strive or make efforts to achieve better results.[18]

Zeno bin Jamil said that *Aqidah* also means following the five pillars of Islam, namely the creed, prayer, *Zakat*, hajj, and fasting.[19] The creed is the reading of the profession of faith as a sign of Islam. The creed consists of two sentences, namely *La ilaha illa Allah*. There is no one to worship except Allah (*s.w.t.*). *Muhammadar Rasulullah*, Muhammad (*s.a.w.*) is the Messenger of Allah (*s.w.t.*). Prayer consists of performing five daily prayers, namely Fajr, Dhuhr, Asr, Maghrib, and Isha, at the appointed time. *Zakat* is an obligation for Muslims if they have 85 grams of gold or equivalent wealth. So, every year 2.5% of the value of the wealth has to be paid as *Zakat*.[20] Hajj is for those who are physically and financially able to travel to the Holy Land. Fasting in the month of Ramadhan means not eating, drinking, and restraining the desires that break the fast from dawn to sunrise.[21]

Strong *Aqidah* inspires a sense of confidence that all that is commanded by the Creator and all that is forbidden is delivered through an intermediary, namely the Prophet Muhammad (*s.a.w.*). Strong *Aqidah* always relies on the action of its horn following the example of the life of Prophet Muhammad. All problems of life can be solved. There is a way out for every problem. Every way out is the best for the people.

Aqidah becomes a bridge of relationship or inner bond between a being and the Creator. People who have a strong *Aqidah* have a clear vision. The vision of achieving the long-term goal of salvation in the hereafter, without ignoring the achievement of short-term goals, is the success of life in this world. People who have a strong *Aqidah* will be aware that a long-term vision can be achieved by implementing the mission of living in the world as God's representative on earth. For this reason, everything that is done must always be beneficial and good for you, your family, your descendants, and for many people.

In realizing this vision, it is not possible for someone to hurt, oppress, or harm others. People who have a strong *Aqidah* believe that social relations between people are expressions of service to their Creator. Therefore, interaction with others is essentially worship and adoration of the Creator.

Umar RA also said: "One day when we were sitting near the Prophet Muhammad (*s.a.w.*), suddenly a man who was dressed in very white appeared and his hair was very black. He did not appear to be a trace from a long journey and no one among us knew him. Then he sat in front of the Prophet PBUH, then slammed his knees against the Prophet's knees, and put his hands on his thighs, then said:" "O Muhammad, explain to me about Islam."

Then Rosululloh (*s.a.w.*) replied: "Islam, namely: let you testify that there is no worship that is worshiped except Allah and indeed Muhammad is the messenger of Allah. You should establish prayer, pay *Zakat*, fast on the month of Ramadan, and do the hajj to the house of Allah if you are able to do it." The person said: "You are right." We were surprised, because he asked, and he justified it.

The person asked again: "Then explain to me about faith." (Rasululloh) replied: "You must believe in Allah, believe in His angels, His books, His messengers, the Last Day, and you must believe in good and bad *taqdir*." The person said: "You are right." Then the man asked again: "Then explain to me about *ihsan*." (He) replied: "You should worship Allah as if you saw Him. Even if you cannot (worship as if) see Him, surely, He sees you."

The person said again: "Tell me about the Day of Judgment." (He) answered: "The person who was asked did not know more than the one who asked." The person then said: "Tell me the signs." (He) replied: "If slaves give birth to their masters, and you see Bedouins who are barefoot, those who are poor are sheep herders competing for the building."

Then the person left, while I stayed for a while. Then the Prophet PBUH said: "O Umar, do you know the person who asked that?" I replied: "Allah and His Prophet know better." Then he said: "He is the angel Jibril who came to you to teach your religion" (Narrated by Muslim).

Shari'ah is the law and rules of human life both in the world and in the Hereafter; it contains commandments and prohibitions which Allah (*s.w.t.*), the

Creator, has imposed on His servants. That is, the *Shari'ah* is the guide to life, the manual, the guidance, the rules, the regulations, or the rules of the game from Allah (*s.w.t.*) given to all people through their apostle Muhammad (*s.a.w.*). The main source of the *Shari'ah* is the Qur'an and the Hadith. The *Shari'ah* regulates two cases, namely worship and *Muamalah*.[22] *Shari'ah*, which governs the course of worship, was ordained by Allah (*s.w.t.*) through the Messenger of Allah (*s.w.t.*). It must be implemented in accordance with Allah's provisions. If someone performs a ritual of worship that is not regulated by Allah (*s.w.t.*), the ritual is classified as *Bid'a* (Al Imran, 2009).[23]

Sometimes, when performing the *Shari'ah*, a translation from experts or scholars is required to understand it. The translation referred to is called *Fiqh* (Nyazee, 2003).[24] Fiqh is an operating procedure (SOP), a working instruction, a script arrangement, an orderly administration, operational guidelines, technical guidelines, references, etc.

Shari'ah and *Fiqh* regulate problem-solving (troubleshooting). These are references in the maintenance process; references in carrying out corrective action; references for taking preventive action against things that can cause misdirection in life. These are also references to doing a life improvement process (improvement) for the better; references for determining the direction of strategic management to achieve the goal of salvation in the hereafter and success of life in this world.

The analogy to the above conditions is that when a product is manufactured, the factory must hand over the products together with the manuals. The manual explains the important components of the product, how to operate the product, what prohibitions should not be made on the product, how to maintain the product, what to do if the product has a problem, and where to contact the dealer for customer service. The more sophisticated the product, the more detailed the explanation in the manual.

Likewise with the creation of the universe. Allah (*s.w.t.*), as the Creator, created the universe with manuals as detailed and complete as those contained in the *Shari'ah* (al-Quran and Hadith). The *Shari'ah* explains who the man is. What is the purpose of his life? Where should it begin? Where will it end? When will it begin? When will it end? How do you realize your vision and mission? And why should you fight for the vision and mission?

Akhlaq, in language that is easier to understand, is ethics, even though the scope of *Akhlaq* is much broader than ethics. Ethics is understood as a standard of moral behaviour, that is, behaviour that is accepted by social life as truth over error behaviour (Nickels, 2002).[25] In the field of business, ethics is interpreted as a moral standard of someone in activities to achieve their business goals. Nash (1990)[26] stated that business ethics is closely related to three basic things in decision-making. The first is the legal basis on which decisions should be made and whether the law should be followed. The second is decisions about economic and social issues that lie outside the legal realm. The third is deciding on the priority of personal interests over the interests of the company.

In business, legality is the most important ethical standard. Ethical conduct involves two things, knowing what is right and what is wrong and behaving accordingly. The manager should behave ethically. When he decides, he should be able to distinguish whether the decision is legal or not in terms of the things agreed upon. If he takes the right decision in accordance with the common provisions, it means that he has behaved ethically. If he makes a wrong decision that is not in accordance with the common provisions with the stakeholders, it means that he does not behave ethically.

Li (2010)[27] emphasized that business ethics is the most important issue for people who do business. He argues that business ethics is the soul of a business. When Arthur Andersen broke up, the whole world was astonished. Arthur Andersen is a public accounting firm that sets honest and law-abiding accounting standards. Arthur Andersen made ethical culture something to be proud of and implemented compactly in the company.[28] Arthur Andersen built the company through a lot of team building and ethics training.

But unfortunately, the ethical culture applied by Arthur Andersen was an ethical culture based on money and wealth and not spirituality. The ethical culture did not have the power to strike at the heart of the individual. Arthur Andersen was dissolved in 2002 because of ethical violations by its managers.

Islamic teachings emphasize that *Akhlaq* is an activity to apply the shari'ah of a believer. Of course, a believer is expected to always behave according to the shari'ah in daily life so that it can give a flavour to social life or colour it according to the requirements of the *Aqidah* and the *Shari'ah* guidance. That is, *Akhlaq* is ethics, morals, behaviour, attitudes according to the requirements of the *Aqidah*, and the *Shari'ah* guidance.

Up to the level of support and its implementation, *Akhlaq* and ethics are the same. Both are attitudes and behaviours based on a certain standard of reference. Yet, there are very prominent differences between the two. Ethics is the level of attitudes and behaviours that relate to man-made rules or laws. A rule and law that is highly dependent on place and time. *Akhlaq* is the level of attitudes and behaviour that relates to the *shari'ah* based on the *Aqidah*. *Shari'ah* and *Aqidah* were established by the Creator of the law. Therefore, *Akhlaq* is objective and does not depend on place and time, while ethics is subjective because it depends on place and time.

In the language used by Nasution (2009),[29] *Akhlaq* cannot ignore the transcendental value, while ethics only talks about universal values. Although there are many theories and approaches in ethics, ethics is sometimes difficult to apply because of its normative nature.

Akhlaq in the language of management is all the activities of applying the *Shari'ah* in daily life, both in domestic life and in the life of people, both in personal life and in social, political, economic, legal, and other activities. To behave according to the *Shari'ah* is a must for a believer. Violating the *Shari'ah*, whether intentionally or unintentionally, will bear its own consequences.[30]

For this reason, a believer must always conduct an internal examination for himself as to whether his daily conduct in the family, community, organization, or government is in accordance with the shari'ah. The manifestation of a believer's reverence towards his Creator has implications for *Akhlaq* in everyday life. Nata (2008)[31] stated that a person who has a strong faith is again truthful and performs worship with full sincerity and solemnity should ideally have a moral or moral character.

Aqidah, Shari'ah, and *Akhlaq* are three important aspects in Islam. People who do not have *Aqidah,* also do not have an obligation to apply shari'ah. Conversely, it can be said that someone who does not apply the shari'ah does not have *Aqidah. Akhlaq* is an important factor in proving that the person in question has *Aqidah* and *Shari'ah* (Nasution, 2009).[32]

The relationship between *Aqidah, Shari'ah,* and *Akhlaq* can be associated with a race. *Aqidah* is a vision, a mission, and the goal of being a champion of a race. *Shari'ah* are maps or racecourse plans, GPS, operating manuals for race cars, racing rules, and conditions. Morale is the ethics of the drivers' behaviour when they race from start to finish.

A racer with a winning mentality will have the vision and mission to win the race, whoever the opponent is, wherever the race is held, and whatever the conditions of the racing environment. A driver with a winning mentality will always be guided by the rules in place. Regarding the race car he uses, he always refers to the manufacturer's manual. Communication is always with both the navigator and the team at the pit stop. Champion drivers are drivers whose behaviour complies with the race rules. Behaviour before the start of the race, behaviour at the starting position, behaviour when overtaking the opponent, and so on.

The interpretation of *Aqidah* and *Akhlaq* is relatively unchanging (constant) in time and place. In the language of mathematics, it can be said that the interpretation of *Aqidah* and *Akhlaq* is not a function of place and time.[33] However, the conditions of understanding and applying it to a person may change according to the situation in which that person finds himself. Al-Ghazali in Zidan (1997)[34] says that a person's *Akhlaq* can change or be changed by their actions. Therefore, they should always try to suppress anger, lust, and evil.

The interpretation of *Shari'ah* (*fiqh*) always changes according to the need and is very dependent on the standard of living or human civilization where they are. In the language of mathematics, it is said that the interpretation of *Shari'ah* is a function of place and time.[35]

The application of the three aspects of Islam, as explained above, is essentially a person applying the system of Islam to Allah (*s.w.t.*) as Creator, to his fellow human beings, and to other creatures of Allah (*s.w.t.*). In the context of organization, the application of Islam means the application of Islamic values in the behaviour of the organization to the Almighty, who gives sustenance to the members and to the environment.

The interaction between the organization with God, the Creator, the organization with the stakeholders, and the organization with the environment (Figure 6.2) is to achieve salvation in the afterlife and success of life in the world. It can be said that the activity of doing good to Allah (*s.w.t.*), the Creator, the stakeholders, and the environment is a cause for achieving the goals of life (consequence).[36] This principle leads to the understanding that the salvation in

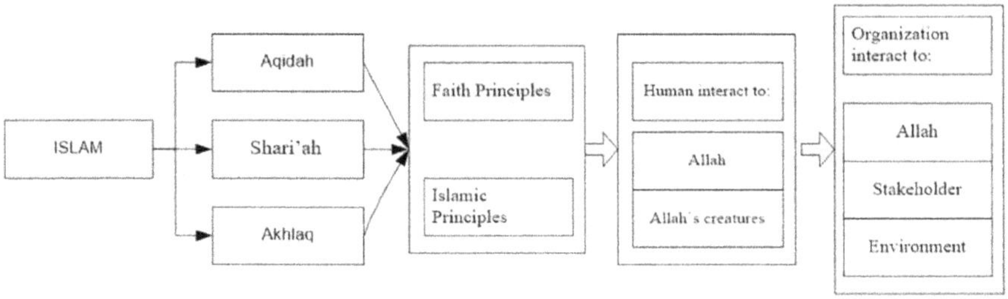

Figure 6.2 The Basis and Application of Worship Orientation.

Source: Processed data

the hereafter and the success in the world cannot be achieved if it does not do well to Allah (*s.w.t.*) the Creator, to stakeholders, and to the environment.[37]

(*Al-Nafs*) – Internal Process Orientation: *The View of the Protection and Preservation of the Soul*

As al-Ghazali explained, man is made up of two components, namely a body, which has a physical dimension and a spiritual dimension which is nonphysical. The body is a part of the human being that can be physically seen or felt. The soul, on the other hand, is not material and cannot be perceived with the five senses. These two components play an important role for a human being. The body is the identity of a human being, while the soul makes the body live, grow, and develop.

The same can be explained for the organization. The bodies in the organization are infrastructure, IT, equipment, machines, materials, money, buildings, distribution channels, etc. The souls of the organization are systems, values, strategy, core competencies, work culture, and brand image. They are all affected by all the internal processes of the organization. These processes can be broadly classified into three process groups. Main or core processes, support processes, and prevention and sustainability processes.

Material or physical resources are the bodies of the organization. On the contrary, non-material or non-physical resources are the souls of the organization. The body and soul of the organization and the body and soul of a person are like a rice field that becomes a place for farming. The yield of cultivation is not only for one's own benefit but also for the benefit of the community. The body and soul of the organization must play a role, both economically and socially, for the stakeholders.

The body and soul of the organization must be nurtured and developed, not only to survive in the world but also to find redemption in the hereafter. An instance of this is an Islamic Financial Institution that manages the finance of its clients. In achieving its goal, the institution seeks not only the highest profit but also the blessings of Allah (*s.w.t.*), the Owner of the Last Days.

Figure 6.3 Spiritual Energy Flows from Worship Orientation to Internal Process Orientation.

Source: Firdaus (2017: 92)

To achieve this, the soul of the company must be purified. One thing that must be done is to get out of the interest system. The interest system can destroy the ownership system. It has a detrimental effect on the property system. *Maqasid al-shari'ah* guarantees that the organization provides services that can avert harm.

Soul cleansing can only occur when the organization is able to meet the needs of the worship orientation. The worship orientation, as the energy centre, transmits spiritual positive energy to the entire *Maslahah* orientation of the organization. All orientations respond to the energy of the worship orientation. The internal process orientation has the least inertia compared to the other orientations. The internal process orientation responds faster to the worship orientation than others (Figure 6.3). The worship orientation makes the soul of the organization become calmer, gentler, more patient, more optimistic, and so on. And finally, the internal process orientation is fulfilled.

The needs of the organization's soul must be met for the organizational life to be balanced. Chapra (2007)[38] described 12 soul needs that must be fulfilled at the macro level, namely: dignity-respect-human fraternity and social equality; justice; spiritual and moral upliftment; security of life-wealth rights and honour; freedom; education; good governance; need satisfaction; employment and independent work; balance of income and wealth distribution; marriage and childcare; and family and social solidarity.

Fulfilling these 12 needs creates an environment that can fulfil the 13th need, which is lowering the crime rate. When all these 13 needs are met, it can be assumed that the 14th need, spiritual peace and happiness, will also be met.

At the micro level, Rampersad (2006)[39] found that there is a relationship between employee well-being and organizational performance. There is also a strong relationship between employee satisfaction and employee retention. A satisfied workforce would increase the retention of workers in the organization.

Rampersad pointed out that a lack of employee retention and satisfaction causes high litigation costs and affects the performance of the company. This naturally leads to dissatisfaction among customers. Rampersad explained that individual retention occurs through the alignment between personal scorecards and the organizational scorecard.[40]

Meeting the needs of the soul of the organization can be done in various ways. Ibn 'Ashur (1998)[41] stated that organizations should fulfil their basic needs through activities to promote human welfare, prevent corruption, maintain justice, and preserve stability and harmony. Fulfilling the soul of the organization is necessary to support the sustainability of the organization.

The needs of the organizational soul are rooted in the internal processes. Organizations must be able to recognize internal processes through the design of work systems and work processes. The design of work systems and work processes is done through value chain analysis methods.[42] Porter (1998)[43] introduced the concept to explain internal business processes. Value chain analysis was based on the view that the organization is a compilation of various machines, equipment, people, money, materials as well as methods. By systematically arranging all the resources and a set of activities, value could be created that was needed by the customer.

Porter distinguishes between main processes and supporting processes. The main process is an activity that is directly related to the value delivered to the customer. The main process is divided into five main areas, namely input logistics, operations, expenditure logistics, marketing, and sales and services. Each of the main processes is associated with a supporting process that promotes the effectiveness and efficiency of the main activities. The supporting process consists of four main areas, namely procurement department, technology development including research and development, human resource management, and infrastructure, i.e., systems for planning, finance, quality, or information management, etc. The detailed value chain analysis can be seen in Figure 6.4.

Referring to the value chain analysis, a work system and work process are designed for the organization based on the *Maqasid al-shari'ah* as shown in

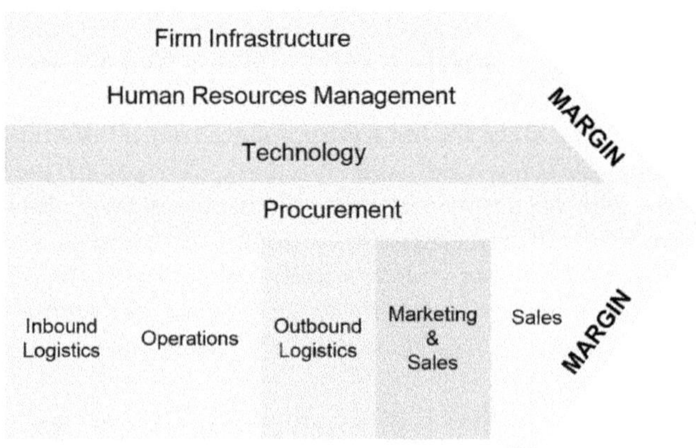

Figure 6.4 Value Chain Analysis.

Source: Michael Porter (1998: 10)

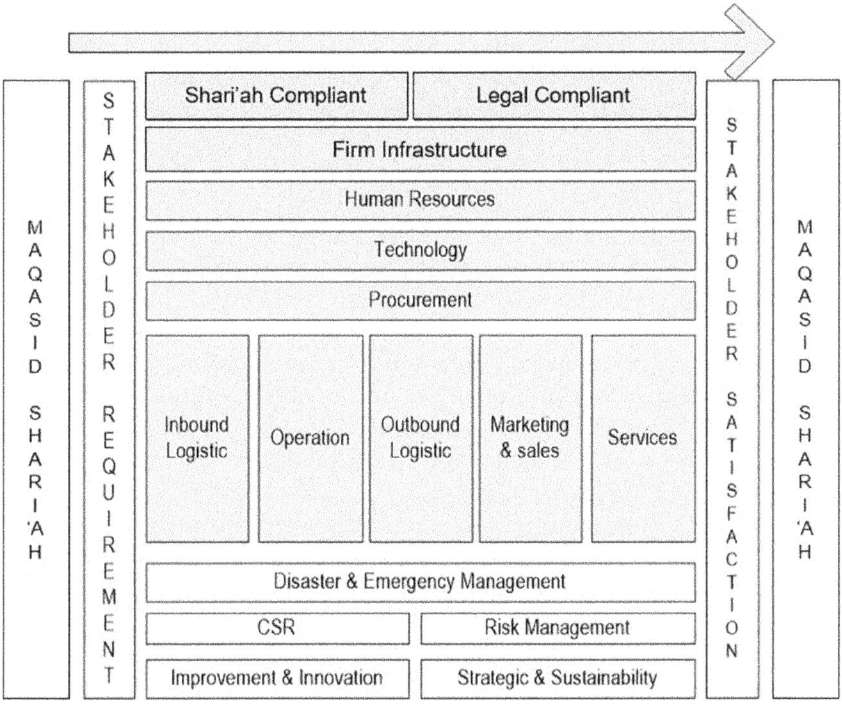

Figure 6.5 Design of Internal Process Orientation.

Source: Processed data

Figure 6.5. The design is generic and can be adopted for different types of organizations, both services and manufacturing, both for-profit and not-for-profit. The difference between the two types of organizations can be seen in the main processes. They are the input logistics, the operational processes, and the output logistics.

Maqasid al-shari'ah becomes the most important basis for the design of work systems and work processes.[44] In organizations that are not based on *Shari'ah*, the work system is controlled by the requirements of the stakeholders to achieve the satisfaction of the stakeholders. In organizations based on *Shari'ah*, the work system[45] is controlled by the requirements of the stakeholders who are based on *Shari'ah* to achieve the satisfaction of the stakeholders who are also based on *Shari'ah*. This means that the stakeholders' requirements are the basis for determining the work processes within the organization, but these requirements must be aligned with *Shari'ah*.

If the stakeholder's requirements are not consistent with shari'ah then it is grouped into requirements which are rejected by shari'ah. This is because the intended goal is the stakeholder's satisfaction which is aligned with shari'ah. If the stakeholder's satisfaction is not aligned with shari'ah, it is grouped into satisfaction rejected by shari'ah.

Shari'ah provisions that form the basis of stakeholder requirements can be derived from the Al-Quran, the Hadith, the fatwas of the ulama, the input from *Shari'ah* supervisory board, etc. *Shari'ah* provisions form the basis for determining whether the stakeholders' requirements are in accordance with *Shari'ah* or rejected.

Stakeholder requirements are determined through customer satisfaction surveys, supplier satisfaction surveys, job satisfaction surveys, supplier–customer regulations and feedback, mid-term plans, annual plans, past business results, improvement and innovation processes, audit results, or management review meetings.

As stakeholder desires and expectations change, so do their requirements. Regulatory changes can negatively impact products and services, as well as the methods used to distribute products and services. Technological changes affect the acceleration of product cycles. If a company does not respond wisely and appropriately, it will be let down by its stakeholders. The sustainability of the organization is then naturally at risk.

The core process or main process is a process within the organization that has a direct impact on creating value for the stakeholders. For an Islamic life insurance company, the core process includes the underwriting process, the actuarial process, and the claims process. For a manufacturing company, the core process includes the quality control of the input process, the production inspection process, and the quality control of the output process. For a college, the core process includes the student and faculty recruitment process, the academic process, the alumni management process, the library management process, and the research management process.

Supporting processes are processes within organizations that support the core processes or key processes in creating value for stakeholders. For an Islamic life insurance company, supporting processes include the processes of financial management, human resource management, marketing, and information technology management. For a manufacturing company, supporting processes include procurement processes, financial management processes, human resource management processes, customer service processes, and information technology management processes. For a college, supporting processes include financial management processes, human resource management processes, and information technology management processes.

To ensure that the entire process in the organization always refers to *Maqasid al-shari'ah*, the organization must establish a process specifically tasked with planning, monitoring, and evaluating the application of shari'a in all processes within the organization. The main purpose of the existence of the process is to maintain the adherence to shari'ah.

Compliance is not limited to *Shari'ah* only. Since the organization is in a region, it can be established that there are provisions or regulations in the region that govern the activities of the organization. As an entity in the region, the organization must comply with the rules and regulations. Therefore, the organization must establish the process that will ensure the implementation of the compliance process.

Natural disasters, as well as other unexpected events such as fires or losses, can result in tangible and intangible losses to the organization. Worse is the threat to the sustainability of the organization. Organizations need to manage natural disasters and emergencies in such a way that the extent of damage and losses can be controlled.

The organization operates in an uncertain environment. Something that happens to the organization due to uncertainty is called risk. Sometimes the risk matches the expectations, and sometimes, it does not. Risk is a certainty. It means that the risk can happen exactly. For risk to be properly controlled, the organization must establish a process that is responsible for managing the risks that occur. The investment management function has risks related to non-realization of investment returns. The production process function has risks, the occurrence of production results that do not meet customer expectations. The product development function has risks where the product is not accepted by customers.

Organizations have a social responsibility to the communities around the organization. Like an organism living in a habitat, an organization should be able to interact with the environment. A special function is needed in the organization to manage the social life of the organization. CSR is a function created in organizations to manage the social responsibility of the organization. Islamic organizations consider CSR not only to improve the social functions towards the environment but also to manifest the human functions as Allah's *Caliphs* on earth.

Organizations must be flexible to change. Therefore, they must be innovative and creative. To achieve this, organizations must establish a process to guide the management of improvement and innovation. Sustainable improvement is achieved using quality policies, quality objectives, audit results, data analysis, corrective actions, preventive actions, and effective management reviews. Corrective actions are taken to eliminate the cause of nonconformity so that similar incidents do not recur. Preventive actions are taken to address root causes that could potentially lead to nonconformances.

Organizational sustainability is a goal that the manager of the organization strives for. Of course, sustainability can only be achieved through a strategic planning process that is carefully structured and applied according to the plan. The results of the implementation of strategic planning are also properly monitored. For this reason, organizations need to manage the strategic planning process and sustainability.

From the above description, the internal process orientation is a view on the preservation of the soul (*al-Nafs*). This aspect is the answer to the question: "How should organizations manage internal processes so that salvation in the hereafter and the success of life in this world are sustainable?"

(*Al-Nasl*) – Talent Orientation: *The View of the Protection and Preservation of the Talent*

وَٱلَّذِينَ يَقُولُونَ رَبَّنَا هَبْ لَنَا مِنْ أَزْوَٰجِنَا وَذُرِّيَّٰتِنَا قُرَّةَ أَعْيُنٍ وَٱجْعَلْنَا لِلْمُتَّقِينَ إِمَامًا

> And those who say: "Our Lord, grant us from among our wives and offspring comfort to our eyes and make us a leader [i.e., example] for the righteous."
>
> (QS Furqan 25: 74)

Firdaus (2012a)[46] explained that in the business context, achieving business benefits is highly dependent on the fulfilment of employee orientation to explain the education and maintenance of offspring *(al-Nasl)*. Managing the workforce for the sustainability of leadership is done by placing the workforce in a high position.

Islam is very concerned about the position of the employees in the organization. Before the employees start their work, they must know how much wages they will receive.[47] Wages must be paid as soon as possible.[48] Rasulullah (*s.a.w.*) threatened the managers of the organization who did not pay the wages of the workers. Allah (*s.w.t.*) classifies *Dzalim* acts against workers in a group of big sins.[49]

Choudhury (1986)[50] explains that individual wages must be in proportion to the amount of work and the categories of work done by workers. The amount of work is usually calculated in terms of hours worked. However, the categories of work are specific to each occupation. This explains that the wages of workers are related to labour productivity.

The management of an organization should be aware that Allah (*s.w.t.*) has chosen the employees as *Caliphs* of Allah (*s.w.t.*) to run the organization when they have joined or become part of the organization.

There are three groups of people who will be my enemies on the Day of Judgment. Whoever is my enemy, I am hostile to him. **The first** is the person who swears allegiance to Me and then breaks it. **The second** is a person who sells free people (not slaves) and then uses the money from the sale price. **The third** is a person who employs a worker but does not give him wages after the work is done (Narrated by Ibn Majah).

The above doctrine differs from the capitalist understanding. Capitalists equate labour with commodities. Ricardo (2004)[51] stated that labour is like other objects (other things) that are bought and sold, and their quantity may increase or decrease. There are fair prices and market prices for labour. The fair price for labour is the price necessary for workers to earn a living among themselves and maintain a working group without the number of workers increasing or decreasing.

Ricardo stated that the number of labour groups must be maintained. When the number of labour groups increases, the supply of labour increases, so labour market prices decrease. When the number of labour groups decreases, the supply of labour decreases, so labour market prices increase. To maintain the number of workers, workers' wages should not be too far from the fair price. In other words: When workers do well, workers' families grow. The number of workers increases, keeping the price low in the labour market. Labour suffers. When workers are not doing well, the number of workers' families decreases. The number of workers decreases, making the price in the labour market high. The entrepreneurs suffer.

The labour needed to support oneself and one's family does not depend on the amount of salary but on the amount of spending on food, needs, and pleasures. They all depend heavily on spending habits. Thus, according to Ricardo, the just wage of workers depends on the price of food, necessities, and pleasures necessary for the maintenance of the workers and their families. This view shows that the cost of labour does not depend on labour productivity but on external factors. When the price of food and necessities rises, workers' wages rise; when the price of food and necessities falls, workers' wages fall.

The question is whether the entire workforce can be a representation of the *Maslahah daruriyah* organization, that is, a descendant (*al-Nasl*), as intended by al-Shātibi? Organizational sustainability is interpreted as the sustainability of the benefits of the organization to the stakeholders of the organization. The benefit of sustainability is very important. When someone dies, the opportunity to do something good ends. There is no other activity that can be done to increase the benefit except for three things, namely charity, useful knowledge, and pious children who always pray for their parents.

> From Abu Hurairah RA, he said: "The Messenger of Allah said: 'When the son of Adam - who is a human being - dies, his deeds will be ending - that is, he cannot increase his reward -, but from three kinds of things, namely: charity or usable knowledge or righteous children who like to pray for them.'"
>
> (Narrated by Muslim)

It can be said that the three practices are the real passive income for people to achieve salvation in the hereafter and success of life in the world. It can also be said that the three practices mentioned above are machines that generate rewards. The machine continues to produce rewards even if the owner of the machine is non-productive in producing goods. In the context of the organization, the organization must have rewards even if the founder/manager of the organization is deceased. To achieve this, the organization must do three things, do a lot of charity, learn a lot, and build a good talent system.

The sustainability of organizations depends heavily on the offspring or next generation of organizations (*Dhurriyyah*)[52] that can satisfy others. A successful successor generation consists not only of manpower but also of talented employees who can please and bless others. The next generation has a vision and a mission that are consistent with the vision and mission of the organization that established them. They inherit the noble ideals of the organization's founder/leadership. It traces the lineage (*Nasab*)[53] of organizations. Talent orientation is an improvement process carried out to prepare the next generation of organizations that are compliant and pious so that the leadership relay of the organization runs smoothly.

Talented employees are produced by good human resource management. Coyle[54] explained that talented employees emerge from an ignition process in an organization called hot talent. The ignition process is done through master coaching by deepening the practice. To produce talented workers who represent the essence and attitude of the *Caliph* of Allah (*s.w.t.*) on earth, fuel is needed, which comes from worship orientation and internal process orientation.

The worship orientation as the central energy sends positive spiritual energy to all components of the organization. The spiritual relationship between the organization and the Supreme Giver *Rizk*, between the organization and stakeholders, and between organizations and the environment provides a good aura for the attitude and behaviour of talented workers. Work is revered by a talented workforce not only at the level of philosophy or concept but also at the level of application.

On the other hand, achieving internal process orientation also gives positive energy to talented employees. Working relationships between superiors and subordinates become better and more harmonious. Talented employees frequently conduct self-assessments. Awareness of their potential and important role to the organization increases. This undoubtedly has a positive effect on increasing the capacities and capabilities of talented employees (Figure 6.6).

The capacity of the workforce is identical to the vessel, capacity, the measure of how much *Aqidah, Shari'ah, Akhlaq*, insight, knowledge, skills, education, and experience the workforce can absorb. Capacity is synonymous with content: *Aqidah, Shari'ah, Akhlaq,* insight, knowledge, skills, education, and experience that the labour force possesses. An example: capacity is a cup, while ability is the water that fills the cup.

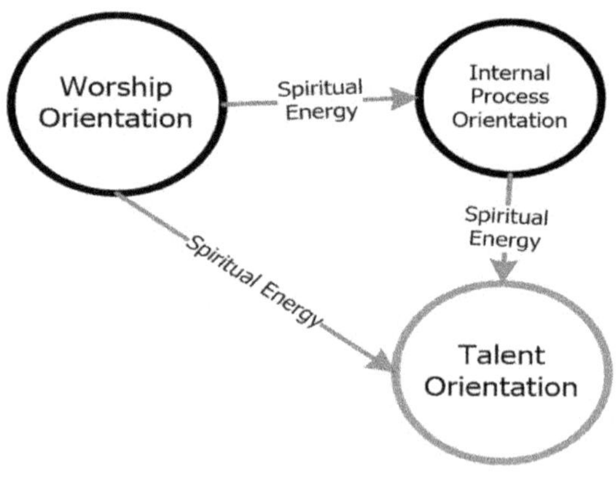

Figure 6.6 Spiritual Energy Flows from Worship Orientation and Internal Process Orientation to Talent Orientation.

Source: Firdaus (2017: 101)

Figure 6.7 Talented Workforce Capabilities and Talent Capacities.

Source: Firdaus and Yusuf (2014)

Talented workers are always happy at work. They are energetic and innovative in their work. This condition occurs not only in the workforce but also in their domestic harmony. Innovative and spiritually minded talented employees influence the agility of the organization. This promotes the sustainable improvement process, both in individuals and organized organizations. Organizations are flexible to environmental changes. Organizational managers are increasingly aware of the important role of talented employees in organizational sustainability (Figure 6.7).

Talented workers are workers who possess the skills of insight, knowledge, skill, education, and experience that match the capacity of organizational management competencies. At the same time, talented workers must have the capabilities of *Aqidah, Shari'ah,* and *Akhlaq* that are consistent with the capacity of worship orientation.

Organizational management competence is the total measure of insight, knowledge, skills, training, and experience. Competence in terms of worshipful orientation is the total measure of *Aqidah, Shari'ah,* and *Akhlaq*. These two competencies are expected to be able to motivate talented workers who, when they work, are basically not only earning a living but serving as a means of fulfilling their duties as *Caliphs* of Allah (*s.w.t.*).

As *Caliphs* of Allah (*s.w.t.*) in the management of the organization, talented workers must naturally have a strong *Aqidah*. This is necessary so that talented workers can behave according to the requirements of the *Aqidah* and in accordance with the guidance of the *shari'ah*. This will enable talented employees to perform their duties and responsibilities according to the moral principles of Prophet Muhammad (*s.a.w.*).

As managers of an organization, talented employees must have insight into the scope of work. Talented employees must also have knowledge of job descriptions. They must be able to do the work according to their workload. They must also be able to do the work without having to be given instructions. Therefore, talented workers are required to have a level of education that is commensurate with the scope of the work. Talented workers also need to be able to develop in many ways by gaining experience to be able to solve new tasks. Without all this, talented workers cannot increase their capacity and skills.

It is very interesting what was Chowdury[55] found out. He explained his views about the characteristics of organizations that will exist in the twenty-first century. Only organizations led by talented workers will exist at that time. Chowdury explained that talented workers are not only able to perform routine tasks but also understand the importance of the task or work in the value chain of the organization.

Chowdury assumes a shift from the industrial age to the information age. In the industrial age, physical assets were considered the most important buffer for competitive advantage. But in the information age, it is the non-physical assets that are unquantifiable as the main buffer. The main pole for non-physical assets that cannot be calculated is in the talented workforce.

Chowdury's statement is consistent with the findings of a McKinsey & Company study. In 2000, McKinsey[56] conducted a study of 13,000 managers from 112 large companies in the United States. The research showed that talented workers determine who wins the competition. McKinsey stated that in the manufacturing industry, the best factory manager was able to increase profits by 130%. In the service industry, the best managers managed to increase profits by 80%. While in the financial services industry, the best portfolio manager achieved a growth rate in returns (earnings) of close to 50%.

There are several qualities that talented workers possess, including a high level of initiative. Talented workers initiate something new. They do not like it when something is procedural or established. You could say talented workers become the locomotive of change in the company. They do not like the status quo. The principle they believe in is change or die.

An inspiring story comes from Edward Deming when he first introduced the PDCA idea to Japanese Scientists and Engineers (JUSE)[57] in 1951. At the time, his brilliant idea was not selling well in his home country, the United States. But when he explained it to Japanese government engineers and scientists, the idea met with a positive response. So PDCA is identical to the Japanese TQC.

Talented workers are always innovative and can teach innovation to other workers. Japanese companies have a good system to find talented workers. Through the culture of Gemba Kaizen, employees are encouraged to always be innovative in their work environment.

The talented employees inspire and motivate other employees. A talented workforce is a workforce that does not just want to make the proposed changes itself. He hopes that other workers will do the same with him. The talented worker likes to share with other workers. But remember that not all talented workers can easily implement their brilliant ideas or can do so.

The entire description above explains that talent orientation is a perspective for the preservation of the progeny (*al-'nasl*). This aspect is the answer to the question: "What activities should be carried out for talented workers so that salvation in the Hereafter and the success of life in the world are sustainable?"

(*Al-'Aql*) – Learning Orientation: *The View of the Protection and Preservation of the Intellect*

Al-Ghazali defined intellect in four terms, namely:

- i The quality which distinguishes man from animals, so that by its man can understand and acquire theoretical (*Nazaiyah*) and abstract (*Fikriyah*).[58]
- ii The word intellect is used to understand axioms, or understand possibilities that could occur, or understand the impossibility of something that cannot possibly occur. For example, intellect can understand that two should be greater than one. It is impossible for one to be greater than one. Another example: If someone is present in one place, then it is impossible for him to be present in another place at the same time.
- iii The word intellect is used for both science gained through experience (empirical) and science gained through education.
- iv The word intellect is used when the power of instincts develops more than usual. Generally, people who have such instincts can see the end of something.

Intellect is created by Allah (*s.w.t.*) so that humans can find the reason for their creation. Allah (*s.w.t.*) has created human beings as *Caliphs* on the earth. Allah (*s.w.t.*) shows the signs of human caliphate by creating the universe. Therefore, to understand the universe (*Kauniyah*), humans must use their minds. Allah (*s.w.t.*) also writes these signs in the al-Quran and the hadiths. Therefore, intellect should be used to ponder over the written verses (*Kauliyah*) in al-Quran and the Hadith.

Allah (*s.w.t.*) has described the importance of intellect in human beings in many verses of the Al-Quran.[59] The Al-Quran explains the people who use their minds by saying, "They are people who have minds" or "Verily, in this case there is a lesson for those who have minds."[60] For people who do not use their intellect, the Al-Quran states: "Have you no mind?," "Do you not think?"[61]

Al-Ghazali explained that intellect is the source of knowledge. Knowledge is always emanated from the intellect. The diffusion of knowledge through the intellect is like the light emitted by the sun, like the fruits produced by plants, the sight that emanates from the eye. It is also the intellect that makes dark situations bright, from ignorance to understanding, from not knowing the problems to knowing the problems.

But the intellect has limitations. The intellect can only allow things that can be activated by the mind. In life, there are many things that cannot be explained by the intellect. To discuss such things, the way is faith. The intellect is an instinct that Allah (*s.w.t.*) has created for man to obtain various kinds of information to support reason. Moreover, Allah (*s.w.t.*) created the heart to tackle things that are not possible with the intellect.

It is obvious that giving nourishment to a balanced intellect and a balanced heart is necessary for an optimal learning process. It is not overdoing it with each other. Too serious a learning process proves fatal to the organization. The case of the dissolution of Arthur Andersen in 2002 became a valuable lesson for all of us.

Andersen (Smith and Quirk, 2004)[62] was the largest professional firm in the world with 85,000 employees in 44 countries. Andersen's revenue reaches more than USD 9 billion. Andersen sets standards for honest and law-abiding accounting. The existing slogan "There is an Andersen way and there is a wrong way." The Andersen philosophy is implemented throughout the world through various team-building activities and various morale improvement exercises. One Andersen employee received 135 hours of transition training.

The ethical culture employed by Andersen is one that promotes reason over the heart. Such a culture does not have the power to reach the heart of Andersen employees. Andersen also dissolved in 2002 because its managers violated ethics.

For the heart to be a companion to the intellect in the learning process, the heart must be given nourishment. If the heart does not receive nourishment, the heart may die. The food of the heart is science and knowledge gained through the intellect. Man needs proper synergy between intellect and heart in the process of learning. Allah (*s.w.t.*) has prepared the duet between intellect and heart for human beings to perform their duties and responsibilities as *Caliphs* on earth.

Fulfilment of the needs of the learning orientation results from the flow of positive spiritual energy emanating from the worship orientation. Spiritual energy makes it easy for the intellect and the heart to fulfil its nourishment. The intellect always thinks and ponders about Allah's creations. The heart can easily believe it.

Moreover, the learning orientation can be fulfilled when the talent orientation is fulfilled. The talent orientation can produce workers as learners. Individual learners and learning organizations are individuals and organizations that are able to control their intellect and heart to control their actions and behaviour according to the competencies of worship orientation and organizational management competencies (Figure 6.8).

Individual learners cannot have much impact on the organization if individuals are not properly mobilized, managed, and packaged. Organizations should organize different kinds of organizational resources to make learning in organizations as organizational culture. Learning culture as organizational work culture can be achieved by incorporating learning objectives into the vision – mission and goals of the organization. This is done so that all learning activities can be understood and carried out continuously by using different medium in the organization both individually and collectively.

Figure 6.8 Spiritual Energy Flows from Worship Orientation and Talent Orientation to Learning Orientation.

Source: Firdaus (2017: 107)

The main object of the learning process, then, is human capital and organizational capital. Human capital arises from the intellect and the heart. Intellect and heart create competencies for worship orientation and competencies for organizational management. Worship orientation competency is the total of *Aqidah, Shari'ah,* and *Akhlaq*. Organizational management competence is the total amount of insight, knowledge, skills, experience, and training.

Insight is a person's view of a matter. Insight depends on education, family background, environment, length of work, life experience, etc. In the field of work, a manager's insight is usually broader than an operator's, but an operator's insight is not always narrower than a manager's. The breadth and narrowness of insight of managers and operators depend greatly on the field of work or educational background.

Knowledge is a variety of symptoms and phenomena that humans encounter and acquire through intellectual observation. In simpler terms, knowledge is something generated by the intellect. Food sense is thinking, and the result of thinking is knowledge. Without thinking, intellect cannot produce knowledge. In the context of work, knowledge can be gained from problems found, information from subordinates or supervisors, customer feedback, benchmarking with competitors, standard books, SOP manuals, regulations, etc.

Skills are abilities that a person possesses. Skills are usually acquired through experience, work hours, training, and education. Someone acquires the ability to drive a forklift after attending a forklift operator training course. One acquires the ability to spin wool yarn after working for one year. One acquires welding skills when one performs welding work.

Experience is something that one has lived through or experienced. An operator has been working on a CNC machine for five years. This means that the operator has been operating CNC machines for five years.

Education is a planned system to teach someone. A manager's position requires at least a bachelor's degree, which means that a manager's position must be filled by people who have gone through at least the bachelor's level education system.

Jacobson and Roos (1997)[63] explain that there are five main categories of intellectual capital. The five categories are human capital, customer capital and relationships, and organizational capital. Organizational capital consists of two sources, namely business process capital and repeat business and development capital.

Meanwhile, Kaplan and Norton (1996)[64] found that the learning and growth perspective of organizational performance depends on three factors, namely human resources (employee capabilities), information systems (information systems capabilities), and organizational resources (motivation, empowerment, harmony). Kaplan, therefore, used three objectives for the learning and growth perspective, namely human capital, information capital, and organizational capital.

The role and function of organizational capital can be determined in terms of work systems and work processes. As explained in the orientation to internal processes, work systems and work processes are designed and implemented by breaking down all the processes in the organization. The work system and work process begin with the understanding of the *Maqasid al-shari'ah* (Figure 6.9).

In addition, the organization must receive work system inputs and work processes that emerge from stakeholder requirements. The design of the work system and work processes is done by considering processes that are core competencies, supporting processes, improvement and innovation systems management, strategic planning and sustainability, regulatory compliance, disaster management and emergencies, risk management, and social organization engagement in the environment.

The whole above description explains that learning orientation is a way to maintain intellect (*al-'Aql*). This aspect is the answer to the question, "What

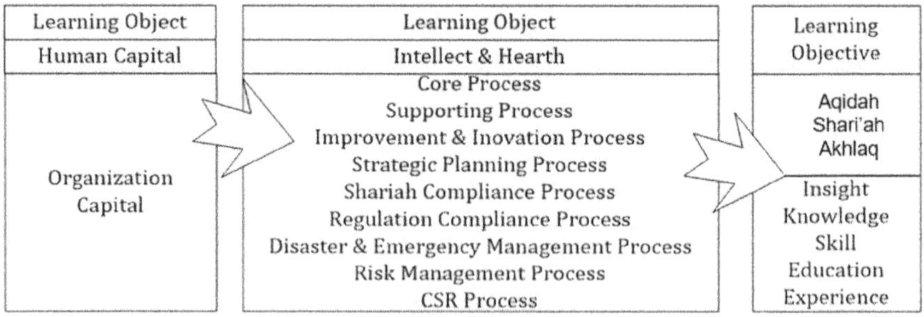

Figure 6.9 Scheme of Learning Object and Learning Objective.

Source: Firdaus and Yusuf (2014)

learning activities should be carried out so that salvation in the hereafter and the success of life in this world can be sustained?"

(*Al-Mal*) – Wealth Orientation: *How to View Explanation of Wealth*

O you who believe, do not consume each other's wealth unlawfully, but only [in lawful] transactions by mutual consent. And do not kill yourselves (or each other). Verily Allah (*s.w.t.*) is ever merciful to you (QS al-Nisā 4: 29).

Wealth (*al-Mal*) is everything that is loved by humans.[65] The verse explains that people love things that are material in nature, such as women, children, and wealth consisting of many kinds of gold, silver, horses, cattle, and rice fields. Wealth is needed for activities. Without wealth, humanity cannot perform its activities optimally.

Unfortunately, there are many mistakes in the perception of wealth. Wealth is often seen as the main purpose of life. There are various ways and strategies to acquire wealth. But often, the process of obtaining wealth is not considered *Halal* and *Haram* boundaries are ignored. However, the procedure for obtaining wealth has implications for the blessings of wealth.

The blessing of wealth is obtained when the asset is used in the right (*Halal*) and good way. *Halal* means how to obtain wealth and spend it according to the rules of *Shari'ah*. The meaning of good means how to obtain wealth and spend it in a way that is good in accordance with the rules of social ethics.

Wealth that is not blessed causes unexpected expenses. Wealth that is acquired can be consumed without leftovers. This is because wealth is reversible. Quite a few people who are rich in wealth have lost their wealth. Corrupt government officials also happen. The rest of the old days must be spent in jail. On the other hand, if one follows the rules given by Allah (*s.w.t.*) in acquiring and using wealth, then Allah (*s.w.t.*) will replenish his supply.

Islamic teachings teach that wealth is used as a means or tool to achieve goals. The two short-term goals are the success of life in this world and the long-term goal of salvation in the Hereafter. Islam regulates the position of wealth as follows:

- i Wealth deposited by Allah (*s.w.t.*)[66] does not belong to human beings. Human ownership of wealth is relative (not absolute). Consequently, the possession of principled wealth is prescribed or billable in the Hereafter.
- ii The process of obtaining and spending wealth must be in accordance with *Shari'ah*.[67] The procedure of obtaining and spending wealth has implications on the blessing of wealth.
- iii The perspective of using wealth is not only for worldly purposes but also for *Ukhrowi*.[68]

Islam is a religion that has many rules regarding the acquisition of wealth. Trade and business are really controlled by *Akhlaq*. The results of trade and business should serve the public interest. Any transactions that are against the law or *Akhlaq* and public interest are considered illegal and unlawful.

Islamic teachings teach that organizations must be able to create wealth. With this, organizations can improve the welfare of stakeholders, *Zakat, Infaq, Shadaqoh, Waqf, Qurban*, corporate social responsibility (CSR), *Hajj* for labour, and stakeholders, or other social activities such as improving healthcare, education, community welfare to improve economic function, and social organization.

As for acquiring wealth, Buang (2008)[69] has pointed out different ways of acquiring wealth, namely *Ihya 'al-Mawat* or acquiring wealth from land that was not inhabited or land that was not used or abandoned by the owner or had never been inhabited by anyone else. *Al-sayd* or hunting is the hunting of wild animals or fishing, spoils of war (*Ghanimah*) which are the result of war victories, etc. With human civilization, the procedure of acquiring wealth is done in a more civilized manner. Trade and business are the main ways to attain wealth.

Dahan *et al.* (2012)[70] explains that according to the Shari'ah, there are three stages of wealth management, namely the acquisition of wealth, the preservation of wealth, and the distribution of wealth. The acquisition of wealth is the process of acquiring wealth. Preserving and spending wealth is the process of spending wealth on the most important needs. Distribution of wealth is spending wealth for other purposes. Dahan holds that wealth management must be in accordance with *Maqasid al-shari'ah*. Dahan uses the strategy of deep allocation of wealth.

The same opinion was also expressed by Sulaiman (2011).[71] Sulaiman explained wealth management with the approach of Islamic financial planning. Wealth management consists of wealth creation, wealth enrichment, wealth purification, wealth protection, and wealth distribution.

Wealth creation is a process that is carried out to obtain wealth. Treasures in Islam are gifts given by Allah (*s.w.t.*) and not just Allah's love for them. Efforts made by humans are considered processes that result in negative or positive outcomes. Everything on earth was created by Allah (*s.w.t.*) for human life, but still Allah (*s.w.t.*) is the owner.[72] Sulaiman explained that the creation of wealth is not based on human effort alone, but on Allah (*s.w.t.*) who made it possible.

The recreation of wealth is the process of developing existing wealth into greater or more. Islam strongly supports the development of wealth. Islam even forbids leaving wealth unused. For this reason, wealth must be reinvested.[73] Islam regulates the process of developing wealth according to *Shari'ah*, namely avoiding the development of wealth from the factors of *Azalim, usury, Maysir,* and *Gharar.*

> It is narrated from Abu Said al-Khudri, he said: "Rasulullah (*s.a.w.*) sat in the pulpit and we sat around him, then he said, 'Indeed, one of the things I fear for you is that which will be what I will open for you, all of the beauty of the treasures of the world and its ornaments - that is, this overflow of wealth among the people of Muhammad (*s.a.w.*) is greatly feared, because it can harm religion if it is not vigilant to control it.'"
>
> (*Muttafaq'alayh*)

The purification of wealth is the process of cleansing or purging wealth of something to which it is not entitled. The purpose of purification or cleansing is to cleanse the income of illegal things and to give rights or parts of eight *Asnafs*.[74] This process is a very important activity in Islamic financial planning[75] and can even be considered as a distinguishing feature from conventional financial planning. The benefit of paying *Zakat* is the promise of Allah (*s.w.t.*) that *Zakat* will multiply wealth many times over.[76]

Wealth protection is the process of asset allocation that aims to manage potential risks. One way to do this is through insurance (*Takaful*). Risk management in Islam is highly recommended because humans cannot predict tomorrow. Only Allah (*s.w.t.*) knows the events of tomorrow.

There was an incident in the time of Rasulullah (*s.a.w.*), namely, there was a friend who left his camel without tying it to anything, e.g., a tree, a pillar, etc., and then left it behind. He (*s.a.w.*) asked, "Why do not you tie it?" He replied, "I have put my trust in Allah." Rasulullah (*s.a.w.*) could not approve of the person's way of thinking and then said: "This means bind yourself first, then put your trust." In conclusion, resignation without prior effort is wrong and false according to Islamic view (*Riyaduṣṣaliḥīn Imam Nawawi*).

Wealth distribution is the process of distributing property when someone dies. Islamic law stipulates that when a person dies, the assets left behind should be distributed according to the provisions of QS al-Nisā 4: 11–12.[77] These provisions are implemented when all the obligations of the deceased are fulfilled, such as repayment of debts, third-party claims, etc.

Dahan *et al.* (2012), Sulaiman basically divided the two main processes of wealth management, which are the acquisition of wealth and the expenditure of wealth. The strategy adopted by Sulaiman in spending the wealth is also the same as Dahan *et al.* (2012), namely wealth allocation strategy.

In the context of the process of spending wealth, Al-Ghazali in Ghazanfar and Islahi[78] that the first thing to be done in spending wealth is to meet basic needs, namely food, clothing, and shelter. Next, wealth is distributed to meet other needs such as education, health, transportation, religious obligations, refreshing activities, etc.

In the context of the process of spending wealth, Al-Ghazali explained in Ghazanfar and Islahi that the first thing to be done in spending wealth is to meet basic needs, namely food, clothing, and shelter. Next, wealth is distributed to meet other needs such as education, health, transportation, religious obligations, refreshing activities, etc.

To attain blessed wealth, the most important key is to achieve worship orientation. Focusing on worship as the centre of spiritual energy sends positive energy into the overall direction of the organization's benefit. The positive energy of worship orientation affects individuals and organizations to always keep their attitudes and behaviour in line with the requirements of the *Aqidah* and the *Shari'ah* guidelines. Similarly, in the attitudes and behaviour of obtaining wealth, individuals and organizations always uphold the *Akhlaq* taught by Prophet Muhammad.

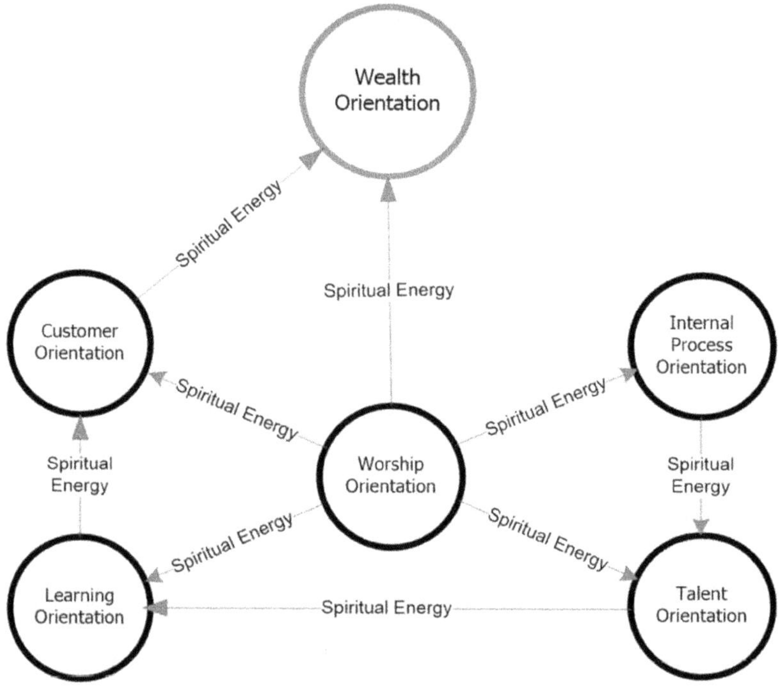

Figure 6.10 Spiritual Energy Flows from the Worship Orientation and Customer Orientation to Wealth Orientation.

Source: Firdaus (2017: 121)

On the other hand, learning orientation creates awareness, desires, hopes, and aspirations to improve the organization's utility not only for managers but also for the stakeholders and the environment. This is a manifestation of the caliphate. Customers become satisfied with the services provided by the organization. Finally, old customers remain loyal to the company and new customers get to know the organization better (Figure 6.10).

To derive blessings from asset purchase, wealth allocation strategy is the most important key. Properly acquired wealth is allocated by meeting customer needs, learning orientation, talent orientation, internal process orientation, and worship orientation (Figure 6.11).

Basically, the orientation to wealth is the cycle of how to obtain wealth and how to spend wealth in accordance with *Maqasid al-shari'ah*. Of course, what is meant by the cycle of how to obtain wealth and how to spend it is not that the orientation towards wealth is only process-oriented without considering the results. Just from this cycle, wealth orientation is result oriented. It is not possible to spend wealth if the cycle of wealth orientation does not lead to a result.

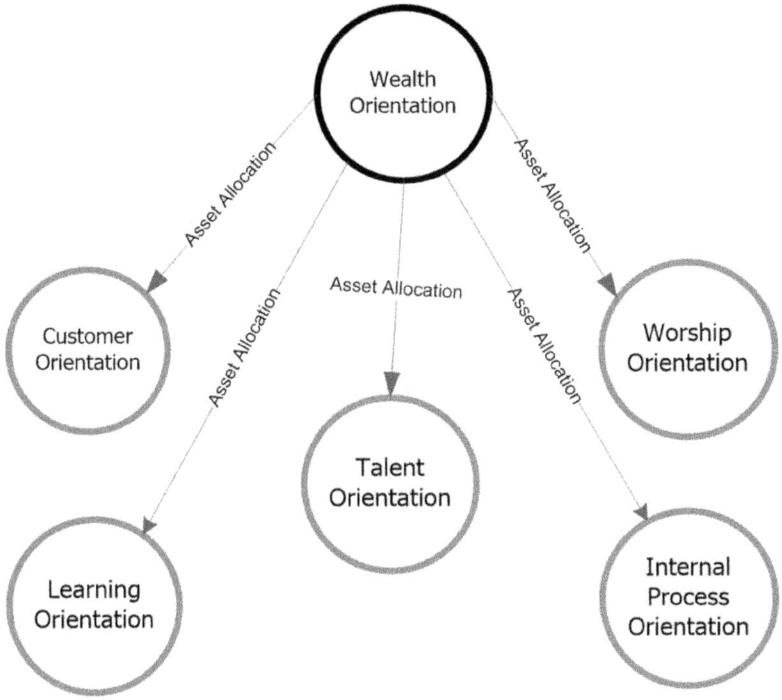

Figure 6.11 Wealth Allocation to Fulfil the Needs of *Maslahah* Orientation.

Source: (Firdaus, 2017: 122).

The cycle of acquiring and spending wealth is the "pull" cycle. This means that the process of spending interesting wealth is the process of acquiring wealth. That is, Islam requires people to acquire good and proper wealth to fulfil all their needs. "Pull" in the context of Islam is a need to fulfil all basic needs or *Maslahah daruriyah* which includes religion (*al-Din*), soul (*al-Nafs*), offspring (*al-Nasl*), wealth (*al-Mal*), and reason (*al-'Aql*). Above these needs, fulfilment is conditional. On the other hand, fulfilling something luxurious and excessive can be categorized as wasteful. This, of course, is forbidden in Islam.

The reason why one should focus on results was also taught by Siti Hajar when she ran seven times from *Shofa* and *Marwah* Hill. Siti Hajar only focuses on finding a spring for her son Ismail to drink from. Siti Hajar did not care about the efforts she was making. There was no trace in Siti Hajar's mind that she had to walk seven times first to find a spring.

The entire above description explains that orientation towards wealth is a perspective for the preservation of wealth (*al-Mal*). This is the answer to the question: "What efforts should one make to acquire and spend wealth so that salvation in the Hereafter and the success of life in the world may be permanent?"

Summary

Worship orientation is the view of the protection and preservation of the religion. Internal process orientation is the view of the protection and preservation of the soul. Talent orientation is the view of the protection and preservation of talent. Learning orientation is the view of the protection and preservation of the intellect. Wealth orientation is how to view the explanation of wealth.

Notes

1 Ahmad, S. F. (1991). *The Ethical Responsibility of Business: Islamic Principles and Implications.* Islamic Principles of Business Organization and Management. *Journal of Objective Studies*, Vol. 3, No. 1: 74–90.
2 Nata, A. (2008). *Kajian Tematik al-Quran tentang Fiqih Ibadah.* Bandung: Penerbit Angkasa.
3 Al Imran, A. bin M. (2009). *Tahifatu al Muslim Fil Aqīdah wal Sīrah.* Riyadh: Dar Ibnu Atsir.
4 QS al-Shūrā 42: 11–12, QS Hūd 11: 6, QS al-An'ām 6: 59, QS Luqmān 31: 34.
5 QS Maryam 19: 65, QS al-Baqarah 2: 255, QS al-Ḥashr 59:22–24, QS al-Shūrā 42: 49–50.
6 QS al-A'rāf 7: 180.
7 QS al-Anbiyā 21: 26–27.
8 QS Qaf 50: 17–18.
9 QS al-Ḥadīd 57: 25, QS al-Māidah 5: 44, 46, QS al-Ḥijr 15: 9.
10 QS al-Nisā 4: 165.
11 QS al-Zumar 39: 68, QS al-Anbiyā 21: 104.
12 QS al-Mu'minūn 23: 102–104, QS al-An'Ām 6: 160.
13 QS al-Sajadah 32: 17, QS al-Ṭalāq 65: 11.
14 QS al-Kahfi 18: 29.
15 Zeno bin Jamil, S. M. (September 1996). *The Pillars of Islam & Iman & What Every Muslim Must Know about His Religion.* Jeddah, Saudi Arabia: Darussalam Publications.
16 Shaikh Muhammad said that there are four levels of destiny, namely believing that Allah (*s.w.t.*) is all-knowing, knows what has happened, what will happen, and how it happened. Writing believes that Allah (*s.w.t.*) has written everything that happens until the end of the day, in *Lauhun mahfudz*. The will is the belief that what happens in the heavens and earth depends on His will, what He wants will happen, and what He does not want is impossible. Creation is the belief that God creates everything. Maintaining His creation, whatever is between heaven and earth belongs to Him.
17 QS al-Haj 22: 70.
18 QS al-Ra'd 13: 11.
19 From Abū Abdirrahman Abdullah bin Umar bin Khaṭṭab Raḍiyallahu 'Anhuma, he said: "I have heard Rosululloh shollallohu" alaihi wasallam said: "Islam was built on five cases, namely: Testifying there is no god but Allah and indeed Muhammad is the messenger of Allah, upholding prayer, issuing alms, doing the pilgrimage to Baitulloh, and fasting on the month of Ramadan" (Narrated by Bukhari and Muslim).
20 The author does not discuss in more detail about zakat, hajj, and fasting. An explanation of the pilgrimage of hajj and fasting can be seen in the literature on the pilgrimage of hajj and fasting.
21 From Abū Abdirrahman Abdullah bin Umar bin Khaṭṭab Raḍiyallahu 'Anhuma, he said: "I have heard Rosululloh shollallohu" alaihi wasallam said: "Islam was built on five cases, namely: Testifying there is no god but Allah and indeed Muhammad is the messenger of Allah, upholding prayer, issuing alms, doing the pilgrimage to Baitulloh, and fasting on the month of Ramadan" (Narrated by Bukhari and Muslim).

22 Worship meant here is worship carried out by humans to Allah (*s.w.t.*) the Creator in worship rituals such as prayer, paying zakat, hajj, and fasting, while *Muamalah* is the interaction or relationship between humans and others in living activities such as economics, politics, social, and other societies.

23 Al Imran said that *Bid'ah* in language is derived from the word *al-Bid'u* which means creating something without an example. In the sentence "Allah created the earth and the heavens," this is called creating because the example of the earth and the sky did not exist before God created it, while if you make something that already exists, an example is called find.

24 Nyazee, on page 18, says that *fiqh* is used literally to mean "understanding" and "differentiation." On page 24, Nyazee mentions the real difference between *sharī'ah* and *fiqh*: *sharī'ah* is the law itself while *fiqh* is knowledge from the law or commonly called jurisprudence.

25 Nickels, W. G., James, M. and Susan M. (2002). *Understanding Business*. New York: McGraw-Hill.

26 Nash, L. (1990). *Good Intention Aside; a Manager's Guide to Resolving Ethical Problem*. Boston: Harvard Business School Press.

27 Li, Yo. (October 2010). The Case Analysis of the Scandal of Enron. *International Journal of Business and Management*. Vol. 5, No. 10: 37–41.

28 Arthur Andersen was founded in 1913 by Arthur Andersen with Clarence DeLany. It was originally a small auditing company in the centre of Chicago. In 1918, DeLany resigned, and the company changed its name to Andersen & Company. Andersen has provisions in hiring employees. Only graduates from top universities receive it. Arthur Andersen then teaches the new employee with the slogan, "think straight and talk straight." This slogan is a value that is always held firm by the company.

29 Nasution, M. E. (2009). Islamic Spirit and Morale in Economics. *Journal of International Development and Cooperation*. Vol. 15, No 1–2: 113–124.

30 Accidental adherence to *sharī'ah* intent is someone who has known a certain law but does not obey, does not apply or violate the law with his own awareness. Inadvertent disagreement with the meaning is someone who does not know a particular law so that he does not obey, does not apply or violate the law or someone who has known a certain law but because the situation is urgent or in an emergency does not apply or violate the law.

31 Nata, A. (2008). *Kajian Tematik al-Quran tentang Fiqih Ibadah*. Bandung: Penerbit Angkasa.

32 Nasution, M. E. (2009). Islamic Spirit and Morale in Economics. *Journal of International Development and Cooperation* Vol. 15, No. 1–2: 113–124.

33 The relationship or relational between *Aqidah* and *Akhlaq* can be written in mathematical language as f (*Aqidah* and *akhlaq*) ≠ f(x, t).

34 Zidan, A. (1997). *Al-Ghazali"s* Ihya' Ulum al-Din *Revitalization of the Sciences of Religion*. Cairo, Egypt: Islami Inc. for Publishing and Distribution.

35 Relational *sharī'ah* can be written in mathematical language as f (*sharī'ah*) = f(x, t).

36 QS al-Baqarah 2: 25, 58, 112.

37 QS al-Baqarah 2: 59, 81, 85.

38 Chapra, M. U. (September 2007). *The Islamic Vision of Development in the Light of Maqasid Al-Sharī'ah*. Jeddah: Islamic Research and Training Institute Islamic Development Bank.

39 Rampersad, H. K. (June 2006). *The Personal Balanced Scorecard; the Way to Individual Happiness, Personal Integrity and Organizational Effectiveness*. Greenwich, CT: Information Age Publishing Inc.

40 Personal scorecard is an individual employee scorecard that explores vision, mission, key personal roles, success factors, goals, performance measurement, and employee personal improvement actions. Rampersad argues that the causes of employees are not happy at work because they are not given the opportunity to explore their personal scorecard.

41 Ibn 'Ashur, M. al-Tahir. (1998). *Maqasid al-Shari'ah al-Islamiyyah*. Kuala Lumpur: al-Basa'ir.
42 Value Chain Analysis is an analysis that views organizations as a sequential process of an activity to create value. Starting from the process of obtaining raw materials to the delivery of finished products to customers.
43 Porter, E. M. (1998). *Competitive Advantage, Creating and Sustaining Superior Performance*. New York: The Free Press.
44 The elements of the work system include strategic objectives, performance measures, organizational structure, workforce, management systems (BSC, ISO 9001, ISO 17025, ISO 14001, etc.), risk assessment, quality manuals, procedures, policies, etc.
45 Work systems and work processes refer to the value chain analysis (Porter, 1998).
46 Firdaus, A. (15 September 2012). *Maslahah Scorecard,* Business Performance Measurement System Based on *Maqasid Shariah*. Call for Paper 2012 Islamic Banking & Finance Conference. Islamic Economy Revivalism: Between Theory and Practice, Faculty of Economics and Business Syarif Hidayatullah UIN, Jakarta.
47 The Prophet forbade the employment of a worker before it was clear the wages he would receive (Narrated by An-Nasaa'i).
48 Give the workers their wages before drying their sweat (Narrated by Abu Ya'la).
49 Committing dzalim to wages for workers including major sins (Narrated by Ahmad).
50 Choudhury, M. A. (1986). *Contributions to Islamic Economic Theory, a Study in Social Economics*. New York: St. Martin's Press.
51 Ricardo, D. (2004). *The Principles of Political Economy and Taxation*. New York: Dover Publications Inc: 52.
52 QS Al-Furqan 25: 74, QS al-Saffah 37: 77.
53 QS Al-Furqan 25: 54.
54 Coyle, D. (May 2009). *The Talent Code, Greatness Isn't Born, It's Grown, Here's How*. New York: Bantam Dell.
55 Chowdury, S. (2005). *21st Century Organization*. Jakarta: Index Publishers.
56 McKinsey & Company. (April 2001). *The War for Talent. Organization and Leadership Practice*. New York: McKinsey & Company.
57 Watson, G. H. and DeYong, C. F. (2010). Design for Six Sigma: caveat emptor. *International Journal of Lean Six Sigma*. Vol. 1, No 1: 66–84.
58 QS al-Isrā 17: 70.
59 QS Yūsuf 12: 111; QS al-Shu'arā 26: 28; QS al-Ṭolāq 65: 10; QS al-Māidah 5: 58, 100; QS al-Baqarah 2: 179, 197; QS Ṭōhā 20: 54, 128; QS Hūd 11: 78, 87; QS Āli 'imrān 3: 7; QS al-Zumar 39: 17, 18, 21, 43; QS al-'Ankabūt 29: 35; QS Ibrāhīm 14: 52; QS al-Jāsiyat 45: 5; QS al-Rūm 30: 28; QS al-Fajr 89: 5; QS al-Ra'd 13: 19.
60 QS al-Zumar 39: 18, 21; QS Yūsuf 12: 111; QS al-Shu'arā 26: 28; QS al-Thalāq 65: 10.
61 QS al-Māidah 5: 58; QS al-Jin 72: 4.
62 Smith, C. N. and Quirk, M. (2004). From Grace to Disgrace: The Rise & Fall of Arthur Andersen. *Journal of Business Ethics Education*. Vol. I, No. 1: 91–130.
63 Göran J. and Roos, J. (1997). Measuring your Company's Intellectual Performance. *International Journal of Strategic Management*, Special Issue on Intellectual Capital. Vol. 30. No. 3: 413–426.
64 Kaplan, R. S. and Norton, D.P. (July-August 2007). Using the Balanced Scorecard as a Strategic Management System. *Harvard Business Review*. July-August 2007: 1–14.
65 QS Ali ran Imran 3: 14.
66 QS al-Nur 24: 33, some of the verses say, "and give to them a portion of the inheritance of Allah that has been given to you."
67 Qal-Nisa 4: 29, Surah al-Nahl 16: 114.
68 QS al-'Discount 29: 64.
69 Buang, A. H. (2008). Appreciation of Syari'ah Principles in Property Management in Contemporary Malaysia Society. *Shariah Journal*. Vol. 16: 555–566.

70 Dahan, M. H., Ahmad, N., and Basir, F. A. M. (12–13 March 2012). Factors Inhibiting Islamic Will Adoption: Focus on Muslim Community. *Paper presented at the 3rd International Conference on Business and Economic Research (3rd ICBER 2012)*, Bandung, Indonesia.

71 Sulaiman, R. (2011). Realizing Maqasid Al-Shariah in Islamic Financial Planning. *The 4E Journal*. Vol. 11. No. 1: 13–17.

72 Surah al-Nahl 16: 80 which means, "and Allah made you your houses as dwellings and He made for you houses (tents) from the skin of cattle that you felt light (carry) in your time walking and the time you settle and (for Him also) from fleece, camel hair and goat's hair, household utensils and jewellery (which you use) to (certain) times."

73 In the Book of *Bulughul Maram Min Adillatil Ahkam, Al-Hafidz Ibn Hajar Al-Ashqolani* explained:

> "The 142nd Hadith, From Urwah, from 'Aisha Radliyallaahu' anhu that the Prophet Sallallaahu 'alaihi Wa Sallam said: 'Whoever prospers land that is not owned by anyone then he is more entitled to the land.' Urwah said: Umar imposed the law during his khilafah (Narrated by Bukhari)."
> "143rd Hadith, From Said Ibn Zaid Radliyallaahu 'anhu that the Prophet Sallallaahu' alaihi Wa Sallam said: 'Whoever revives dead land, then the land belongs to him.' History of Imam Three. Hashad Hadith, according to Tirmidhi and he said: the hadith was narrated with mursal and there was a dispute about his friend. Some say (his best friend is) Jabir, some say 'Ayesha, and some say Umar. The strongest is the first."

74 It is the people who have the right to get zakat as explained in QS al-Tawbah 9: 60 "Verily the zakat is only for the needy, the poor, the administrators of *Zakat*, the converts who are persuaded by his heart, to (freeing) slaves, those who owe, to the ways of Allah and those who are on the way, as a decree that is required by Allah; and Allah is Knower, Wise."

75 Threats and punishments will be imposed on people who do not pay zakat, as explained by Rasulallah (narrated by Bukhari) in his hadith.

Abu Hurairah *r.a.* said, "The Messenger of Allah said, 'Whoever is given wealth by Allah, but does not issue zakat, then the wealth will be made like a bald male snake (because of its many poisons and old age). The snake has two fangs that cover its neck on the Day of Judgment. Then the snake stung him with his fangs, he gripped his jaws by saying, 'I am your treasure, I am your savings.' Then he recited the verse: 'Do not be miserable with the treasure that Allah has given them from His grace, thinking that the evil is good for them. But the evil is bad for them. The treasure that they possess will be wrapped around their necks. On the Day of Resurrection, belongs to Allah, all inheritance (that is) in the heavens and on earth, Allah knows what you do.' '(In one way narration with an editor that reads: 'One's treasure from you tomorrow will be a bald male snake, and the owner runs away from him. But the snake chases after saying,' I am your treasure. 'For Allah's sake, the snake continued to chase it. So, he spread his arms, then the snake chewed it with his mouth.' He said next, "If the owner of the livestock does not give his rights (zakat), surely the livestock will be authorized on the Day Then, will trample his face with the soles of his feet. '8/60)."

76 In Surah al-Baqarah 2: 261, it is explained that "the parable (the income issued by) those who spend their wealth in the way of Allah is like a seed that grows seven grains, in each grain: one hundred seeds. Allah multiplies (rewards) for whom He wants. And Allah is the Most Extensive (His gift) is the Knower."

77 Allah (*s.w.t.*) instructs you about (the distribution of inheritance for) your children. Namely: "the portion of a boy is equal to the portion of two daughters; and if the child is all more than two women, then for them two-thirds of the wealth left behind; if the girl is one, she gets half of the wealth. And for two mothers, for each one-sixth of the wealth left behind, if the deceased has children; if the person

who dies does not have a child and he is inherited by his mother (only), then his mother gets one-third; if the deceased has several siblings, then the mother gets one-sixth. (Distribution of the above) after being fulfilled the will he made or (and) after the debt was paid. (About) your parents and your children, you do not know who among them is closer (much) to your benefit. This is a decree from God. Lo! Allah is Knower, Wise" (Surat al-Nisa 4: 11).

"And for you (husbands), half of the wealth left by your wives if they don't have children. If your wives have children, then you get a quarter of the wealth left behind after they have fulfilled the will they made or (and) after their debt was paid. Wives get a quarter of the wealth that you leave if you don't have children. If you have children, the wives get an eighth of the wealth that you leave after being fulfilled the will you made or (and) after you paid your debts. If someone dies, both male and female, who do not leave their father and do not leave the child but have a brother (a thousand) or a sister (just a thousand), then for each of the two types of brothers is one-sixth treasure. But if there were more than one thousand brothers and sisters, then they fellowship in the third, after they had fulfilled the will made by him or after they had been paid their debt without giving harm (to the heirs). (Allah establishes that as a Shari'a which is truly from Allah, and Allah is Knower, Most Merciful" (Qur'an 4: 12)).

78 According to Al-Ghazali, in Mohammad S. Ghazanfar and Abdul Azim Islahi. "Economic Thought of Al-Ghazali (450–505 AH/1058–1111 AD)," Islamic Economics Research Series, King Abdulaziz University (1997) that all economic activities are carried out in meeting three basic human needs, namely food, clothing (clothing), and residence (shelter). These three basic needs are flexible and inclusive depending on the conditions of place and time must also be consistent with Islamic Shari'a.

7 Customer Orientation and Preservation of Customer Relationship

Becoming the Medium of Allah in Delivering *Rizq* to Others

وَٱللَّهُ فَضَّلَ بَعْضَكُمْ عَلَىٰ بَعْضٍ فِى ٱلرِّزْقِ ۚ فَمَا ٱلَّذِينَ فُضِّلُوا۟ بِرَآدِّى رِزْقِهِمْ
عَلَىٰ مَا مَلَكَتْ أَيْمَـٰنُهُمْ فَهُمْ فِيهِ سَوَآءٌ ۚ أَفَبِنِعْمَةِ ٱللَّهِ يَجْحَدُونَ

> And Allah has favored some of you over others in provision. But those who were favored [i.e., given more] would not hand over their provision to those whom their right hands possess [i.e., slaves] so they would be equal to them therein.[1] Then is it the favor of Allah they reject?
>
> (QS an-Nahl 16: 71)

The customer is a very important and very crucial factor for the organization. The customer represents the number of needs (demand). There is no organization if there is no demand. Therefore, there is no organization if there are no customers. The size of the organization and its ability to be sustainable are also highly dependent on the customers. Based on these considerations, it is necessary to adapt the application of the concept of *Maslahah* to the organization, namely by adding customer orientation.

The customer is an intermediary for the sustenance that Allah (*s.w.t.*) has given to the organization. The number of customers is directly proportional to the revenue the organization receives. Being closer to the customer naturally increases the organization's chances of receiving *Rizq*. However, the customer is only an intermediate medium to download *Rizq* which has been determined by Allah (*s.w.t.*) as the giver of *Rizq*. Allah (*s.w.t.*) is the determiner of the size of *Rizq* received. So, it can be said that the customer is one of the opening doors for *Rizq* that Allah (*s.w.t.*) has given to the organization.

If Allah (*s.w.t.*) has imparted *Rizq* to the organization through the customers, it does not mean that Allah (*s.w.t.*) cannot give the *Rizq* directly. Allah (*s.w.t.*) uses the medium of the customer to convey *Rizq* with the aim that the organization can interact with or be kind to the customers. The interaction between the organization and the customer is not just a transactional economic relationship between the one who needs the product or service and the one who provides the product or service. Allah (*s.w.t.*) has also designed the interaction between the two as a social relationship to fulfil human duties as deputies of Allah (*s.w.t.*).

DOI: 10.4324/9781003390947-9

It is narrated from Anas, "There were two brothers at the time of Rasulullah (*s.a.w.*), one of them came to the Prophet and the other worked. The one who was working complained to Rasulullah (*s.a.w.*) about his unemployed brother and he said, "Perhaps you have been given sustenance by Allah for helping your brother whom you gave food and so on.""

(Narrated by Tirmidhzi)

Customers and marketing are two things that are closely related. The principles that apply in marketing based on Islamic values emphasize the importance of combining the concept of value maximization and the principles of justice for social welfare (Hassan *et al.*, 2008).[1] With this principle, marketing has the importance of creating value as well as trying to raise the standard of living of people in general through commercial activities.

Social welfare through the process of maximizing fair values can be created if the organization meets the orientation needs of customers. Its realization can be created when the worship orientation needs are met.

The worship orientation provides positive spiritual energy in every alignment for the benefit of the organization. Spiritual energy that can straighten out the intentions, mentality, and motivation of the people in the organization. Service to the customer is performed according to the requirements of the *Aqidah*. It is a service that always refers to the guidance of Allah (*s.w.t.*) and is performed with good morals (Figure 7.1).

At the same time, fulfilling the internal process orientation gives direction to the management to place customer requirements as orders to be fulfilled. The requirements are derived from the desires and expectations of customers. These requirements are recorded and well documented by the organization. The

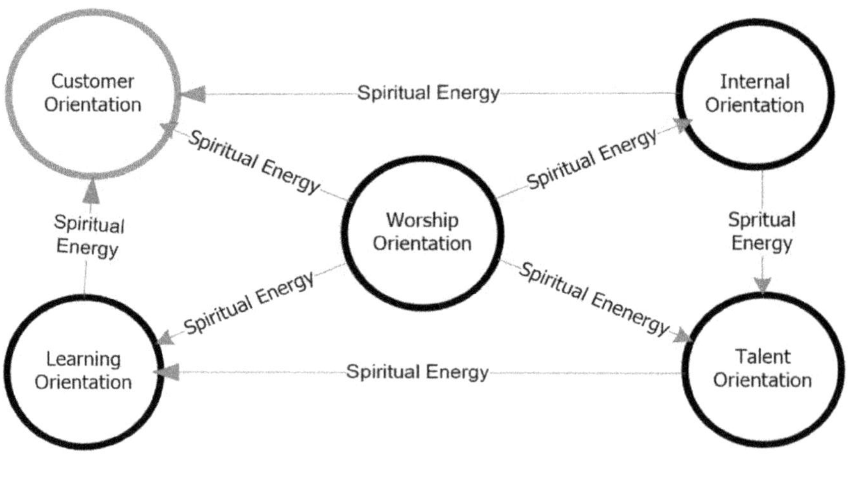

Figure 7.1 Spiritual Energy Flows from Worship Orientation and Learning Orientation to Customer Orientation.

Source: Firdaus (2017: 111)

organization then mobilizes its resources to meet these requirements. Failure to meet customer requirements is an embarrassment to the organization that must be corrected immediately. Organizations feel ashamed when they fail to meet customer requirements. This happens because the organization is fully aware that the customer is a medium for Allah (*s.w.t.*) to bestow His blessings upon them.

The customer requirements must be stated in written down when designing the work system design and work process. The statement is anchored in the stakeholder requirements as one of the sources of input process. Other process inputs can be derived from the *Shari'ah* provisions, *Fatwas*, input from *Shari'ah* supervisory board, core competency, analysis of organizational strengths and weaknesses, opportunities and challenges of the environment, customer requirements, regulatory requirements, input from suppliers and partners, long-term plan, medium-term plan, annual plan, employee satisfaction surveys, workforce satisfaction surveys, past organizational performance, improvements and innovations, audit findings, management review meetings, and customer feedback.

The subsequent customer requirements are met by the organization through a set of work processes which are divided into the main processes, supporting processes, innovation and process improvement processes, disaster and emergency management processes, risk management processes, CSR processes, *Shari'ah* processes, and legal compliance processes. All processes perform their respective functions and tasks to create value. The process of value creation also generates an output, namely stakeholder satisfaction, including customer satisfaction, which is referred to as *Maqasid al-Shari'ah*.[2]

Resource management to achieve customer satisfaction is also in line with ISO 9001: 2015 Quality Management Principles or QMP (ISO.org, 2015).[3] The clause QMP 1 Customer Orientation states that the focus of quality management is to meet customer requirements and strive to exceed customer expectations. This means that there is a cycle of work that needs to be carried out to achieve customer orientation, namely identifying customer requirements and meeting the provisions of customer requirements to achieve customer satisfaction.

To increase the number of customers, several development strategies are known, namely market development, market penetration, product development, and diversification (Kotler and Armstrong, 2012).[4] Market development is the growth strategy of the company by identifying and developing new market segments for its current products. Market penetration is a strategy for a firm's growth by increasing sales of current products in current market segments without changing products. Product development is a strategy for the growth of the company by offering modified products or new products for the current market segment. Diversification is a strategy for business growth by seeking business outside the existing products and markets.

The above four development strategies are basically the development strategy of the business by retaining loyal customers or old customers and by attracting new prospects or customers.[5] Both become targets of market development. That is, potential customers and old customers are expected to be the medium of *Rizq* that Allah (*s.w.t.*) gives to the company.

On the other hand, fulfilling the talent orientation creates talented employees who always devote their energy and intellect to meeting customers' needs and expectations. A talented workforce with the ability of worship orientation and the organizational management skills they possess can explore all the needs of their customers. With their ability, talented staff can get other staff to do the same with themselves. This has been done to satisfy the customers.

Positive energy is also gained by fulfilling the learning orientation. Learning orientation creates people in organizations who can use their minds and hearts in service to customers. At the same time, organizations can use all their capital, both human capital and organizational capital, to meet customer needs. The organization always checks its own system to prevent any incompatibility with customer requirements. When something happens, the company always takes corrective, preventive, and improvement measures with its capabilities.

Do You Want to Become the Medium of Allah in Delivering *Rizq* to Others?

"Mr. Adi, where are you?" a manager asked his staff. "Yes, sorry sir, I am still in the mosque, I got caught in the rain, the rain was heavy sir," said Mr Adi on the other side. "The agent recruitment data from yesterday, where was it sir, I have to report it to the marketing director now!" the manager said with a tone of voice that started to rise. "Oh yes sir, I have put them in the employee file, but I am sorry sir, I am bringing the locker key sir," Mr Adi replied in a flat tone without guilt.

"How can?." "Please come to my room immediately," the manager ordered angrily. A few minutes later, Mr Adi hurriedly came to the manager's room. "Sorry sir, this is the agent recruitment data you need," Pak Adi said. "Mr. Adi, please sit down for a while, I want to talk to you," said the manager.

"What do you think Allah intends to do with the rain?" asked the manager. "As a means to provide *Rizq* to the inhabitants of the earth, sir," replied Adi. "I see, are you sure that there is *Rizq* in the rain for the people?" asked the manager.

"Yes sir," replied Mr Adi.

"Who gets *rizq* from the rain?" "Farmers, motorcycle washers, car washers, coffee sellers, umbrella *ojek* (umbrella rent providers), umbrella repairers and many more people" Mr Adi replied.

"Now you understand." "Rain is a medium for *Rizq* for umbrellas *ojek*, why do not you want to be part of Allah's media to convey *Rizq* to an umbrella *ojek* worker." "Do you consider rain as a hindrance to work?." "You should consider yourself lucky, with the rain you can become an extension of Allah's hands to give *Rizq* to the umbrella *ojek*."

"Mr. Adi, please understand that when you asked the umbrella *ojek* to take you to the office, you prayed all the way from the mosque to the office. Compared to you staying in the mosque during *Zikr* waiting for the rain to stop." "I hope you have understood my explanation and now please continue working."

As explained above, the customer is the intermediary for the *Rizq* that Allah (*s.w.t.*) has given to the organization. This view is from the perspective of the organization. However, from the customer's perspective, this is not the case. Nowadays, customers still see the organization as a party that provides them with the value they need. The customers' motivation is transactional and commercial. Customers only get the value they need.

One day, there will be a situation where the customer sees himself as the medium of Allah (*s.w.t.*) in conveying *Rizq* to the organization. The customer will position himself as Mr Adi has positioned himself as the medium to deliver *Rizq* to the umbrela *ojek*. The client voluntarily becomes the medium of Allah (*s.w.t.*) in transmitting *Rizq* to the organization. This happens with organizations that maintain the performance of *Maslahah*.

Voluntary does not mean that the customer does not have to or is not allowed to make a complaint. For example, in the case of Hajj/Umrah pilgrims, Hajj is part of the pillars of Islam, while Umrah is a religious service that is highly recommended. People who perform the Hajj/Umrah want to worship the Creator. Nevertheless, pilgrims as customers of the Ministry of Religion or travel companies cannot escape the feeling of satisfaction or dissatisfaction with the services of Hajj/Umrah managers.

Therefore, the Hajj/Umrah manager must always give priority to the satisfaction of the Hajj/Pilgrims. Hajj/Umrah managers must not adopt the principle that the pilgrims are holding a religious service. Therefore, if something bad happens to the Hajj/Umrah pilgrims, they must endure the test given by Allah (*s.w.t.*). The poor service of the Hajj/Umrah manager is not just a test of Allah (*s.w.t.*) for the worshippers. On the contrary, the very poor service of Hajj/Umrah is a test of Allah (*s.w.t.*) for the Hajj/Umrah manager. The poor service of Hajj/Umrah is the proof of management mistakes committed by the Hajj/Umrah managers.

The ideal relationship that exists in Hajj/Umrah service is that the manager of Hajj/Umrah is the medium of Allah (*s.w.t.*) to serve the guests of Allah (*s.w.t.*). In contrast, the pilgrims of Hajj/Umrah are the medium of Allah (*s.w.t.*) to convey *Rizq* to the managers of Hajj/Umrah. This ideal relationship always applies to a variety of services for customers.

زُيِّنَ لِلَّذِيْنَ كَفَرُوا الْحَيٰوةُ الدُّنْيَا وَيَسْخَرُوْنَ مِنَ الَّذِيْنَ اٰمَنُوْا ۘ وَالَّذِيْنَ
اتَّقَوْا فَوْقَهُمْ يَوْمَ الْقِيٰمَةِ ۗ وَاللّٰهُ يَرْزُقُ مَنْ يَّشَاۤءُ بِغَيْرِ حِسَابٍ

> Beautified for those who disbelieve is the life of this world, and they ridicule those who believe. But those who fear Allah are above them on the Day of Resurrection. And Allah gives provision to whom He wills without account.
>
> (QS al-Baqarah 2: 212)

Islamic Bank is Allah's media for customers in managing their finances. Instead, the customer is Allah's medium to convey *Rizq* to the management of the Islamic bank. Islamic insurance is Allah's medium for the participants in anticipating the risks that may arise. Instead, the insurance participant is

Figure 7.2 Organizational Management and Customer Relationship.

Source: Firdaus (2017)

Allah's medium when it comes to transmitting *Rizq* to the insurance manager of Islamic insurance. The *Zakat* institution is Allah's medium for obligatory *Zakat* in managing assets belonging to third parties and attributable to him. On the other hand, obligatory *Zakat* for the *Zakat* institution is Allah's medium in distributing wealth to the inhabitants of the earth, especially to eight groups of people who receive *Zakat*.

Organizational Management and Customer Relationship

The following Figure 7.2 explains the relationship in managing an organization in the face of uncertainties. This is very important for sustainability.

The whole above description provides an explanation that customer orientation is a way to maintain customer relationships. This aspect is the answer to the question, "What activities should be done for customers so that salvation in the hereafter and success of life in the world can be sustained?"

Summary

The customer is an intermediary for the sustenance that Allah (*s.w.t.*) has given to the organization. Product producer or service provider is the medium of Allah (*s.w.t.*) to serve the customer. Because the customer is the intermediary for the *Rizq* enlargement that Allah (*s.w.t.*) has bestowed upon the organization. This view is from the perspective of the organization.

Notes

1 Hassan, A., Chachi, A. and Abdul Latiff, S. (2008). Islamic Marketing Ethics and Its Impact on Customer Satisfaction in the Islamic Banking Industry. *JKAU: Islamic Econ.* Vol. 21, No. 1: 27–46.
2 If there are inputs or outputs from the work system and work processes that are not in accordance with the topic *Maqāṣid al-shari'ah*, then the input and output are included in the group that is rejected by the *Shari'ah*.
3 International Organization for Standardization. (2015). *Quality Management Principles*. Geneva, Switzerland.
4 Kotler, P. and Armstrong, G. (2012). *Principles of Marketing*. 14th ed. New Jersey, US: Pearson Education. Inc.
5 Old customers are customers who already use goods and services, while potential customers are people or parties who are targeted by new customers.

Part III

Managing *Maslahah*-Based Organizational Performance System

Organizational performance system based on *Maslahah* or *Maslahah* Performa (MaP) is a system of organizational performance used to realize the human vision of redemption in the hereafter and success of life in the world. This vision can be achieved by fulfilling the mission of human life as Allah's *Caliph* on earth. Vision and mission can be achieved if the basic needs of organizations are equally fulfilled. The basic needs of organizations consist of fulfilling worship orientation, internal process orientation, talent orientation, learning orientation, customer orientation, and wealth orientation (Figure 8.1).

Therefore, the fulfilment of the *Maslahah* orientation of any organization is always based on the vision and mission of human life. For this reason, it is impossible for the fulfilment of the *Maslahah* orientation to bring lasting benefits to the organization if the fulfilment process does not relate to the vision and mission of human life.

Satisfying the basic needs of the organization by giving the highest priority to the fulfilment of the worship orientation is the necessity of the organization in the daily application of religion, i.e., interaction with Allah (*s.w.t.*) as the giver of life, stakeholders, and the environment. All these interactions are carried out by the organization as part of worshipping Allah (*s.w.t.*), the Creator.

The next priority for fulfilling the basic needs is internal process orientation, i.e., fulfilling the needs of the soul of the organization in the form of internal process management within the organization. The third priority for meeting the basic needs is talent orientation. Talent orientation is meeting the needs of talented employees as the next generation in the leadership of the organization. The priority of meeting the basic needs is meeting the intellectual needs of the organization, i.e., in the form of managing learning activities to become a learning organization.

The next level of meeting the basic needs of the organization is meeting customer orientation. Customer orientation is the fulfilment of customer needs, both old and new customers. Fulfilment of customer needs is reflected in customer satisfaction. Customers are not the only reason for organizations because Allah (*s.w.t.*) is the Livelihood Giver. Nevertheless, Islam believes that customers are the medium that carries *Rizq* from God to the company. So, the more

DOI: 10.4324/9781003390947-10

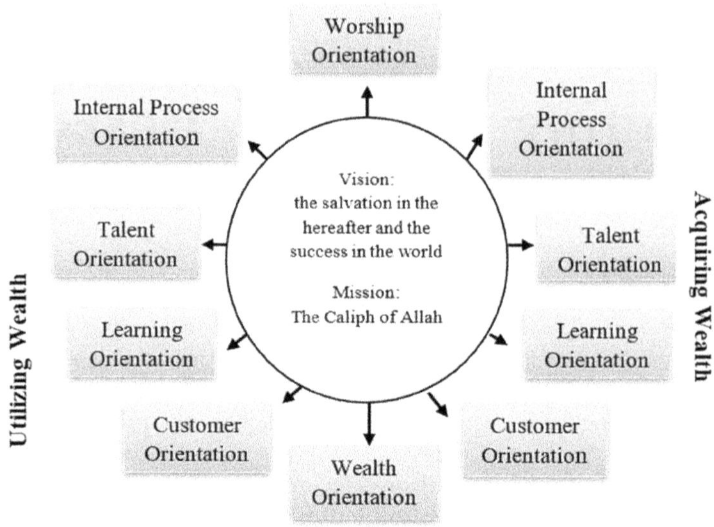

Figure 8.1 The Cycle of Acquiring and Utilizing Wealth.

Source: Firdaus (2017: 126)

customers, the greater the chance of receiving *Rizq*. The more customers are loyal to the company, the greater the chance for the company to receive *Rizq*.

The final priority of meeting basic needs is meeting the wealth orientation. Wealth orientation is the fulfilment of the basic needs of the organization in its effort to acquire and spend wealth. Organizations acquire wealth through the cycle of orientation fulfilment: worship, internal processes, talent, learning, and customers. Organizations spend wealth through the allocation of assets in the following areas: customers, learning, talent, internal processes, and worship. The organizational performance system of *Maslahah Performa* (MaP) is an organizational performance system that assumes that wealth is not the main purpose in creating organizations but that wealth is a means to accomplish the main goal of human life, which is salvation in the hereafter and life success in the world. This vision can be achieved by man fulfilling his life mission as God's representative on earth. This part covers four chapters.

8 PDCA Cycle of MaP Performance System

PDCA's Step Is Developed into Eight Steps of MaP Performance

The PDCA cycle is identical to the Japanese management system. There is no denying that, even though the initiator of the PDCA cycle is the American Edward Deming, it was the Japanese who popularized it. In the aftermath of World War II, Japan was devastated by the Allied atomic bomb on Hiroshima and Nagasaki. The Japanese learned the lesson of the PDCA cycle from Deming through lectures to Japanese scientists and engineers in 1951, after which they applied the PDCA cycle to quality control (QC) and total quality control (TQC) in business, especially in manufacturing.

Thanks to the application of the PDCA cycle, the Japanese overcame the adversity of World War II. Japanese industry began to explore the world. Japan rose in all walks of life. By the 1970s, Japanese industries had truly dominated the world. We still remember that in the 1970s, various Japanese products overwhelmed the world. At that time, Japan was accused by Indonesian students as the ruling country of the Indonesian economy. The highlight was the visit of Japanese Prime Minister Tanaka Kakuei to Jakarta from 14 to 17 January 1974. Students led by Hariman Siregar greeted him with a demonstration in Halim Perdanakusuma. The event is then known as Malari (Plagues of the Fifteenth of January).

Americans began to adopt the PDCA cycle in the 1986s through lectures by Deming. Americans' interest in applying the PDCA cycle in all walks of life, especially in industry and business, is inseparable from Japan's success in adopting the PDCA cycle. This means that America, as a developed country, was 30 years behind Japan at that time.

The application of the PDCA cycle in industry and business is basically the application of scientific and technical methods in both fields. PDCA cycle is a four-step cycle for problem-solving that includes the following steps: Plan, define problems and hypothesize causes of problems and propose solutions. Do, implementing the solutions. Check, evaluating the results. Action, taking improvement actions and standardizing and improving. PDCA emphasizes the process of preventing the repetition of the same mistakes.

DOI: 10.4324/9781003390947-11

The standardization step can be compared to a transition from one PDCA cycle to the next PDCA cycle. It is carried out to ensure that the process of improvement and increment goes in the desired direction.

The PDCA cycle is a general management approach. The PDCA cycle has the advantage that it can be applied to all types of activities. The steps in the PDCA cycle are developed for performance management (Qing-ling, 2008) into eight,[1] namely: analyse current conditions to find problems, conduct an analysis of the causes of performance problems, identify the main cause, sign a performance contract, implement performance, performance appraisal, prepare feedback and apply the results of the assessment. Also, the development of a Six Sigma management system with the phases of the DMAIC model (Define – Measure – Analyze – Improve – Control) cannot be separated from the PDCA cycle.[2]

The PDCA cycle is applied as a method to implement MaP performance as follows: performance planning, performance implementation, performance evaluation, and performance action. The MaP performance system is implemented using the cycle methodology shown in Figure 8.2.

Performance planning is developed into five steps of planning. Performance implementation is carried out in one phase. Performance evaluation is done in one stage. Performance action is applied in one stage. Thus, there are eight steps in the MaP performance system.

The first step of performance planning is the development of strategic planning. Strategic planning is the process of setting corporate goals and

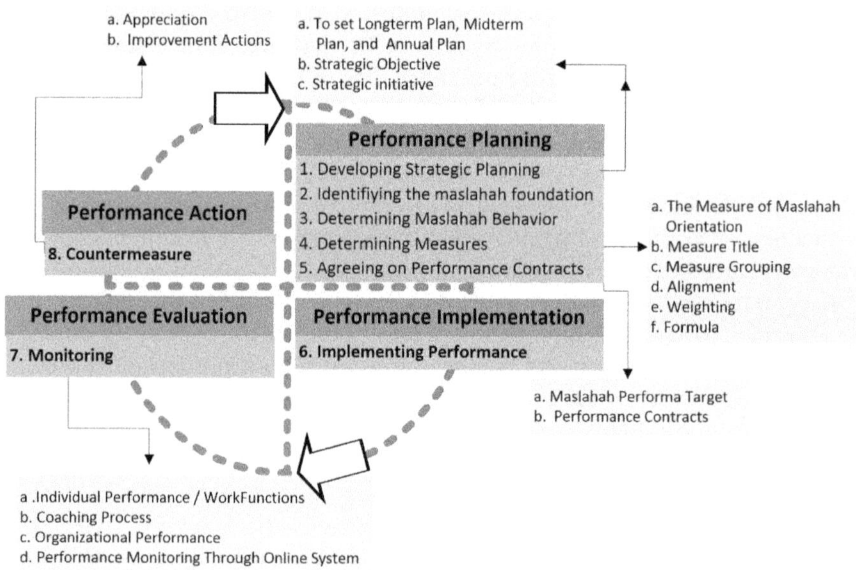

Figure 8.2 PDCA Cycle of *MaP* Performance System.

Source: Firdaus (2018)

objectives. It includes a long-term plan, a medium-term plan, a short-term plan, a strategic goal, and a strategic initiative. The planning process is strategically set in the form of a grand strategy.

The second step of performance planning is to identify the fundamentals required to achieve the *Maslahah* orientation. This step identifies the *Maslahah* infrastructure that must be provided to achieve *Maslahah* alignment.

The third step of performance planning is to determine the behaviour required for each *Maslahah* orientation. *Maslahah* behaviour is the attitude, characteristics, behaviours, and values that the organization must possess as a fundamental asset to provide benefits to all stakeholders' behaviour.

The fourth step of performance planning is the establishment of measures. The measure is an indicator that shows the success or achievement of the organization in achieving the strategic objectives. While the formula approach, formulas, or ways to calculate performance measures.

The fifth step in performance planning is to agree on a performance contract. There are several stages in creating a performance contract, namely setting target and contract design. Target can take the form of time, percentage, number, frequency, ratio, etc. Target should be quantitative. Target can be qualitative, but to be easily understood by all work units and employees, target should be arranged in a range or interval.

The sixth step of the MaP performance system is the implementation of the performance system. In this stage, all performance plans are implemented. Of course, it is expected that all set targets can be achieved.

The seventh step of the MaP performance system is performance monitoring. Performance monitoring is done by monitoring the performance of the individual and the work function, the implementation of the coaching process and the organizational performance.

The eighth step of the MaP performance system is the follow-up, which consists of two sub-activities, namely awarding and implementing improvement activities.

Summary

Maslahah performa is a cycle of getting and spending good wealth, so the approach in implementing it must be cyclical. PDCA is a great tool for implementing *Maslahah* Performa. PDCA is developed into eight activity steps.

Notes

1 Qing-ling, D., Cao Shu-min, Ba Lian-liang, Cheng Jun-mo. (2008). Application of PDCA Cycle in the Performance Management System. *Paper presented at 4th International Conference on Wireless Communications, Networking and Mobile Computing WiCOM '08*: Dalian, China, 12–17 October 2008. https://doi.org/10.1109/WiCom.2008.1682

2 Watson, G. H. and DeYong, C. F. (2010). Design for Six Sigma: Caveat Emptor. *International Journal of Lean Six Sigma*. Vol. 1, No. 1: 66–84.

9 Performance Planning

Developing Strategic Planning

Following the PDCA (Plan – Do – Check – Action) cycle, the first step of the MaP performance system is to develop strategic planning. Strategic planning is the process of setting the organization's goals in the form of a grand design for the long-term, medium-term, and short-term achievement of the organization's vision, mission, and objectives.

The long-term vision of the organization is to accomplish salvation in the hereafter and success of life in the world. The long-term mission of the organization is to accomplish the organization management as a manifestation of the *Caliph* of God on earth. The long-run objective of the organization is the realization of the organization conferring benefits. Through strategic planning, organizations can ensure that all resources are utilized to achieve the organization's vision, mission, and goals.

Setting Long-term Plan, Mid-term Plan, and Annual Plan

The long-term corporate plan is a picture of the grand design of the organization's ideals to realize an organization that is well-suited. The great aim of achieving salvation in the hereafter and success of life in the world can be realized by harmonizing the organizational management tasks as the implementation of the duty of the vicegerent of Allah (*s.w.t.*) on earth.

The medium-term corporate plan is the objective and goals of the organization for a period of five years. The medium-term plan gives the direction of development that you want to achieve in the next five years. Of course, the resources you have must support the direction of this development. The medium-term plan also explains the policy and strategic priorities. The medium-term plan must ensure that the five-year organization's planning is clearly linked to the long-term plan.

The annual plan is a measurable program of work to be achieved within one year. The annual plan is an operationalization of the medium-term plan. For the medium-term goal to be achieved, the organization must divide the medium-term goal into an annual goal. The main objective of the annual plan

DOI: 10.4324/9781003390947-12

is to facilitate the achievement of the medium-term objectives as described in the medium-term plan. The annual plan must ensure that the routine activities of the organization are clearly linked to the medium-term plan. Thus, the routine activities of the organization are essentially directed towards a clear and organized goal, namely the achievement of the annual plan, the medium-term plan, and the long-term plan.

Pearce and Robinson[1] mentioned that for short-term goals to be effective and have a certain quality, they must have the following characteristics: (1) measurable; (2) list of prioritized goals: while all short-term goals are important, considering time and degree of importance, short-term goal preparation must be selected based on priority; (3) connected to the medium-term objectives.

Some important aspects in preparing strategic planning are:

- Excellence is determined by *Shari'ah* (*Maqasid al-shari'ah*) not by the customers. This is a strategic view of organizational excellence that focuses on conformity to the *Shari'ah*. Stakeholder satisfaction is indeed very important, but conformity to the *Shari'ah* is the most important thing. Conformity with the *Shari'ah* is to ensure the sustainability of the integrity of the organization.
- Improved performance, including innovation processes at the individual, work unit, and organizational levels that contribute to the productivity, growth, and competitiveness of the organization as a whole. Development of operational capabilities such as processor speed, responsiveness, agility, and organizational flexibility.
- Learning process both at the individual, work unit, and organizational level. Learning is necessary to respond to various irregular environmental changes (turbulence).

The strategic plan is the result of an analysis of the potential and the problems facing the organization. The potential is an elaboration of the core competencies that the organization possesses. This includes the internal conditions of the organization and the organizational capabilities. Potential analysis is the process of analyzing the strengths that the organization possesses. The core competencies are the most important assets of the organization in achieving the strategic goals and objectives.

Challenges analysis refers to the process of identifying various weaknesses. The weaknesses of the organization must be immediately supported by various strategies so that they do not become a weakness of the organization. The challenges faced by the organization must be solved so that the strategic objectives and goals can be realized. The challenges faced by an organization can come from both the internal organization and the organizational environment.

Challenges from the internal organization may be in the form of limited resources or technological constraints. Challenges from the organizational environment may be in the form of regulatory changes, changes in the natural environment, competition from old and new competitors, technological changes, changes in consumer behaviour, social change, limited access, political change, etc.

Assessing the external environment of the organization is an important step. As we know, the environmental situation of the organization is dynamic. From the physical point of view, the entropy of a system is always positive. This causes the environment to change rapidly. Change is double-edged in the organizational environment. Change can be an opportunity or hope if the organization is willing to manage it. On the other hand, change becomes a threat in the organizational environment if the system faces it unprepared.

The results of the analysis of the potential and the problems faced by the organization become a consideration for organizations to develop various alternative strategies. The strategy is based on the matrix of each component of SWOT (Strength – Weakness – Opportunity – Threat). The first strategy is designed for a state where the organization has the power and connects with the opportunities that exist in the environment. The second strategy is designed for a state where the organization has the strength and combines with the threats that exist in the environment. The third strategy is arranged for a state in which the organization has weaknesses and combined with opportunities that exist in the environment. The fourth strategy is arranged for a state in which the organization has weaknesses and combined with opportunities in the environment.

The Grand Design is structured by a description of the strategic steps that must be taken to achieve the organization's vision. The Grand Design describes everything related to the resources needed to achieve the organization's vision. From the variety of strategies available for selection, the organization must determine one strategic priority as the main strategy. The determination of the main strategy is done in a way that determines the rank of all the proposed strategies. The strategies that rank the highest become the main strategy. In determining the ranking, various factors may be considered, such as the degree of importance, the costs incurred, the sources of manpower, the time required, or the degree of difficulty in applying the strategy (see Table 9.1).

Table 9.1 Strategy Priority Assessment

	Consideration						
Strategy	*Interests*	*Cost*	*HR*	*Time*	*Difficulty*	*Score*	*Rank*
Strategy 1	4	3	1	2	3	13	3
Strategy 2	3	4	2	3	4	16	1
Strategy 1	3	3	4	2	2	14	2
Strategy 2	4	2	3	1	2	12	4

Note: Value 4 indicates very influential considerations; value 3 indicates influential considerations; value 2 indicates consideration has no effect; value 1 indicates that consideration has no effect.

Strategic Objective Setting

Strategic objectives are intermediate goals on the way to the main goal. A strategic goal serves as a steppingstone to a series of benefits. A climber has the main goal of reaching the top of the mountain. To achieve this main goal, he had provided several intermediate goals while climbing. The intermediate goal in climbing is required as a kind of strategy that combines various resources to achieve the goal of climbing.

Climbing to the summit of Mount Lawu (Karanganyar Regency, Central Java, Indonesia) can be done by setting the goal of climbing in two different bases, namely Cemorokandang in Tawangmangu, Central Java, and Cemorosewu, in Sarangan, East Java. Ascent of Cemorosewu via two sources, namely Sendang Panguripan and Sendang Drajat.

Climbing Ciremai, the highest mountain in West Java, can be done from the east via Linggarjati, from the south via Palutungan and from the west via Maja. Of the three lines, the Linggarjati and Palutungan lines are the paths recommended by Perhutani (State Forestry Public Company) as the administrator of the Gunung Ciremai forest area.

Strategic targets have several characteristics. Pearce and Robinson, Jr.[2] stated that these characteristics are: (1) acceptance, i.e., acceptable by the underlying organization or work unit; (2) flexible, i.e., the strategic goal must be able to adapt to environmental changes; (3) measurable, i.e., strategic goals must be measurable. Among things that should be measurable are the time of achievement and the amount or number of its achieved; (4) motivation, the strategic goal that should hopefully be able to motivate individuals within the organization and work unit to be able to achieve it; (5) appropriate, the goal and the strategy must be appropriate with other strategic goals or mutually supportive. It is not possible to agree on a strategic objective that conflicts with the others. It is understandable that the strategic objectives must be understood by all people and work units. To be achieved, the strategic objectives must be within the range that can be achieved by the organization.

Some strategic objectives for organizations based on *Maslahah* including:

1 The achievement of a visionary organizational manager.
Visionary organizational managers have a clear vision of life, a long-term vision to achieve goodness in the world and goodness in the afterlife.[3] To attain this goodness, they always obeys all the commandments and keeps away from all the prohibitions of the Creator, the Almighty Regulator, the Happiness Giver.[4] Visionary organizational managers can adapt to changes in their environment if these changes do not conflict with *Shari'ah*.

Strategic ends embody organizational managers who are visionary and aim to create people involved in organizational activities as people who have a long-term vision, not only the success of life in the world but also salvation in the hereafter. People who have a vision for life in the world and the Hereafter will always maintain their actions as prescribed by the *Shari'ah* and required by the Islamic *Aqidah*.

2 Realization of the social functions of the organization.
Strategic goals to realize the social functions of the organization take a high priority in embodying the function of the caliphate of the organization, i.e., bringing benefits to the stakeholders. A program to realize the social functions of the organization is through corporate social responsibility (CSR) activities and partnerships.

3 Improving economic function.
Organizations must be able to anticipate all forms of change, both those emanating from internal and external organizations. Internal or external organization changes have an economic impact on the organization. Therefore, organizations must design work systems and work processes and implement them consistently. The design and implementation of work systems and work processes must make an economic contribution to the organization.

The realization of the economic role of the organization is reflected in the increase in the efficiency of production costs. Efficiency means reducing the level of errors, eliminating waste of time, reducing waste of goods errors, increasing the number of suggestions for improvement, reducing non-value-added activities, and reducing production process costs.

4 Realization of justice.
Justice means a balance between rights and obligations. Appreciation should be given for employees' performance according to their achievement. Justice is fairness both for the organization and for the employees; fairness to the company and also fair to suppliers; fairness for the organization and also for customers; fairness for the organization and also fair for the environment.

5 Creating high productivity.
Productivity means increasing the volume of production or service. Productivity also means producing efficiently; the number of defective products decreases, the cost of quality goes down, and the company's profits increase.

6 Ensuring leadership sustainability.
Gifted manpower who has competencies in worship orientation and organizational management become recipients of leadership in the management of the organization. Gifted manpower is the basic capital for sustainable leadership in the management of the organization. This is a solution to the problems that occur currently. Especially in Indonesia, where the development of *Shari'ah* financial institutions is not accompanied by the growth of talented workers who have skills in worship and organizational management.

7 Increasing the satisfaction of talented employees.
A conducive environment is one that can awaken a motivated, talented workforce so that they always feel happy to be at work. The feeling of happiness comes when they are satisfied at work. Therefore, the satisfaction of the talented workforce is a strategic goal that the company must achieve.

8 Enhancing employee ownership.
One method to increase workers' work motivation is to involve them in decision-making or other activities according to their authority and responsibility. Employees are encouraged to make suggestions or proposals to the management, which are then followed up by the management. In the quality management system, suggestion submission activities are referred to as suggestion schemes.

9 The establishment of a learning work culture.
The learning work culture leads to a situation where workers are gifted to be creative and innovative. Talented workers become accustomed to an environment where the process of repair and improvement is also emphasized in terms of achieving goals (goal attainment). An indicator of learning success is a large number of suggestions for improvement. Method development in the implementation of the work, continuously do. The number of productions increases, the error rate decreases. The time of task execution (tack time) becomes faster. Non-value-added activities can be reduced. The response of talented employees to customer dissatisfaction becomes faster. This affects stakeholder satisfaction, especially customer interest, and the amount of compensation also decreases.

10 Integration of IT infrastructure as a learning media.
Michael Wade and John Hulland (2004)[5] found that the power of the source information system can be an important driver for the organization to create a competitive advantage and long-term performance, if it is unique and valuable and cannot be copied by competitors. On the other hand, Maris Martinsons, Robert Davison, and Dennis Tse (1999)[6] explain that the use of information systems can increase the productivity of individuals.

In their application, the performance of information systems must be measured by two things: First, the efficiency of activities related to the development and operation of information systems. Second, the contribution of information systems to increasing individual productivity. They say that efficiency is related to internal processes, while effectiveness is related to organizational values and user orientation.

11 Establishment of learning-oriented reward system.
The most important thing in the application of Kaizen is a discordant system (Jacobson *et al.*, 2009).[7] This system is one of the characteristics or features of a Kaizen culture. Brainstorming systems can enable everyone involved to solve problems. Every suggestion gets a response and every success in implementing the suggestion is rewarded. This spurs everyone to make improvements.

12 Increase customer satisfaction.
Customer is a medium conveyed by God to send *Rizq* to the organization. Therefore, the increase in the number of customers is directly proportional to the *Rizq* delivered. The more customers, the higher the chance of receiving *Rizq*.
On the other hand, an increase in the number of customers must also be accompanied by an increase in customer satisfaction for the organization. The more satisfied a customer is, the more loyal they are to the company. Loyal customers will not switch to other companies. Loyal customers can become a marketing medium that is good for the company. The customer will recommend the company to other potential customers.

13 Customer empowerment.
Empowerment of customers means that customers can determine the input, process and output of the organization's work system. The most important thing in the process of customer empowerment is the willingness of the customer to be involved in the process of customer participation.
It is unlikely that an organization will conduct an empowerment process for its customers if the customers do not desire to be involved in the process. Customer involvement increases when the organization responds quickly to the customer's expectations.

14 Double gain.
The cycle of getting and spending wealth gives you the lesson that the best situation is one in which income is greater than expenditure. In an organizational context, an excess of income over expenses means profit. This situation is a driving force for organizations to always focus on a surplus of two times between income and expenses.

15 Realizing the cleanliness of wealth.
The acquired wealth needs to be purified through a purification process, namely *Zakat*.[8] *Zakat* is not only a sanctuary but also serves as leverage of income.[9] This happens because zakat can increase the blessings for the wealth left behind. In this case, zakat payments can not only be a strategic goal but also serve as a strategic initiative.

16 Realization of an efficient organization.
When using wealth, organizations need to prioritize the spending items that have high priority. Meeting basic needs is the top priority when spending wealth. Not only being wasteful but also being too stingy is a trait that is repeatedly taught by Rasulullah (*s.a.w.*). Organizations should be efficient and effective in managing expenditure items.

17 Realizing an obedient and consistent organization.
This strategic objective aims at making individual managers obedient organizations to *Shari'ah* as well as regulatory organizations. Obedience, of course, belongs to consistent or continuous compliance, not temporary compliance. Do not obey because of certain desires but obey for the sake of Allah (*s.w.t.*).

18 Creating organizations that have flexibility and dexterity towards change. Flexible and dexterous is the attitude of the organization that responds well to all forms of change and implements them quickly. The change may be caused by regulatory changes, competitive environment, customer requirements, changing stakeholder expectations, etc. To respond to change, organizations need to be both flexible and adept at managing change. Flexibility without dexterity will cause the organization to fail at accommodating changes in the environment.

Of course, to create a well-organized organization, it is not enough to only set strategic goals as described above. There are other strategic objectives that can be agreed. This depends on the nature and form of the organization.

Strategic Initiative

Abu Ishāq al-Shāṭibi explained that the upholding of religion is done in two strategies, namely, first, the creation of conditions that facilitate worship, and second, the performance of worship itself. The first initiative of Abu Ishāq al-Shāṭibi called *al-Wujūd*. It is applied through the implementation of peace, prayer, *Zakat*, fasting, and hajj.[10] *Syahadat*, prayer, *Zakat*, fasting, and hajj were undertaken to increase the intensity of worship within oneself. The second initiative is *al-'Adam*, which is a preventive-proactive initiative in terms of content. It is applied through the decree of jihad to protect the religion.[11]

Zaharah (1958)[12] uses the term *al-Muḥāfizatu 'alā al-din* or religious security guarantees, which are carried out by preventing the emergence of slander and salvation in religion and by anticipating impulses of desire and actions that lead to utter destruction. As the Hadith of Prophet Muhammad reminds mankind to always preserve the religion one possesses by restraining the desires to vie for the wealth of the world.[13] Zaharah considered that preservation of religion is done by encouraging from within by restraining the passions of the world which can make one forget the religious interests. This is an initiative to generate soul/*Ruhiyah*.

Stating the same opinion as Zaharah, Chapra (2007)[14] said that the maintenance of religion is through the purification of the soul.[15] This is the basis for Chapra to put the order of fulfilment of soul care first in order to fulfil the basic needs. After the needs of the soul are fulfilled, the initiative to maintain the religion is to maintain the behaviour and value system in daily life, to promote motivation in the practice of religion, and the third initiative is to educate. On close examination, the three initiatives described by Chapra are the awakening of the soul in the form of maintaining behaviour and values in daily life, providing motivation, and habituation or standardization of education.

Kamil *et al.* (2010)[16] stated that the initiative that must be taken to uphold the religion are the rituals of worship or ibadah, forgiveness or *al-'Afw*, belief in Allah (*s.w.t.*) and dhikr, remembrance of Allah (*s.w.t.*) or *Dzikrullah*. Performing acts of worship such as *Solat, fasting, Zakat,* and *Hajj* will improve the spiritual relationship between people and Allah (*s.w.t.*) and the relationship between individuals. If the ritual activities are not performed regularly, the spiritual relationship will become weak. Allah (*s.w.t.*) has prescribed worship through daily activities, for example, five daily prayers; weekly activities, for example, Friday *Solat*; and yearly activities for examples *Ramadhan* fasting. This will strengthen and increase confidence and purify the heart from faults and sins.

Dzikrullah is the activity of remembering Allah (*s.w.t.*) by the employees in the work environment to strengthen the spiritual bond between the workers and Allah (*s.w.t.*) so that Allah's intervention is included in various decisions at work. *Taubah* and forgiveness refer to granting tolerance, removing blame, and repaying evil with good so that people who make mistakes receive forgiveness from Allah (*s.w.t.*). Operational belief in Allah (*s.w.t.*) means loyalty to Allah (*s.w.t.*) at work, along with efforts to achieve the goal of one's work.

To achieve the strategic goal of worshipping Allah (*s.w.t.*), some initiatives can be carried out which are the strategy of *Dzikrullah*. As explained by Kamil *et al.* (2010), this is the activity of remembering Allah (*s.w.t.*) by praying together with the employees in the work environment. Such activities can be done by reciting the Holy Quran before work. The *Dhikrullah*'s activities aim to increase the passion of workers for spirituality in the work environment. This is necessary to sustain the spirit of worship in the work environment.

Strategic initiatives integrate the performance appraisal system with the Spiritual Quotient (SQ). Elements that can be integrated into the performance appraisal include memorization of several Quranic verses or hadith, *Sunnah fasting, Tahajud prayer, Duha prayer, I'tikaf, Infaq, Sodaqoh,* etc. The nature of the element is adapted to the conditions in the work area. The purpose of integrating worship activities into a performance appraisal system is so that worship activities can become established habits of the workforce.

The strategic employee empowerment initiative aims to improve the social function of the organization. The programs can be implemented directly by the organization but can also partner with other social service agencies. The programs can be in the form of education, health services, counselling, socialization, scholarships, entrepreneurship, community development, mentoring, etc.

While to protect the soul, Zaharah (1958)[17] explains the initiatives that need to be carried out. Zaharah uses the term *al-muḥāfizatu 'alā al-nafs* or a guarantee of security of life, which is a guarantee of security for the right to live a life that is honourable and noble. The guarantees of salvation include guaranteed security of life, limbs, and guaranteed human dignity such as freedom of choice, freedom of thought and expression, freedom of speech, and freedom to choose a place of residence.

According to al-Shāṭibi, the needs of the soul can be guaranteed by creating the conditions for survival through the *al-Wujud* approach, which is fulfilled by meeting the needs for food with nutritious food, maintaining health, the needs for clothing, and the needs for a place to live. Also, with the *al-'Adam* approach, namely through *Jinayat* such as *Qisas, Diyat, Had,* and *Ta'zir.*

To realize justice, the company has taken the initiative to introduce new products that are *Riba* free. As a result, customers have a wide choice. It also strengthens the bargaining position of the company vis-à-vis its competitors. It should not be forgotten that products that are free from riba are an implementation of *Maqasid al-shari'ah*.

Some large companies enforce a policy for suppliers. Goods received today are paid two or three months later. Of course, this policy is very troublesome for suppliers, especially small capital suppliers. Standardization of payments to suppliers considering equity elements should also be done.

In the area of employment, the hiring of outsourcing employees must also be included as a strategic initiative to achieve equity. Currently, outsourcing is an important issue in employment, especially in Indonesia. Workers believe that outsourcing is a scourge for employment in Indonesia. A scourge for workers is the lack of a policy to hire permanent employees for outsourcing workers who have worked long enough. This is perceived by workers as an injustice.

The strategic initiatives to implement the cost reduction program target the sources of cost wastage. These include production costs, supporting costs, print procurement costs, overtime costs, operating costs, etc. As far as production costs are concerned, the main program aims at reducing the error rate in the process. This is reflected in a lower percentage of products that are rejected. In the service process, the reduction in defects may be reflected in higher customer satisfaction, lower compliance, or lower customer dissatisfaction.

The cost reduction program focuses on controlling quality costs in accordance with established goals. Quality costs are costs incurred in managing or controlling quality. When defective products occur, i.e., products that do not meet requirements/standards, the organization must inspect the product, find out the cause of the problem, and take corrective and preventive action.

When defects occur in the work area, the organization shall ensure that similar products still in the work area shall be re-tested. Products that are already at the customer's premises must be taken back. All costs resulting from the above process are grouped under quality costs. In service-oriented organizations, quality costs may be incurred when a product does not fit, and the customer is dissatisfied. The organization then must replace similar services for the service dissatisfaction. Quality costs are not only in the form of tangible costs but can also be intangible, such as brand image or brand. Poor service has a negative impact on the brand image of the company.

Strategic initiatives integrate the recruitment and selection system with skills development, which is carried out in relation to medium-term planning. It includes information about the capacity and skills of the talent needed, including the type and amount of work that needs to be prepared by the organization.

In addition, the organization specifies the characteristics that the future talent must possess. These characteristics are described in the job description,[18] which includes a description of the main tasks, job descriptions, job specifications, and competencies. The characteristics of worship orientation are reflected in the provisions of *Aqidah, Shari'ah*, and *Akhlaq* that must be fulfilled by talented workers, while the characteristics of an organizational leader are reflected in the knowledge, skills, education, and experience of talented workers according to their position and function.

The compatibility or fit between the competencies of potential talents and the specified requirements is very important, because the selection of potential talents is basically not only about finding talents that meet the requirements of capacity and ability to lead the organization, but also about the vision, mission, values of management and work culture of the organization.

Candidates for talented employees who are recruited and selected can come from internal organizations or from external organizations. Internal sources are from workers who have already worked in the organization. After they have gone through observations and have sufficient skills, they are given the opportunity to expand their capability. Other internal sources come from workers who are in outsourcing status, but after the observation process, they are found to have criteria that match the requirements for the talent needed, so they are given preference in the recruitment and selection process.

Sometimes, organizations cannot conduct their own recruitment and selection processes for certain positions. Because the position is very specific or requires a lengthy process, or for other reasons, the recruitment and selection process may be conducted with the help of an independent third party or consultant. This is to maintain the credibility and professionalism of the recruitment and selection results.

The strategic talent management initiative aims to continuously develop and nurture talented employees. This is done to ensure that talented employees are always in a happy and enjoyable work situation. Developing and empowering talented employees aim to ensure that talented employees can achieve the company's key objectives. Lockwood (2006)[19] pointed out that organizations that do not link their organizational goals to talent strategies can say that the organization does nothing. Such organizations focus only on resource activities and not on impact or outcomes.

Talented employees feel tied to the organization. They develop a sense of ownership as the caliphate. The system for developing and empowering talented employees must be able to encourage talented employees to continuously improve themselves to achieve better work results. Dissemination and brainstorming systems are used in various activities to solve problems. These activities affect the mentality of talented workers. Capable workers increasingly feel involved in various decision-making processes.

Strategic initiatives determine the career system and performance of the gifted workers. They are carried out to promote the performance of the talented workers so that they are always better than the previous period. The management of talent is controlled by a good system and always adapts to all forms of change. Undoubtedly, the development of talented workers' performance must include a fair system of rewards and punishments and stay away from misconduct.

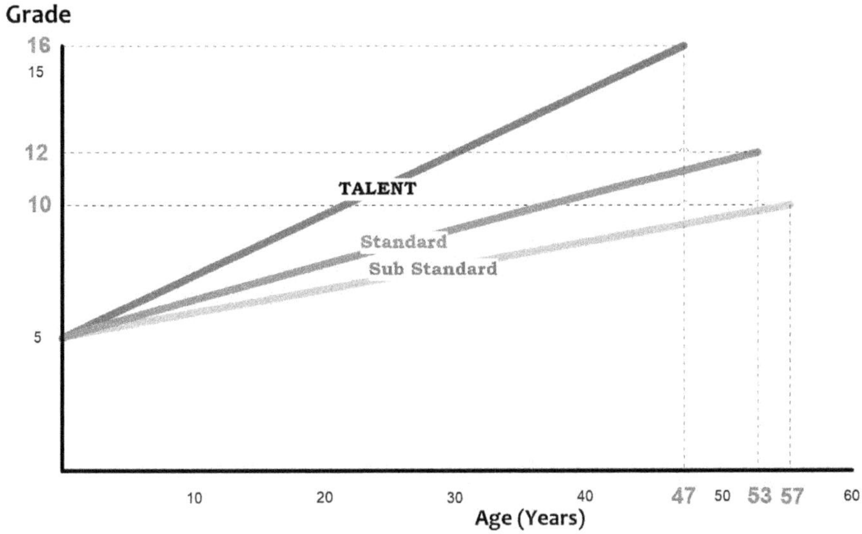

Figure 9.1 Career Development for Workforce.

Source: Processed data.

The governance of the compensation and benefits system is designed to provide benefits to both talented employees and their families while promoting the principle of equity for the organization. The normal rights of talented workers, such as wages, should be paid on a time basis. The right to recreational leave shall be granted in accordance with the regulations. All activities culminate in a state where talented workers feel happy and feel attachment to their jobs, as stated by Chapra and Rampersad.

As for the career system for talented workers, the following is an example of how to determine the career of talented workers. All workers are classified into three groups, namely talented workers, standard workers, and inferior workers. Talented workers have the opportunity to advance from one grade to another for at least two years, while standard workers have the opportunity to advance for four years. Underperforming workers can advance to a higher grade at least every six years.

Talented workers have career acceleration that is two times faster than standard workers and three times faster than non-standard workers (Figure 9.1).

Assumption of talented workers:

- a Fresh graduate, Bachelor's Degree, start working at the age of 25 with grade 5.
- b Opportunities for promotion to higher grades every two years.
- c The talented workers reach the highest career in grade 16.
- d The highest-grade 16 career was achieved at the age of 47 years.

Assumption of standard labour:

- a Fresh graduate, S1, start working at the age of 25 with grade 5.
- b Opportunity for promotion to a higher grade every four years.
- c The standard workers reach the highest career in grade 12.
- d The highest-grade 12 career was achieved at the age of 53 years.

Assumption of substandard labour:

- a Fresh graduate, S1, start working at the age of 25 with grade 5.
- b Opportunities for promotion to higher grades every six years.
- c The standard workers reach the highest career in grade 10.
- d The highest-grade 12 career was achieved at the age of 55 years.

Strategic initiatives to implement the Total Quality Management System (TQM) also needed to be done. TQM is a strategic management system that involves all levels of work within the organization. TQM involves a management process based on quality, teamwork, productivity, and customer satisfaction. TQM aims to continuously improve the organization's performance at each level of operation or process by using available human resources and capital.

Adawiyah (2011)[20] studied the application of the TQM principle in an Islamic bank in Central Java. They found that the application of TQM has a great impact on management commitment. Spiritual values in the workplace can link employee engagement with empowerment, organizational engagement, and customer service. For this reason, Adawiyah recommended that the Islamic bank should apply TQM.

Individual learners need to develop themselves. Everyone should realize that self-development and empowerment are not only the needs of the organization but also the basic needs of the individual to realize himself as the *Caliph* of Allah (*s.w.t.*). Self-development can be done by developing conscience, caring, courage, and self-confidence to achieve a goal. This is done by getting used to one's appearance, expressing opinions, writing, arguing correctly, etc.

Worker's development is carried out through the right training program. Training is carried out through the PDCA cycle. Training is carried out through the PDCA cycle. Training planning starts with Training Needs Analysis (TNA). Training needs can be derived from individual employee performance evaluation, management policies, customer feedback, risk analysis, audit results, etc. Training can be delivered through internal training, on-the-job training, external training, internships, mentoring, group discussions, etc.

Evaluation of training activities is done by assessing responses, i.e., evaluation of materials, teachers, methods, etc. Learning evaluation is done by comparing the understanding of the participants after the training activities with the understanding of the participants before the training activities. Participants should have experienced a change after the training. Behavioural evaluation is done to see how the training affects the implementation of daily work. The training should have a better impact on the work of the participants. It is expected that after the training, the participants will perform their work faster and more carefully.

The training is conducted with the aim of changing the insight, knowledge, skills, education, experience, and behaviour to be better than before. The training also aims to improve *Aqidah*, *Shari'ah*, and the morale of the participants so that they are better than before the training.

Strategic initiatives to improve customer satisfaction are carried out by integrating inputs, feedback, and complaints through online facilities that customers can access directly. The company's response to inputs, feedback, and customer complaints has a great impact on the level of customer satisfaction. Online facilities are required to maximize customer access to service products and services of the company. Online facilities also become a source of knowledge for customers to find other information about the company. Maximizing the function of online networks is an urgent need for the organization.

To improve customer satisfaction, the organization reviews all service procedures. The review is done on ineffective procedures. Procedures that hinder service time are shortened. An overly bureaucratic procedure is reviewed for simplicity, etc. This is done to simplify and streamline the procedures and provide convenient, reliable, and fast service to the customers.

Without a customer satisfaction study, it is not enough for the organization to assess whether the services are good or still bad for the customers. Organizations must be able to measure customer satisfaction through customer satisfaction surveys. The survey can be conducted by the organization itself, but it can also be done in collaboration with third parties, namely consultants. A third-party survey is conducted to ensure the credibility of the survey results. Clearly, surveys conducted by third parties have a higher level of credibility in terms of trust in the results of the survey compared to surveys conducted by the organization itself. When the survey is conducted by a third party, the brand image of the consultant also has a great impact on the trust in the survey results.

Customer empowerment is done by designing products according to customer needs and trends that occur in the community. The products are properly socialized to the customers. All the advantages and disadvantages of the product should be communicated to the customers.[21] Contracts or *aqds* are also made complete but as simple as possible so that customers do not feel that they are being ripped off. The handling of complaints and dissatisfaction is properly managed. Customers can voluntarily give input, feedback, advice, etc. The initiative that can be taken is to increase customer mobilization activities and build a customer community.

Customer mobilization is an activity carried out with the aim of gathering customers through various activities. This is a good means of communication between companies and customers. Forming a customer community creates a sense of belonging and increases customer loyalty towards products and services.

Several strategic initiatives have been implemented to achieve double win. Double bottom line is a profit target that is double the previous period. Of course, this target is lofty. The milestone states that annual net profit must increase by 40%. For this reason, it is necessary to improve the process, which is a big improvement, not just a small improvement. One of the suggestions is to have a Business Process Re-engineering (BPR) process for the channel system.

Strategic initiatives to realize the purification of wealth are carried out through the payment of Zakat. Zakat payments are expected to double compared to the previous year. This is an extraordinary target. The amount to be distributed is very high. It could be that the organization will collaborate with Amil Zakat Institution (LAZ) to channel the productive Zakat, where the distributed Zakat will be used for productive purposes and not for consumption. The cooperation with LAZ is through the formulation of productive work programs in the real sector.

The strategic objectives of making an organization into an efficient one are realized through the creation of a Grand Design that links the vision, mission, goals, objectives, and action plans to the budget. The Grand Design is monitored on an annual, semi-annual, quarterly, and monthly basis.

Strategic initiatives establish a Code of Conduct to guide the direction and policies of the organization. The Code of Conduct includes provisions regarding compliance (*Shari'ah compliance*). The Counterpart team developed the Code of Ethics with input from DPS. The Code of Ethics is approved by top management and then socialized to all levels of the company. Socialization took the form of indoctrination, i.e., teaching lessons to the entire workforce, especially at the management level, since the Code of Ethics is usually violated at that level.

Strategic initiatives are development programs designed to help an organization's leaders anticipate and adapt to various forms of organizational change. The programs are aimed at all employees, especially the talented employees of the organization. This program aims to increase the capacity and skills of employees. The part that needs to be considered in the development process is covering the worship orientation competencies, namely *Aqidah*, *Shari'ah*, and *Akhlaq*, and the organizational management competencies, which consist of insight, knowledge, skills, experience, and training.

The competency development program is created by comparing the need for worship orientation competencies and organizational management competencies in the future (need) with existing worship orientation competencies and organizational management competencies (Figure 9.2).

The competency development program is structured not only for the existing employees but also for the new employees through management development programs. The HR department hopes that the employees who are accepted will have competencies in worship orientation and high organizational management competencies, but in reality, it is not easy to find employees with such qualifications. Therefore, a program to develop worship orientation and organizational management competencies for staff is needed.

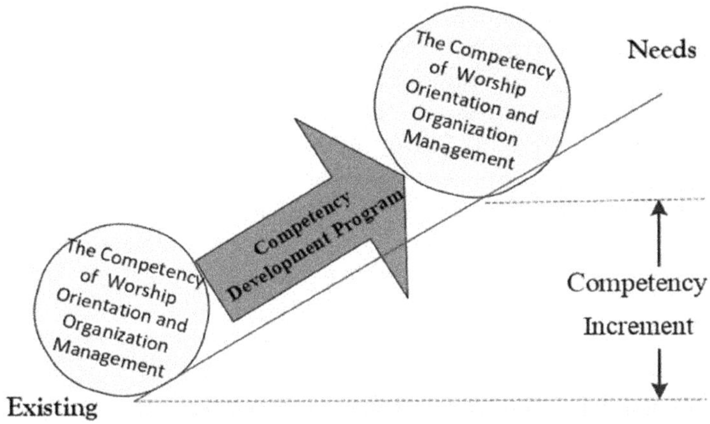

Figure 9.2 Competency Development Program.

Source: Firdaus (2017: 148).

Identifying the *Maslahah* Foundation

This step is carried out to identify foundation required for the construction of a *Maslahah* building. Foundation is a very important part of a building. The main function of foundation is to carry the load from a building structure to the ground. Foundation acts as a palm of the building so that the entire structure of the building can stand firmly on the ground, as well as the function of foundation in a building. The foundation of benefit is a vital infrastructure that must be in place. Without a strong foundation, the building of *Maslahah* will not be able to withstand the shocks of life. The *Maslahah* of the building will easily collapse and will not last long.

The foundation for a one-storey house is certainly different from the foundation for a two-storey house, especially for a skyscraper. A less complicated foundation infrastructure is required for one- or two-storey houses. Therefore, the foundation with river stone structure is sufficient. On the other hand, for multi-storey buildings, foundation in the form of piles made of steel or concrete is required. Therefore, to work on the foundation of a multi-storey building, special heavy equipment is required to drive the pile into the ground.

The foundation depends not only on the kind of building to be established but also on the environment where the building is located. If the ground is stable and capable of bearing weight, a simple structure will suffice for the foundation of the building. However, if the surrounding soil is unstable and has poor bearing capacity, the foundation should be more complex in design.

A strong foundation is not only able to support the load of the building and its contents but also able to withstand natural shocks such as earthquakes or other ground movements. Like the building foundation, the foundation of *Maslahah* must also be able to support the weight of the building of welfare, even from shaking caused by circumstances. A firm foundation and strong welfare ensure that the building of prosperity stands firm and can provide sustainability to many people.

The foundation for fulfilling the worship orientation or religious needs of the organization is three aspects of Islamic teachings, namely *Aqidah*, *Shari'ah*, and *Akhlaq*. *Aqidah* means believing in and performing the pillars of faith and the pillars of Islam. *Shari'ah* consists of the main sources of Islamic law, namely the Qur'an and the Hadith, as well as jurisprudence and rules for the administration of the organization. *Akhlaq* includes morality towards Allah (*s.w.t.*), the angels, the apostles, the books, the Last Day, and destiny. *Morality* also has good relations with stakeholders. These include shareholders, customers, employees, partners, suppliers, the government, etc. *Akhlaq* also has to do with good relations with the environment. These include competitors, society, and the environment.

The basis for meeting internal process orientation or meeting the soul needs of the organization can be physical, which can be counted, or non-physical, which cannot be calculated. The basis of internal process orientation is the suitability of the organization's input and output in relation to *Shari'ah*, the organization's input process, the organization's main processes, the organization's supporting processes, the process of sustainability, disaster management and emergency response, risk management processes, processes compliance with *Shari'ah* and legal and organizational output processes.

The basis for meeting the talent orientation or meeting the inheritable needs for organizations comes from the work and the organization. The foundation that comes from the workers consists of two, namely the skills of insight, knowledge, skills, education, and experience that match the capacity of organizational management skills. Secondly, the skills of *Aqidah*, *Shari'ah*, and *Akhlaq* correspond to the capacity of worship orientation.

The foundation that emanates from the organization is the presence of a favourable environment in which talented employees can develop. Coyle[22] calls the organization a place to formulate talented workers with the term talent hotbeds. The term is used as the process of creating a talented worker is like the process of producing delicious cakes.

According to Coyle, producing a talented employee requires three things, deep practice, ignation, and master coaching. Deep practice has three rules: cut into small pieces, repeat, and learn to interpret feelings.

The basis for meeting the learning orientation or meeting the needs of intellect and heart for organizations comes from human capital and organizational capital. Human beings have capital in the form of intellect and heart. Intellect is used to learn things that are logical or comprehensible. The heart is used to learn things that are not logical or non-comprehensible. The foundations derived from organizational capital are embedded into the work system and processes.

The foundation for meeting the customer orientation or customer needs of organizations comes from existing customers and new or potential customers. The customer needs must be identified by the organization as customer requirements. The customer requirements must be written down. The organization writes them down as determination of customer requirements. Customer requirements written down by the organization are always a reference for organizations in serving customers. The ultimate aim of the services provided by the organization to the customers is customer satisfaction.

The basis for meeting the wealth orientation or meeting the wealth needs of the organization is derived from how to receive wealth and how to spend wealth. The way of acquiring wealth and the way of spending wealth that is in accordance with *Shari'ah* will affect the blessing of wealth. Blessed wealth will be able to grow and develop. The way of acquiring wealth and the way of spending it which is not *Shari'ah* compliance will result in the wealth not being a blessing. The wealth will shrink, and even if the wealth does not shrink, the wealth acquired and spent in a way that is not in accordance with the *shari'ah* will lead to disrespect in the Hereafter.

Determining *Maslahah* Behaviour

Attitude is a way in which one party communicates his feelings to another party. The actions taken to communicate are the behaviour. Attitudes have three levels, namely cognitive or belief or awareness, affective or feeling, and conative or behaviour.

Maslahah behaviour is a value that is upheld by the organization to realize an organization that provides sustainability for stakeholders. Advantageous behaviour means that an organization exhibits behaviour that reflects the depth and strength of its foundation.

Maslahah behaviour is the link of a *Maslahah* performance system. Without *Maslahah* behaviour, the *Maslahah* foundation that an organization possesses becomes merely a concept of performance without a clear and measurable application. Organizational *Maslahah* behaviour is required by the organization to translate the foundation of the organization's *Maslahah* into action.

Worship Orientation

Strong *Aqidah* produces a feeling of closeness to Allah (*s.w.t.*). This feeling arises because Allah (*s.w.t.*) always answers the prayers of those who pray to Him.[23] This makes our soul calm so that we always have positive thoughts about Allah (*s.w.t.*). Whatever you plan to do, if you pray to Allah (*s.w.t.*) before you do it, you will be convinced that the work can be done properly with Allah's help. This naturally inspires a sense of optimism. Optimism can create confidence and keep pointing out that the work can be done with good results.

When a problem arises, remember Allah (*s.w.t.*) and pray for a way out, for Allah (*s.w.t.*) also gives His guidance. Allah (*s.w.t.*) provides the best solution so that the problems can be solved. Through this behaviour, a person gets used to setting goals before performing any work. All efforts are made to achieve the goal. The achievement of the results is completely left to Allah (*s.w.t.*).[24]

A cycle of work is created which consists of planning carefully, praying to Allah (*s.w.t.*), completing the work in accordance with the procedures and morals set by Allah (*s.w.t.*), and checking whether what has been done is in accordance with the planning or not. When this cycle is done consistently, it affects the behaviour of the learner who is constantly improving. A personal learner is a person who can integrate intellectual skills and common sense in tackling all the problems at hand. If so, we will find it easy to find solutions to all problems. Those people have the capabilities to solve all the problems they face.

The strong *Aqidah* will always create the feeling of being watched by the Creator, the feeling of always being watched by the Almighty. Organizational managers become trusting, abide by regulations, avoid bribery activities, stay away from gambling, and share information correctly, not because of the provisions of good governance or others, but because they obey The Lawgiver. Since man is only a creature, he must submit, consistently submit, and surrender to the Supreme Creator.[25]

Organizational managers do all this because they are aware that Allah (*s.w.t.*) is the Creator, The Knower, and The Lawgiver. Organization managers are obedient to Him because they hope for salvation in the Hereafter and success of life in this world from Him. As creatures of Allah (*s.w.t.*) who are destined to be the *Caliphs* of Allah (*s.w.t.*) on earth, people should perform their duties properly in accordance with the guidelines and code of conduct.

If this is done consistently, it can produce people who have high integrity. The integrity between words and actions. What is said always refers to the *Shari'ah* and what is done is what is said. What is done is always written. What is written is always done.

Being close to the Supreme Giver of sustenance has opened our hearts and made us realize that we are not the greatest. If they succeed, it is not because of their intelligence but because Allah (*s.w.t.*) made it easy for them to achieve what they wanted. Positive thinking leads the intellect and heart to realize that they are still far from perfection. There are many external factors that make them successful. What is seen, what is heard, and what is felt can become information that serves as a source for improvement and enhancement.

The behaviour described above has implications for being careful in calculations. Being careful to consider all risks in what they do. Careful about what their responsibility is. Making wrong decisions has bad consequences not only for themselves but also for others; it promotes a strong sense of caring. Managers of organizations take care of the environment, plant trees, provide greenery, take care of exhaust fumes, take care of waste disposal, control hazardous waste materials, save energy, and control the number of industrial accidents, not only because of regulations of the Ministry of Environment, CSR, Partnership and Community Development (PKBL) programs, ISO 14001, Environmental Impact Analysis, regional regulations, or other regulations, but the organizations do this because they love the Creator. They know that Allah (*s.w.t.*) forbids humans to destroy the environment.[26] Environmental damage has a negative impact on human life, flora, and fauna.

The strong *Aqidah* increases patience. In serving, one must be patient. Patience is needed in responding to customer complaints, actively listening to the voice of the customer, always striving to meet customer expectations, trying to always be close to customers, responding to customer dissatisfaction, saying good, polite, courteous, smiling to suppliers, partners, workers, subordinates, or superiors. Those are done not because they want to be appreciated by partners but because those are the regulations set by the Supreme Creator.

Internal Process Orientation

Work systems and work process[27] must create a sense of satisfaction among all employees of an organization. If employees are always happy, this can create a passion for work, so work motivation increases. The state of happiness also affects the ethics, morale, and spirituality of the workforce.

Workers who are always motivated have an impact on the improvement process. This triggers a high level of work innovation. Improvement and innovation are necessary to increase productivity.

In terms of governance and leadership, organizations must be able to design work systems and work processes based on *Maqasid al-shari'ah*, so that they can prevent fraudulent practices such as theft, corruption, or abuse of authority by prioritizing the public interest by avoiding all forms of magrib (*Maysir, Gharar,* and *Riba*) and oppression (*Dzalim*).

Compliance with *Shari'ah*, compliance with regulations, and compliance with standardization systems carried out by organizations such as ISO 9001, ISO 14001, ISO 17025, SMK3, OHSAS, etc., are the main basis of the work system. Compliance and honesty in the management of the organization must be maintained as an embodiment of adherence to the *Shari'ah (Shari'ah compliance).*

In the operational process, including investment, organizations must be able to control risk. Not only that, but the violence of major events such as floods, earthquakes, weather and climate changes, volcanic eruptions, and fires will have an impact on the organization. Organizations need to ensure that such events do not have a negative impact on internal processes. Backing up data and recovering from the worst conditions must be well anticipated. Downtime for disasters and emergencies must be ensured so that service continuity and organizational sustainability are not compromised.

Corporate concern for social problems is evident in CSR activities. Organizations need to improve social functions. Organizational concern for the surrounding community and environment must be controlled by a special function. Foundations engaged in socio-religious activities can be a bridge to realize the socio-religious functions of the organization.

The prevention system is carried out through the process of selecting, determining, and evaluating suppliers, procedures for purchasing raw materials, *Aqd* or work contracts, placing inventory and intermediate products, processing products and services, storing finished products, distributing final products to delivering goods and services to customers.

Two important things that are closely related are improvement activities and innovation and strategic systems and sustainability. Both activities are processes that need to be controlled and developed. Without these two processes, the organization runs in place. Without these two processes, organizations cannot move forward quickly in the competitive environment of their industry. Improvement and innovation move organizations from one position to another, while strategic systems and sustainability provide direction to the organization, namely the direction in which the organization must move.

Talent Orientation

The mastery of worship orientation competencies and organizational competencies becomes the most important asset for talented workers who actively participate in leading the organization. In his engagement, the talented employee brings his full potential, both physical, intellectual, heart and feelings. In today's technological information age, the presence of heart, intellect, mentality, and attention is even more important than physical presence.

Rampersad (2008)[28] pointed out that the lack of employee participation is the cause of the high costs that the company must bear. Not only that, but the lack of employee involvement could also lead to the company not performing as it should. This, of course, also affected customer dissatisfaction. Rampersad reported that in the Netherlands, it was estimated that the mental and thought absences of the workforce in the workplace caused costs of USD 30,000/workforce/year.

The same thing happened in the United States. Rampersad explained that *Optimize Magazine* in April 2005 reported that there was a tendency of morale decrease in work since 1995. The annual report stated that losses in the United States due to managerial and labour non-engagement cost USD 300 billion (TGO, 2005).[29]

However, to improve the performance of talented workers, it is not enough just to rely only on their engagement. An enabling environment is needed for talented workers as representatives of the *Caliphs* of Allah (*s.w.t.*).

Referring to *The Malcolm Baldrige National Quality Award*,[30] there are two areas that influence the performance of talented employees, namely the environment for talented employees and the involvement of talented employees. Engaging talented employees is important to achieve personal success and organizational success. The environment for talented workers is also essential to create an effective and mutually supportive work environment.

A conducive environment is a means of developing talented workers into future leaders. The environment is conducive to supporting and empowering talented workers so that they can achieve excellence at any level or position. A conducive environment must be able to arouse the motivation of talented employees so that they can accomplish personal and organizational ends, namely salvation in the hereafter and success of life in the world. A conducive environment for talented work forces is ever one that supports them to take risks and ever think "outside the box." A favourable environment is a good habitat for the development of good people for the better.

Learning Orientation

There are several learning-oriented behaviours that must be carried out, namely the administration of organizational competencies, the administration of worship competencies, civilization, and the enforcement of punishments and awards. Learning from organizational competency management comes from many sources. Regulatory changes that result in other changes in service to customers are learning materials for maintaining customer loyalty. Information about customer dissatisfaction is input for the organization to develop better products and services for customers. Fire, floods, droughts, and earthquakes are also issues for the organization to control the loss rate.

Risk management of all organizational processes, including investment risk, is carried out to control the level of losses of the organization. The social responsibility activities of the organization for the surrounding community can undoubtedly be used as a learning tool to improve the social function of the organization.

Problems encountered in the work process, audit results, customer satisfaction survey results, and employee satisfaction survey results are the material for corrective action, preventive action, improvement, and innovation. Changes in the work environment, competition from the industry, opportunities for emerging newcomers, technological changes, or changes in customer behaviour are valuable inputs for the organization's strategic decision-making. In this way, organizations become more flexible to change. The sustainability of the company can be well maintained.

Learning competency from the management of worship orientation competencies can be done in various ways. The habit of *Dzikir* institutionalized by organizations can strengthen the spiritual bond between the workforce and Allah (*s.w.t.*). The cultivation of repentance after a mistake can increase the sense of responsibility for tasks and obligations. Forgiveness implies, among other things, loyalty to Allah (*s.w.t.*) in the field of work. Punctual congregational prayers in the workplace increase responsibility for discipline over time. Similarly, the habit of consulting each other unemployed will increase togetherness and solidarity.

Cultivation means habituation, that is, making the management of worshipful orientation and the management of organizational competencies a part that is always done voluntarily. An example comes from a Japanese company. To manage the learning process of new employees, Japanese companies use marking methods. The new staff must wear a red pin on their arm. The red pin is used to identify a new employee for up to a one-month work period. There are certain types of work and certain areas that workers are not allowed to perform. The red pin identification makes it easier to check this rule.

Workers who have exceeded a one-month duty period will receive a yellow pin. There are certain types of work and areas that workers are not allowed to perform for a period of one to two months. The yellow pin identification facilitates the control of these workers.

At the end of the two-month work period, he will be given a green pin. There are certain types of work and areas that workers are not allowed to perform for two to three months. Green pin designation makes it easier to monitor these workers. A three-month worker has a good performance according to the assessment, so he does not have to use a green pin.

Some specific jobs require certain skills. Workers in this position use other signs for identification. Therefore, if there are workers who do not use the designated sign in a special position, they will be sanctioned.

Customer Orientation

The process of identifying customer needs, determining customer needs, and satisfying customers are done through a customer voice management strategy.[31] Two processes that are carried out in managing the customer's voice are listening to customers and involving customers. Figure 9.3 shows the cycle of the process of listening to the voice of the customer. The cycle consists of a planning step, i.e., identifying customers, deciding on the method of listening, deciding on the time and place of listening, and deciding on the team.[32]

Questionnaires, interviews, catalogues, talk shows, etc., carry out the process of listening to customers. The process of understanding the data or information provided by customers is carried out by analyzing and evaluating the data using an appropriate tool. If necessary, statistical analysis methods can be used as a tool to facilitate decision-making.

To take action depends heavily on the content of the information or data provided by customers. If the information or data on customer complaints can be followed up at that time, the assigned official must immediately follow up on the findings. If the information received requires more in-depth analysis,

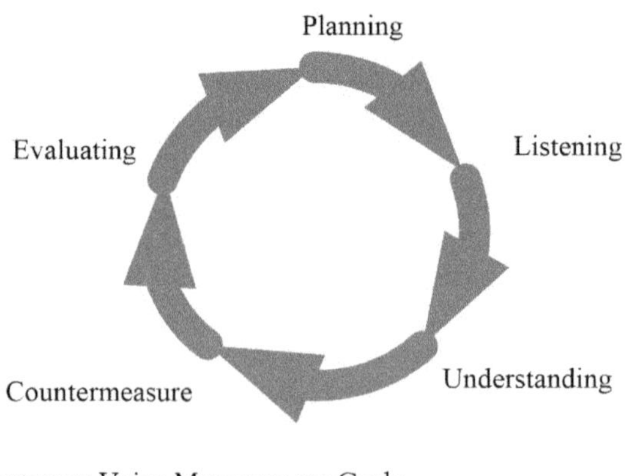

Figure 9.3 The Customer Voice Management Cycle.

Source: Processed data.

it must be completed with the team. The results of listening to customers become a source of input into the design of work systems and operations.

Customer involvement is done by supporting customers and ensuring customer satisfaction. Customer support can be provided by establishing a 24-hour call centre to handle customer services, critics, and complaints. The customer care unit provides services and advice directly to customers and receives and follows up on complaints, grievances, and information from customers. The presence of customer testimonials in magazines, brochures, websites, emails, and social media serves as a communication medium between the company and customers. Direct audience with customers at specific times could also be done. Customer responses and opinions could be conveyed through the company using questionnaires available from customer service unit.

The process of understanding customer complaints or input is done by identifying complaints or feedback so that data on customer expectations is obtained. When complaints or input are received, a decision must be made immediately as to whether they should be investigated or whether they must be forwarded in advance to the appropriate work unit. The speed with which complaints and submissions from customers are responded to has an impact on how customers perceive the company.

The PDCA cycle should be applied to complaints and submissions that require special handling:

a Analyzing problems and finding the main cause of the problems.
b Designing various alternative solutions that can be used to overcome and resolve customer complaints.
c Determining the best solution used to solve the problem.
d Implementing problem-solving solutions.
e Evaluating the effectiveness of the solution by comparing customer responses to services provided.
f Standardizing services and continuous implementation of sustainable improvement processes.

Customer involvement is also done by offering products or services that are quite clear to customers. Customers have the right to receive the clearest possible information about the products or services being offered. Companies should avoid various methods that make customers feel cheated or harassed. Honesty in the sale of goods and services is an organizational obligation that can be fulfilled by achieving a worship orientation.

Customer involvement must be built through a work culture. This means that concern for customer satisfaction is not only embedded in the work system and process, quality policy, or management policy but also implemented and maintained. Concern for customer satisfaction should also be understood and implemented by all levels of the organization, from the lowest working level to top management.

Wealth Orientation

Figure 8.1 explained that the process of acquiring wealth and the process of distributing wealth is a cycle. It begins with alignment to worship orientation and ends in worship orientation as well. This is called the MaP performance cycle, i.e., the effort to acquire wealth and spend it in accordance with the provisions of the *Maqasid al–shari'ah* with *Maslahah* approach.

The way to obtain wealth must fulfil the *Maslahah* requirements, and that is to obtain wealth through the process of fulfilling worship orientation, internal process orientation, talent orientation, learning orientation, and customer orientation. To obtain wealth, one must first ask permission from the One Who Owns Wealth. If one does not ask Him for permission, the action falls under the category of theft. Asking permission is done through prayer. The prayers must be accompanied by efforts because Allah (*s.w.t.*) will not give the wealth directly without making efforts. In doing business, you should naturally cooperate with other people. *Akhlaq* will greatly affect the blessing of business results. You should also remember that there is no instant success in the name of business, Allah (*s.w.t.*) will surely give a test. Therefore, you must continue to pray and make efforts to get the wealth promised by Allah (*s.w.t.*). All the above activities declare the fulfilment of worship orientation.

Improvements in oneself and internal processes must always be evaluated. If the process for obtaining wealth is not consistent or optimal, the blessings ordained by Allah (*s.w.t.*) still feel too far away to be achieved. For this reason, an evaluation process is required for all activities. Has the process of acquiring goods fulfilled the *Halal* and *Thoyib* principles? Which processes still require time, energy, raw materials, labour, and costs? The results of the assessment are then incorporated into corrective actions. These actions aim to improve the process towards a more efficient and effective process.

The efforts to be undertaken obviously require mobilization of the workforce. Their participation is needed to multiply the expected wealth. Companies must try to make them happy. Being happy will motivate the workforce to work better. When the motivation to work increases, the voluntary and sincere workers will participate in the search for the wealth promised by Allah (*s.w.t.*). But it is *Sunatullah* that not all workers have a direct impact on the sustainability of the *Maslahah* of the organization. Only the talented workers have a direct impact on the sustainability of the *Maslahah* of the organization. When this step is completed, the talent orientation has been fulfilled.

Allah (*s.w.t.*) will continue to test people. Can they fulfil the conditions set by Allah (*s.w.t.*)? Therefore, *Muhasabah* or self-reflection for what has been done must always be maintained. Learning from experience and seeking advice from other people and from other sources make human life more meaningful. Striving for wealth is to achieve the noble goal of salvation in the hereafter and success of life in this world. Therefore, we have to stick to the pursuit of wealth in the *Maqasid al-shari'ah*; no other methods. When this step has been reached, the learning orientation has been fulfilled.

The improvement and increase of efforts in the internal processes, the efforts to involve the workforce, and the learning process that is carried out are all aimed at the customers but are actually dedicated to Allah (*s.w.t.*) so that Allah (*s.w.t.*) Will give His blessings. Customers feel respected when their voices are Heard, when they are served with good character, and when complaints are responded to with good morals. When customers feel satisfied, the *Rizq* promised by Allah (*s.w.t.*) can be achieved. When this step is taken, customer orientation has been fulfilled.

When *Rizq* promised by Allah (*s.w.t.*) has been received, we must thank Allah (*s.w.t.*). If the *Rizq* obtained is not in accordance with what is expected, then we must surrender to Allah (*s.w.t.*). Allah (*s.w.t.*) will surely give better *Rizq* at other times and through other media. Up to this point, the cycle of obtaining wealth has been fulfilled.

The way of spending wealth must also be in accordance with the provisions of *Maslahah*. It can be explained that spending wealth is done through a mechanism of wealth distribution, so it is not based on the order of utilization. There are several things that must be done before wealth is allocated, including paying off debts. Debt is sometimes incurred because someone wants to satisfy a need, but at that point the satisfaction is not based on income. Debt is also caused by a person's income being less than their expenses. Remember that debt can lead a person to *Kufr.*[33] Debt can also cause someone to become dishonest.[34]

When someone dies, the obligation that must be fulfilled in addition to paying off his debts is the will he left behind. The distribution of the inheritance is done according to the provisions of QS-Nisā 4: 11–12. The next allocation of the assets is to fulfil the needs of the organization. The fulfilment of the needs of wealth orientation aims to generate wealth: Investments, deposits, savings, current accounts, etc. Meeting the needs of customer orientation includes costs to listen to customer voices, costs to serve customers, costs to manage feedback, and costs to improve customer relationships.[35]

Meeting the needs of learning orientation could be in the form of allocating budget for the cost of training, developing a learning organizational infrastructure is important. Needs of the talent orientation could be in the form of allocating costs of routine salaries, vacation allowance, bonuses, work and family insurance, car allowances, housing allowances, medical expenses, and medical check-ups. Some *Shari'ah*-based companies have even introduced fees for reimbursement of medicines using alternative prophetic remedies *Thibbun nabawi* such as cupping and herbs, as well as holiday allowance (THR) paid two weeks before Eid Fitri, and also time off for employees during the last ten days of Ramadhan.

Meeting the needs of internal process orientation is in the form of allocating budget for production costs, quality costs, risk anticipation costs or insurance, and emergency response infrastructure costs. Meeting the needs of worship orientation includes these three allocations, namely: (1) worshiping Allah (*s.w.t.*) the Most Giving *Rizq*: *Zakat, Infaq, Shadaqoh, Waqf, Hajj, and Qurban*; (2) maintaining relationships with stakeholders: CSR, PKBL, sponsorship, etc.;

(3) maintaining relationship with the environment such as allocating budget for waste control costs, reforestation costs, waste recycling costs, B3 goods control costs, etc. Included in worship orientation fees are costs that must be shared with shareholders (dividend), investment costs, reserve costs, etc.

Determining Measures

The fourth step in the MaP performance system is to determine the measure. A measure is an indicator that shows the success or triumph of an organization in achieving strategic goals as defined in the annual plan. Performance measures are often referred to as Key Performance Indicators (KPI). Performance measures must be clearly defined so that they can be properly understood by all work functions and related individuals. Therefore, performance measures must not be ambiguous, which can lead to confusion regarding the appropriate work function. Performance measures must meet SMART elements, namely: *Specific, Measurable, Achievable, Realistic, and Time bound.*

Specific shows that performance measures can be explained through 5W1H. Who is involved in achieving performance? What should be done? Specific means having time reference. It also indicates identifying requirements or conditions. It is associated with the intent and purpose of the target or benefit of the intended target.

Measurable means that performance measures must be able to be measured. Measurability is a very important aspect of a performance measure. We can only know the achievement of a performance measure by tangible evidence. The evidence should include the acceptance of all parties to the intended measure. For example, to explain the performance of an insurance company in paying claims, the measure "claims will be paid as soon as possible" is used. This measure can be interpreted differently by many people, but if the measure "claims paid within 2 business days" is used, it is certain that everyone will understand and accept the measure.

Achievable means that measure must be able to achieve. Achievable is closely related to measurable. A performance cannot be achieved if it cannot be measured. We can know that a performance measure can be achieved if experience shows that there are others who have succeeded in doing so. Confidence that the performance can be achieved also exists when we have the resources to support achieving the intended performance for some people, letters A in SMART is also defined by the word *Agreed* or agreed upon, which means that the measure of performance must be agreed upon by all parties involved in achieving the goal.

Realistic is related to the question: Do people related to performance have the desire, knowledge, authority, or ability to perform as expected performance? If not, is it possible to set goals? Is the target set too low or, conversely, too high compared to the execution capabilities? Realistic is thus closely related to the belief of the parties associated with the goal to achieve the objectives to be achieved.

Time bound shows that the performance measurement is related to the time limit. When should the assignment start? When should the assignment be completed? How long should the assignment be completed? If the performance measure does not have a time limit, it can be said that the performance measure is subject to uncertainty as to how it will be achieved.

Performance measures must be based on actual data or current data that is fact-based. Therefore, performance measures are not expired data or data based on estimates or perceptions of people or parties involved in performance delivery.

Some principles to consider when establishing measures:

i A clear link to strategic objectives
A measure is an indicator of success in achieving the strategic objectives. Therefore, a measure is something that explains the strategic objectives. It is not possible to make a statement without correlating it to what it has stated. If a company has the strategic goal of creating a company with social value, the performance measure set will naturally relate to the characteristics of the social nature of the organization, such as the amount of CSR funds flowing into net profit, *Zakat* paid, etc.

ii Encourage performance behaviour
The measure should be a clear fence for all involved in the performance so that they always behave in the direction of the desired performance. For example, a non-profit organization sets a strategic goal to increase accountability in managing funds. Therefore, the organization needs to adopt a measure that encourages the behaviour of determining activities based on Pareto interests, i.e., the behaviour of being accountable for fund management, or the behaviour of disclosing information about fund management, etc.

iii Focus on implementation
Performance measures must be easily understood by those involved in performance. A good understanding of the measures will make it easier for organizations to manage and monitor performance.

There are three areas of performance measures, namely:

i Outcome measurement
It measures the result of the service provided. The measurement is usually indicated by numbers or percentages that describe the final performance. For example, customer satisfaction survey results, overall customer satisfaction, gross premiums, etc.

ii The measurement of activities
It measures performance activities. Activities performed to achieve the final output are measured as part of the service delivery. For example, the number of days to process claims, the number of policies closed, the number of customers who visit customer service, the time taken to respond to complaints, etc.

iii Measuring initiatives
It measures initiatives. Initiatives undertaken to achieve final performance are measured as part of service delivery. For example, training centre availability, procurement of comparison suppliers, completion of waste disposal wells, etc.

Performance metrics can be determined in several steps, namely by understanding the performance metrics currently in use, studying the measures that have been used both by the organization and by benchmarking competitors, and evaluating potential measures (Figure 9.4).

The Measure of **Maslahah** *Orientation*

Worship Orientation

In relation to the application of religion, there are several measures used by experts. Among them are Hill and Hood Jr. (1999)[36] that made seventeen measures of the religion application. Those are: the scale of faith and religious practice, the scale of religious behaviour, the scale of worship orientation, the scale of religious development, the scale of involvement and religious commitment, the scale of religious experience, the scale of moral religious values from personal characteristics, the multidimensional scale of religion, the scale of facing and solving religious issues, the spirituality and mystical scales, the God's concept scale, the scale of religious fundamentalists, the scale of viewing death and the end of the day, the attribution scale of religion, the scale of institutionalization religion, and the scale in relation understanding.

Raiya (2008)[37] develops six measures of the religion application within Psychological Measure of Islamic Religiousness (PMIR); these six measures are: Islamic Beliefs, Islamic Ethical Principles and Universality, Islamic Religious Struggle, Islamic Religious Duty, Obligation and Exclusivism, Islamic Positive Religious Coping and Identification and Punishing Allah (*s.w.t.*) Reappraisal. Khraim (2010)[38] put forward three measures of the application of religion to consumer behaviour, namely the current issues of Islam, religious education, and sensitive products.

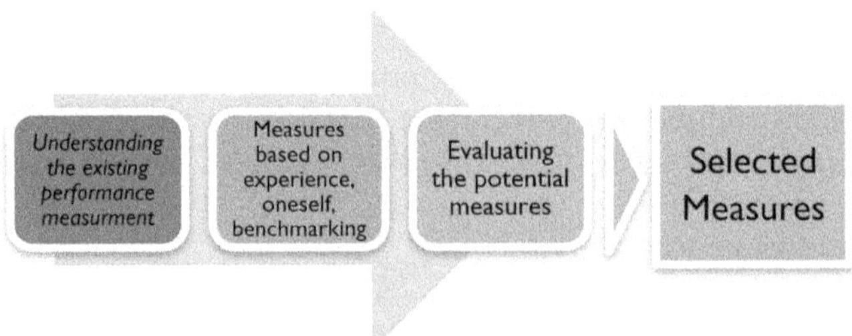

Figure 9.4 The Stages of Determining Performance Measures.

Source: Processed data.

The author develops several measures for worship orientation. The measurements used to measure the achievement of strategic objectives to realize the manager visionary organizations are the number of free-of-interest products. Visionary people are characterized by always displaying behaviour that meets the requirements of behaviour *Aqidah* and *Shari'ah*. Therefore, the increase in products that comply with *Maqasid al-shari'ah* becomes a benchmark for achieving this strategic goal.

Visionary leaders are characterized by always obeying all regulations and staying away from all prohibitions of the Creator, the Almighty Ruler, the Life-Giver. Obeying Him means obeying the organizational regulations if the regulations do not contradict *Maqasid al-shari'ah*. How well the leaders obey *Maqasid al-shari'ah* or other regulations can be seen from the availability of ethical codes for leaders. The content and ethical content of the ethical code must be consistent with *Maqasid al-shari'ah*. The ethical code must have been available before the start of the new fiscal year.

To evaluate the success of the implementation of the Code of Ethics by conducting audits, the measures used to measure the strategic objectives can embody an obedient and consistent organization, with two measures, the availability of the Code of Conduct and the results of the audits.

The strategic objective improves social function through active participation in CSR programs. From an Islamic perspective, CSR is done to share welfare with stakeholders.[39] Islam forbids accumulating wealth without using it. CSR is also not only to improve the functions and obligations of a social organization towards the environment but also to manifest the function of the organization as the *Caliph* of Allah (*s.w.t.*) on earth (Sayd Farook, n.d).[40] Thus, the motivation for implementing CSR lies in devotion to Allah (*s.w.t.*) the Creator (Ashraf Wajdi Dusuki, n.d).[41] The consequence is that the budget allocated for CSR activities does not come from the retained earnings. But rather by allocating CSR as a cost component.

If CSR is part of profit, the CSR budget depends on the amount of profit of the company. If the company achieves high profits, the CSR budget will increase. However, if the company does not make profits or makes losses, then no budget is allocated to CSR. This means that CSR activities are driven by the company's conditions in the previous year.

When CSR is done out of obedience to the supreme creator, CSR will have its own budget. CSR costs are summarized in "compliance costs." The CSR budget is a part of the cost component. This means that CSR costs are determined at the beginning of the year, not at the end of the previous year. Therefore, the variable that can represent CSR activities is the percentage increase in the CSR budget.

Internal Process Orientation

Internal process orientation has the strategic goals of realizing equity, achieving high productivity, and creating flexibility and dexterity to change and improve economic function. Strategic goals realize equity (Zahara, 1958).[42] There are five metrics to measure performance in achieving equity, namely: fairness, products or services produced, efforts made to remove injustice, timing of payment to suppliers or partners, and percentage of outsourced workers hired as permanent employees.

Achieving strategic goals creates high productivity, which can be measured by the size of product and service sales and the failure costs of products and services. The higher the sales value, the better the company's performance. High sales of products and services do not mean that only a certain part of the company is successful but show the success of the whole company. The management costs of defective products occur because there are products that do not meet customer requirements. Strategic goals create organizations that have flexibility and dexterity to change, as measured by the availability of organizational plans (long-term plan, medium-term plan, and annual plan). The strategic goal creates high productivity as measured by two performance measures, product and service sales and product and service failure costs.

The strategic goal of improving economic function is indicated by the efficiency process. The efficiency process is synonymous with cost efficiency, especially production costs. The measure used in the strategic goals of improving economic functions is production cost efficiency.

Talent Orientation

Talent orientation has the strategic goal of increasing the satisfaction of talented employees and ensuring the sustainability of leadership. The achievement of the strategic goal performance is to increase the satisfaction of the talented workforce as measured by the index size of the satisfaction of the talented workforce. This activity is carried out through a survey, which technically can be conducted by companies on their own but also in collaboration with third parties or consultants. The goal of the activity is to find out the extent to which talented workers are satisfied with their jobs. The cost of a talented workforce satisfaction survey conducted by an internal organization is typically lower than the cost of using a third party. However, the results of a talented workforce satisfaction survey conducted by a third party are more credible than those of the internal organization.

Achieving strategic goals ensures leadership sustainability as measured by the number of talented employees who have certification of their expertise. In some organizations, the number of talented employees has met certain conditions that are highly required by regulators or others, such as investment manager qualifications, actuarial qualifications, human resource management qualifications, auditor qualifications, financial manager qualifications, etc. The more these conditions are met, the more the sustainability of the management organization is guaranteed.

Learning Orientation

Some researchers (Chen *et al.*, 2010)[43] use different scales to measure the performance of learning and growth perspectives including: Ellingson and Wambsganss (2001),[44] Libby (2004),[45] and Ullrich and Tuttle (2004)[46] who use employee skill measure for human capital goals. As for Kaplan (2004a),[47] who uses *know-how* for human capital targets.

For organizational capital goals, Kaplan uses two measures, employee knowledge sharing and shared vision. For the information capital objectives, Kaplan uses measures of knowledge management skills and information accessibility. Martinsons, Davison, and Tse (1999)[48] on the other hand use business value, user orientation, internal process, and future-readiness size to measure information system performance.

Learning orientation has four strategic objectives, namely: achieving employee empowerment, building a learning culture, integrating the infrastructure of IT as a learning medium, and establishing a reward-based learning system.

The strategic goal of realizing employee empowerment has a measure: the number of improvements achieved per year. Individual learners are individuals who always learn from the problems they face. Problems encountered become the source of ideas for improvements and enhancements. The ideas for improvements and enhancements should be well managed by the organization to be strong. All ideas delivered are then followed up to improvements and enhancements in the workspace (*gemba kaizen*). Therefore, the number of improvements and enhancements in the workspace is a measure of the success of the learning orientation.

The strategic goals for developing a learning work culture use the amount of knowledge sharing and the number of man-days as performance measures. Knowledge sharing is a culture of sharing knowledge with others in an organization. Knowledge sources can be accessed through training, education, self-development, teaching, reading, writing, etc. Knowledge sharing is not an individual initiative, but must be managed and institutionalized by the organization by making it part of the commitments of employees who receive training, official assignments, project surveys, partner audits, supplier audits, etc. Knowledge sharing should become a work culture within the organization. Man-days are the average number of training days a person receives in a year.

Strategic goals of the integrated IT infrastructure as a learning medium have a measure of customer satisfaction for the IT services. Customer satisfaction and dissatisfaction with IT services may take the form of questions, complaints, suggestions, surveys, or others. This is used as a measure of the strategic goals with the intent of integrating the IT infrastructure with the services to the customer.

The strategic objective of establishing a reward-based learner system is the performance measure of expertise allowances. In learning organizations, workers are required to have certain skills. Each level has a different standard of expertise. If the expertise cannot be met, it affects the individual's annual performance appraisal. It seems that such a system is very burdensome for workers, but the benefits for workers are that those who meet the required criteria receive rewards.

Japanese companies even enforce the Kaizen culture through *small group activities* (SGA). Small teams consisting of three to five people analyze various things in their work area. The team proposes corrective actions. Once these are approved, the repair actions are implemented. All workers are encouraged to conduct SGA.

Within a certain time, the entire SGA group follows the convention, which is the presentation of improvement results by the entire SGA team. Teams that adhere to the panel's evaluations and meet the criteria are awarded by management. Convention activities are conducted on a routine basis. This proves that individual learners should be supported by organizations to develop and empower themselves. Therefore, learning organizations – those which are able to manage learning and link it to the reward system – are then created.

Customer Orientation

Meeting strategic objectives increases customer satisfaction, which is measured by the customer satisfaction index. A survey is conducted to determine the level of customer satisfaction. The level of customer satisfaction is determined based on the following aspects: Understanding of products and services, procedures, service facilities, personnel, and product acceptance.

The strategic objectives are to realize the empowerment of the customer, which is influenced by the organization's response to any input or information from the customer. Thus, the duration of response to customer complaints becomes a measure of success of the strategic objectives to manifest customer empowerment.

Wealth Orientation

The strategic goal of achieving double profit is a state where the net profit has doubled compared to the previous period. Net profit is the profit after paying taxes. Strategic goal achievement, which embodies double profit, is measured by net profit.

Strategic goals to achieve the purity of wealth target the wealth obtained from the rights of others. It is well known that any wealth acquired still actually involves the rights of others. Therefore, the acquired wealth must be purified immediately by paying *Zakat*. The achievement of strategic goals to realize the purified wealth is measured by the amount of *Zakat* payments. This refers to Mohammed and Abdu Razak (2008)[49] and Shaukat (2009).[50]

All activities carried out by the organization must be supported by adequate funding. Planning activities include the budget for the activities that are planned at the beginning of the period. For the funding to be targeted, all these activities must be prioritized. Thus, the availability of work plans and budgets and the monitoring of processes becomes a measure of the success of the strategic goals of making the organization an efficient one.

Measure Title

Each measure must be given a name. The name of the measure serves to simplify the performance monitoring process. Like the naming function, the measure name is used to name performance measures. Examples of performance measure names in worship orientation are reciting the Holy Qur'an, performing *Sunnah fasting*, praying for the Prophets, praying for the parents, etc. Examples of performance measure names in talent orientation are employee satisfaction, human capital readiness, turnover, etc. Examples of performance measure names in learning orientation are man-days training, knowledge sharing, research papers submitted to international journals, etc. Examples of performance measures in customer orientation are customer satisfaction index, customer feedback, customer participation, etc. Examples of performance measures for asset orientation are *Zakat* payments, net profits, operating costs, etc.

Measure Grouping

Referring to the work system and work process design in Figure 9.5, there are three groups of work processes whose performance must be measured. The first group represents *Shari'ah* or regulatory compliance. The second

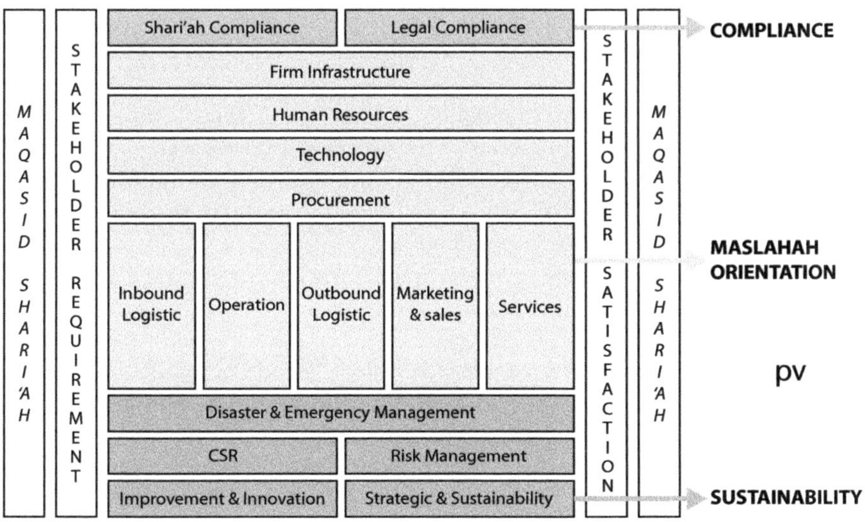

Figure 9.5 Three Groups of Process.

Source: Processed data.

Table 9.2 Performance Measure Grouping

Measure Group	*Measures Type*
Obligatory measure	*Shari'ah* compliance, legal compliance, GCG
Individual measure	Worship, internal process, talent, learning, customers and wealth
Joint measure	Strategic, sustainability, improvement, innovation, risk management, disaster management, emergencies, HSE

Source: Processed data.

group is the input process, core processes, and supporting processes. The third group is the process related to sustainability. Sustainability is related to the improvement process and innovation, strategic, disaster and emergency management, risk management, and CSR.

Compliance is part of the service orientation. However, in this grouping of performance measures, Compliance is included in a separate group outside of the worship orientation. Compliance is mandatory for all individuals/work areas/organizations. Compliance performance is also required. Required means that compliance performance is more than necessary. Even if compliance performance is not implemented or not achieved, the person/work function/organization must accept a reduction in performance value.

Sustainability is part of the internal process orientation. However, when grouping performance measures, sustainability is listed in separate groups outside of the internal process orientation. Sustainability is the performance of individuals/work functions/organizations in supporting a sustainable organization. The output of organizational sustainability performance may (but need not) be a summation of the sustainability performance of individuals/work functions.

The third group is the performance orientation of the outputs that each individual/work function possesses. This group is a performance group that can be different between one individual/work function and another, and it can also be the same. The difference is in the name of the performance measure as well as the performance objective.

Explanation of the three groups of performance measures mentioned above are (Table 9.2):

1 Obligatory measure: A measure that reflects good compliant and fidelity to the *Shari'ah* law and to the laws that supervise the operation of the organization. The obligatory performance measure must be achieved. Failure to achieve the mandatory performance measure will impact the personal evaluation of the organization/performance function/individual owner measure. The owner measure is assigned a negative rating in the form of a penalty Mandatory group of measures related to *Shari'ah* compliance and legality. This group also includes management of corporate governance or good corporate governance (GCG).

2 Individual measure: A measure of performance that belongs to the organization/work function/individual and represents six *Maslahah* orientations, namely worship, internal processes, talent, learning, customers, and wealth. One of the works/individual functions may have the same name as other work/individual functions, but it is probably different.

For example, the claim section has two performance measures on learning orientation in the form of knowledge sharing and training man-days. Similarly, the finance department has two performance measures in learning orientation in the form of knowledge sharing and man-days training. While, the HR section has three individual performance measures in learning orientation in the form of knowledge sharing, training for the management team, and realization of budget training.

3 Joint measure: A measure of performance that is owned by the organization/work function/individual, which is a representation of strategic measure, sustainability, improvement, innovation, disaster management and emergencies, and risk management. Achieving joint measures will have an impact on organizational sustainability. Included in the joint measure group are environmental management and health and safety environment (HSE).

Alignment

This step serves to align the strategy at the organizational level with the strategies at the work and individual function levels (Figure 9.6). The strategy alignment process has several benefits:

1 Ensuring that the achievement of organizational performance is supported by the achievement of performance at all levels of work and individual functions.

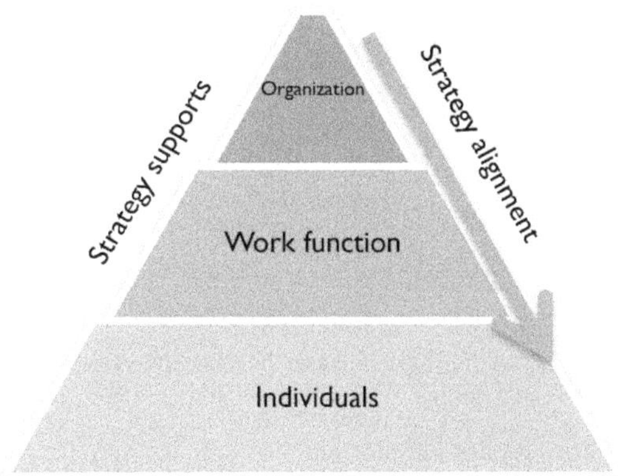

Figure 9.6 Strategy Alignment to Obtain Strategic Support.

Source: Processed data.

2 Creating harmonious, synergistic, and strategic relationships for all work areas and individual functions.
3 Building measurable, structured, and systematic communication performance to achieve the organization's vision and mission.

The process of aligning strategies at the work function level and individual employees at the strategy organization level occurs in a cascading process. The main objective of the cascading process is to ensure performance support at all levels of employees. Therefore, it can be said that cascading is a facility provided by the organization to all levels of employees to contribute to the achievement of organizational goals.

Cascading is done on the performance measures at the organizational level to the performance measures of functional work. Next, the functional work level measure is cascaded down to the individual level performance measures.

Weighting

There are different impacts between a performance area and other performance areas on the overall performance of the organization. Therefore, one performance area has a different weight than other performance areas. The performance area that has a very high importance has the highest weight. In contrast, the performance area with the lowest importance has the lowest performance weight (Figure 9.7).

Formula

A formula is an approach, a formula, or a way of calculating a measure. For example, the wealth orientation has a measure of operating profit. Thus, the

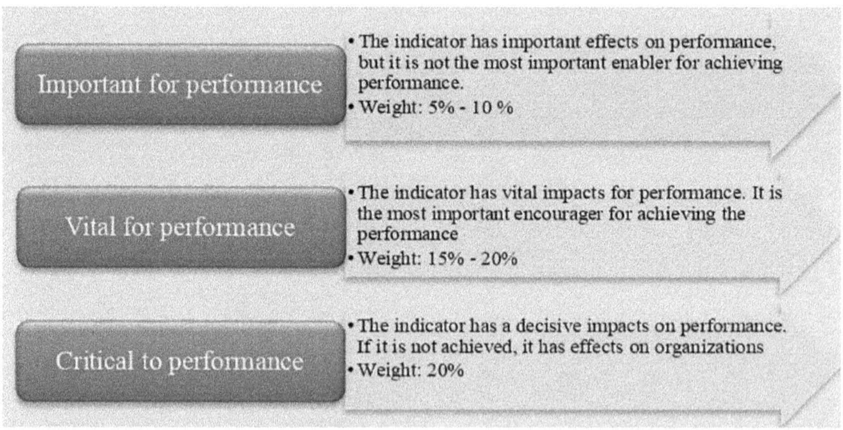

Figure 9.7 Measure Weight Based on Interest Levels.

Source: Processed data.

operating profit formula is the formula for determining operating profit from total revenues minus total costs. Return on assets (ROA) is the ratio used to measure the amount of return or income in terms of net profit relative to the total assets of the company. The formula used is:

$$\text{ROA} = \frac{\text{Earning After Tax}}{\text{Average Total Asset}} \times 100\%$$

Net income or Earning After Tax is the achievement of the net income of the company in the current fiscal year. Total asset is the amount of total average assets listed on the company's balance sheet, which is the total assets at the end of the year plus the total assets of the previous year divided by 2.

It must be understood that the formula is not always referring to the mathematics formula. One of the State-Owned Enterprises (SOEs) Excellence Performance Criteria systems of Key Performance Indicator is the Fulfilment of SOEs Portal update. This KPI has a regularity formula for uploading information to SOEs portals on a regular basis.

The formula used to assess the performance of several products that are riba free is the number of riba-free products divided by total products. The formula used to evaluate the performance of the increase in CSR budget is the percentage increase in CSR budget. The formula used to evaluate the performance of the availability of the Code of Conduct is the date of provision before the new fiscal year begins. The formula for evaluating the performance of follow-up audit findings is the number of follow-up findings.

The formula for evaluating the performance of fair transactions is profit divided by total revenue. Formula to evaluate products or services generated is bad debt divided by total revenue. Formula for valuation of transactions made to eliminate inequities is non-interest income divided by total income.

The formula for evaluating terms for suppliers or partners is maximum 30 days payment duration. This choice is to maintain good relations with the supplier or partner. Of course, the actual period is determined by agreement with both parties to avoid tyrannical attitudes.

The formula used to assess the performance of the outsourcing worker who is appointed as permanent employees is by dividing the number of outsourcing workers who is appointed to become a permanent workforce by the total number of outsourcing workers.

The formula used to assess the performance of production cost efficiency is the total production costs divided by the total costs. The formula used to assess the sales performance of products and services is the volume of sales this year divided by the volume of sales last year. The formula for evaluating the cost performance of defective products and services is the total cost of defects divided by fixed production costs times 10%. The formula for evaluating the availability performance of the organization plan (long-term plan, medium-term plan, and annual plan) is the time of provision before the beginning of the new period.

The index of satisfaction of talented workers is determined by surveys. The processing of survey data is done by the method of descriptive analysis. The formula used for measuring the performance index of satisfaction of the talented workforce is counting the average perception of the talented workforce for variable measurement. $x = \frac{\Sigma(fxi)}{N}$, where x is the value to be calculated, f is the number of frequencies for each variable, i is the category in the concerned variable, and N is the number of respondents. The formula used to measure performance is the number of talented workers who have a certificate of expertise.

The formula used to measure the performance of the number of increases per unit of work per year is one increase per work unit. The formula used to measure the performance of knowledge sharing is number of knowledges sharing per month per unit of work. The formula used to measure the performance Number of man-days is the number of training days times the number of employees who participated in the training divided by total number of employees. The formula used to measure client satisfaction with IT services is the satisfaction index. The formula used to measure the performance of the competency allowances is the number of employees receiving the competency allowance.

The formula used to measure the performance of customer satisfaction is the satisfaction index. The formula used to measure customer complaint response time performance is the number of response days.

The formula used to measure net profit performance is this year's net profit divided by last year's net profit. The formula used to evaluate the performance of the amount of *Zakat* payments is the amount of *Zakat* paid this year divided by the amount of *Zakat* paid last year. The formula used to evaluate the performance of the availability of work plans and budgets and the monitoring process is time of provision before the beginning of the new fiscal year.

Agreeing on Performance Contracts

Determining Maslahah Performa Target

Target is the amount that shows the success of performance achievement by the organization/work function/individual. Targets are set to encourage organizations/work functions/individuals to achieve the organizational objectives set in the long-term plan, medium-term plan, and annual plan. Therefore, long-term, mid-term, and annual performance goals are needed.

Some of the considerations in setting the goal include:

1 Industrial growth
   A company has a market share of 20%, which means that the company contributes 20% to the industry. The company receives accurate data that the industry will grow by 15% in the coming period. For this reason, the company's goal is to participate in the growth of the industry. Thus,

the company aims to increase its market share by 23% compared to the previous period.

2 Core organizational competencies
X life insurance offers a variety of products, including individual products, bundled products, bancassurance, health, and alliance products. Considering that X life insurance's main competency is individual products, management sets premium targets of 60% from individual products, 20% from bundled products, 10% from bancassurance, 5% from health, and 5% from alliance products.
3 The achievement of targets in the previous period
Company Y had a GCG score of 88% in the previous period. With the goal of improving compliance, the company has set a target to achieve a good corporate governance rating of 93% in the next period.
4 Industry benchmarking
A company has an EBITDA ratio of 11%, while the average EBITDA ratio of competitors in the industry is between 20% and 50%. With the goal of improving efficiency, the company expects to increase EBITDA by 17% in the next period.

As the source indicates, the target set can come from the following sources:

1 Set by the shareholders
As the party with the greatest interest in the results of the company's management, the shareholders usually give the target to the company's managers at an early stage. The Ministry of SOEs, as the shareholder of all state-owned enterprises, sets a target for the President director.
2 Cascading or lowering the target at the top level
Cascading is done with the aim of:

   - Synchronizing the vision, mission, and objectives of the company towards targets and behavioural performance at the organizational unit level down to the individual level.
   - Achieving synergies among work units within the organization so that they facilitate and accelerate the achievement of organizational goals and objectives.
   - Ensuring that support from lower levels support the overall performance of the company.

   One company set a net profit target of 4 trillion rupiahs. The target is distributed in four units of its organization, so that each organizational unit charged a net profit target of 1 trillion rupiahs.
3 Survey results
Several polls conducted by independent institutions show that the A candidate has a vote support of about 30% to 40%. Therefore, the A candidate's campaign team is confident enough to set the target of 30% + 1 vote for the A candidate to be elected as the Regent.

4 SWOT analysis
The analysis of the organization's strengths and the expectations it has in the industry competition make the organization confident enough to set high goals. On the other hand, the weaknesses of the organization and the challenges that exist in the industrial environment can be another consideration for the organization to be realistic in setting goals.

Example of breaking down medium-term targets (five years) into short-term targets (annual) is as follows (Figure 9.8):

> Assume that strategic targets embody visionary business leaders have a measure of the number of products that are free of riba. The medium-term performance target that must be achieved is 100%. The five-year target milestone is: year 1 (80%), year 2 (85%), year 3 (90%), year 4 (95%), and year 5 (100%).

Targets are set jointly by the leaders of the organization/work function and the individuals working within. If the performance measure owner objects to the established goal, they are given the opportunity to have a dialog with their superior. However, setting the measure for the performance goal remains the responsibility of the supervisor.

Worship Orientation

Strategic objectives embody visionary organizational managers have a measure of the number of products that are free of *riba* and the target to be achieved is 100% in the fifth year. This means that by the fifth year, the entire product organization will be free of riba. To achieve that target, the organization sets a five-year target of 80% in the first year, 85% in the second year, 90% in the third year, 95% in the fourth year, and 100% in the fifth year.

The strategic objective of improving the social function with a percentage increase in the CSR budget has a target of 25%. To achieve this goal, the organization has set a five-year target of 5% in the first year, 10% in the

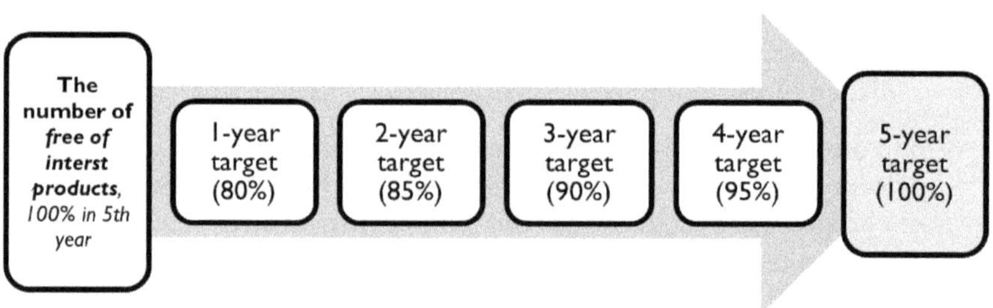

Figure 9.8 Five-Year Target Milestone.

Source: Processed data.

second year, 15% in the third year, 20% in the fourth year, and 25% in the fifth year.

Compliance

The availability of the code of conduct is the strategic objectives to realize an organization that is compliant and consistent in implementing the performance measure. The target is for 100% of the code of conduct to be available before the end of the new budget year. Therefore, the five-year target is as follows: 100% in year 1, 100% in year 2, 100% in year 3, 100% in year 4, and 100% in year 5.

The measure of the performance audit findings is assessed by the number of follow-up audit findings. The target set is 100% in the fifth year. To achieve this goal, the organization sets a five-year goal of 100% in the first year, 100% in the second year, 100% in the third year, 100% in the fourth year, and 100% in the fifth year.

Internal Process Orientation

Strategic objective to realize justice has performance indicators: a fair business, products or services produced, efforts to eliminate inequities, timing of payments to suppliers or partners, number of workers outsourced, labour, and equipment.

Details on the goal for each measure are as follows: Transaction measures that are fair. The target to be achieved is 40% in the fifth year. Therefore, the organization prepares the five-year target as follows: 20% in the first year, 25% in the second year, 30% in the third year, 35% in the fourth year, and 40% in the fifth year.

The measure of the product or service to be achieved by the five-year target to be achieved is 5%. Therefore, the organization sets targets for the following five years: 15% in the first year, 12% in the second year, 10% in the third year, 8% in the fourth year, and 5% in the fifth year.

The scope of efforts to eliminate injustice; the five-year target to be achieved is 100%. The organization sets the following five-year targets: 60% in the first year, 70% in the second year, 80% in the third year, 90% in the fourth year, and 100% in the fifth year.

The measure of the time of payment to suppliers or partners; the five-year target to be achieved is 100% payment to suppliers or partners less than 30 days. Organizations prepare the following five-year targets: 60% for the first year, 70% for the second year, 80% for the third year, 90% for the fourth year, and 100% for the fifth year.

The measure of the outsourced worker in total who become the permanent workforce; the five-year target to be achieved is 30% of total outsourcing staff. The organization sets five-year targets as follows: 10% for the first year, 15% for the second year, 20% for the third year, 25% for the fourth year, and 30% for the fifth year.

Strategic objectives to improve the economic function with a standard of production cost efficiency; the target to be achieved in the fifth year is 100% of the cost of production compared to total costs amounted to 60%. To conclude, the organization is trying to maintain that in the operational process, the production costs remain at 60% of the total cost. The organization sets the five-year target as follows: 60% in the first year, 60% in the second year, 60% in the third year, 60% in the fourth year, and 60% in the fifth year.

The strategic objectives of creating high productivity have two performance measures, namely: product and service sales and the cost of defective products and services. For the volume of product and service sales, which is calculated by comparing this year's sales with last year's sales, the target to be achieved in the fifth year is 15%. Thus, the five-year target is as follows: 10% in the first year, 11% in the second year, 12% in the third year, 13% in the fourth year, and 15% in the fifth year.

For the measure of cost of defective products and services, which is indicated by the ratio of defect costs to production cost maintained at 10%, the target to be achieved is 100%. Therefore, the five-year target is: first year 100%, second year 100%, third year 100%, fourth year 100%, and fifth year 100%.

Sustainability

Strategic objectives create an organization that has the flexibility and dexterity to change the plan for the availability of the actions (long-term plan, medium-term plan, and annual plan). Therefore, the five-year goal is 100% in year 1, 100% in year 2, 100% in year 3, 100% in year 4, and 100% in year 5. Each year the goals must be achieved before the new fiscal year begins.

Talent Orientation

The strategic goal to increase the satisfaction of talented workers has a measure of performance: a talented worker satisfaction index; the expected index value is above 90%. The target to be achieved is 100%. Therefore, the five-year targets are 100% in the first year, 100% in the second year, 100% in the third year, 100% in the fourth year, and 100% in the fifth year.

Strategic goals to ensure leadership sustainability have performance indicators: Number of talented workers who have the qualification certification, five-year targets to be achieved are 15 people. Therefore, the five-year targets are 7 people in the first year, 9 people in the second year, 11 people in the third year, 13 people in the fourth year, and 15 people in the fifth year.

Learning Orientation

The strategic objective of implementing worker empowerment has a performance measure of the number of improvements made by each work unit of 25 per unit per year. The target to be achieved in the fifth year is 25 improvements per work unit. Therefore, the five-year target is as follows: in the first year, as many as 10 improvements per work unit, 12 improvements per work unit in the second year, 15 improvements per work unit in the third year, 20 improvements per work unit in the fourth year, and 25 improvements per work unit in the fifth year.

The strategic objective of establishing a learning work culture is measured by the number of knowledges sharing and the number of man-days. The performance measure for knowledge sharing is assessed by the formula for the amount of knowledge sharing/month/work formula. Therefore, the five-year target is as follows: seven activities/work units/month for the first year, and nine activities/work units/month for the second year. In the following year, the target is 11 activities/work units/month. The target for the fourth year is 13 activities/work units/month, and 15 activities/work units/month in the fifth year.

The performance measure of the number of man-days is assessed by the following formula: number of training days multiplied by employees participating in training per total number of employees. Therefore, the five-year target: 10 man-days in the first year, 15 man-days in the second year, 20 man-days in the third year, 25 man-days in the fourth year, and 30 man-days in the fifth year.

The strategic objective of integrating the IT infrastructure as a learning medium has a measure of customer satisfaction with IT services. The measure is assessed by the satisfaction index formula. The target set for each survey is 90%. Therefore, the five-year target set is as follows: 90% of the first year, 90% of the second year, 90% of the third year, 90% of the fourth year, and 90% of the fifth year.

The strategic objective of building a learner-based reward system has a measure for competency performance allowances. The measure is evaluated using the formula for the number of workers receiving a competency allowance. The target is set at 50% of the workforce receiving competency. The five-year target set is as follows: 30% of the first year, 35% of the second year, 40% of the third year, 45% of the fourth year, and 50% of the fifth year.

Customer Orientation

The strategic objective of increasing customer satisfaction has a performance measure in the form of a customer satisfaction index. The measure is assessed with a satisfaction index formula of up to 90%. The target is that 90% of satisfaction surveys will result in a customer satisfaction index of 90%. Therefore, the five-year target set is as follows: first year 90%, second year 90%, third year 90%, fourth year 90%, and fifth year 90%.

The strategic goal of increasing customer satisfaction has performance indicators such as response time to customer complaints. The indicators are evaluated using a formula that sets a maximum response time of only two business days. The target is 100% of customer complaints responded to within two business days at the latest.

Wealth Orientation

The strategic goal of achieving double profit is measured by net profit performance. The measure is evaluated by the formula in terms of this year's net profit divided by last year's net profit. The target is 200%. Thus, the target for five years is: 120% for the first year, 140% for the second year, 160% for the third year, 180% for the fourth year, and 200% for the fifth year.

Strategic objectives for achieving asset hygiene have a performance indicator of the number of *Zakat* payments. This indicator is evaluated using a formula, namely *Zakat* in this year divided by *Zakat* in the previous year. The target set is 200%. Therefore, the five-year target set is as follows: 120% for the first year, 140% for the second year, 160% for the third year, 180% for the fourth year, and 200% for the fifth year.

Strategic objectives in creating organizations in an efficient organization that has a performance indicator for the availability of work plans and budgets also monitor the processes. The measure will be evaluated using a formula for when it is available before the new fiscal year begins. The target is to have 100% of work plans and budgets and monitoring processes available before the start of the new fiscal year. Therefore, the five-year target set is as follows: 100% for the first year, 100% for the second year, 100% for the third year, 100% for the fourth year, and 100% for the fifth year.

Determination of Performance Contracts

After the target is set jointly between the leaders of the organization/work function and the workers, a performance contract is signed between the supervisors and subordinates. The performance contract indicates that the owner of the performance measures has full responsibility for achieving the agreed-upon goals. The signing is intended to improve accountability for performance (Table 9.3).

For civil servants, performance contracts are regulated by the Government Regulation of the Republic of Indonesia Number 46 of 2011 on the Evaluation of Work Performance of Civil Servants. The evaluation of work performance of civil servants (SKP) is done by comparing the work performed with the target. The evaluation is done in terms of quantity, quality, time, and/or cost.

In the Ministry of Enterprise, Nurhadi (2011)[51] mentioned that there were three periods of development performance assessments. The period of 1958–1989 was a period in which there were no performance benchmarks. The period of 1989–1998 was a period in which the performance of SOEs was evaluated under the coordination of the Ministry of Finance. The assessment is carried out on operational aspects including efficiency and productivity as

Table 9.3 Performance Contract

Measure Group	*Types of Measures*	*Name of Measures*	*Score*	*Monitoring Frequency*	*Target (Year)*	*Quarter Target*			
						Q1	*Q2*	*Q3*	*Q4*
Obligatory	*Shari'ah* compliance								
	Legality compliance								
	GCG								
	CSR								
	Disaster/Emergency Management								
	HSE								
Total score									
Individual	Worship								
	Internal Process								
	Talent								
	Learning								
	Customers								
	Wealth								
Total score									
(Refer to *Table 9.2*, Joint measure)	Strategy								
	Sustainability								
	Innovation								
	Risk management								
Total score									

(Owner of KPI) (Supervisor of KPI Owner)

Source: Data processed.

well as on financial aspects including profitability, liquidity, and solvency. From 1998 to the present, the performance evaluation of SOEs has been coordinated by the Ministry of National Enterprises. The assessment is conducted on five items, namely:

1 State of health (financial aspects, operational aspects, and administration)
2 Level of performance
3 Performance Achievement Indicators
4 Statement of Corporate Intense (SCI)
5 Management Contract (MC)

The SCI is a contract between the board of directors and the shareholders/capital owners, the content of which is, among other things, the promise of the person concerned to achieve the objectives agreed upon when he was appointed as a director of a state-owned company (SOE). Nurhadi explained that SCI is a summary of the company's plan (annual plan) and not a promise made by the prospective SOE director upon his initial appointment. The SCI was later revoked with the issuance of PER-01/MBU/2011.

MC is a contract or promise by a candidate for the SOEs Board of Directors approved by the shareholders/capital owners, when appointed/reappointed as SOE Director. MC contains KPIs, the achievement of which is linked to a reward and recognition system for SOE management. The content of MC includes performance indicators and corporate objectives related to operational, financial, and administrative aspects, a description of roles, tasks, responsibilities, authorities, rights and duties, as well as statements on the application of the principles of the GCG.

Summary

The successful development of a performance plan is critical to the success of organizational performance management. Henceforth spiritual aspects must be complied with to ensure corruption-free organizational practice far ahead of theories only makes a difference.

Notes

1 Pearce, J. A. and Robinson Jr., R. (2007). *Strategic Management, Formulation, Implementation and Control.* 10th Ed. New York, McGraw-Hill.
2 Pearce, J. A. and Robinson Jr., R. (2007). *Strategic Management, Formulation, Implementation and Control.* 10th Ed. New York, McGraw-Hill.
3 QS al-Baqarah 2: 201, that means, "But among them is he who says, 'Our Lord, give us in this world [that which is] good and in the Hereafter [that which is] good and protect us from the punishment of the Fire.'"
4 QS al-Baqarah 2: 124.
5 Wade, M. and Hulland, J. (2004). Review: The Resource-Based View and Information System Research: Review, Extension, and Suggestions for Future Research. *MIS Quarterly.* Vol. 28, No. 1: 107–142.
6 Martinsons, M., Davidson, R. and Tse, D. (1999). The Balanced Scorecard: a Foundation for the Strategic Management of Information Systems. *Decision Support Systems.* Vol. 25. (1999): 71–88.
7 Jacobson, G. H., McCoin, N. S., Lescallette, R., Russ, S. and Slovis, C. M. (2009). Kaizen: A Method of Process Improvement in the Emergency Department. *The Society for Academic Emergency Medicine.* Vol. 16. No. 12: 1341–1349. https://doi.org/10.1111/j.1553-2712.2009.00580.x
8 QS al-Tawbah 9: 103, see Sulaiman, R. (2011). Realising *Maqasid* Al-Shariah in Islamic Financial Planning. *The 4E Journal* 11, No. 1, 1Q: 13–17.
9 QS al-Rum 30: 39.
10 The worship intended by Abu Ishāq al-Shāṭibi is worship in a special sense. Abuddin Nata in the "*Kajian Tematik al-Quran tentang Fiqih Ibadah*" stated that worship in a special sense was all activities whose provisions had been determined by the Quran and as-Sunnah. All worship which in this sense had been perfectly regulated by the text in the Qur'an and hadith and that activity did not accept changes, additions, or subtractions. In worship in a special sense, the principle applies to all acts of worship that are prohibited and invalid except those that have been regulated and determined by Qur'an and hadith.

11 QS al-Haj 22: 78.

12 Zaharah, Muhammad Abū. (1958). *Usul al-Fiqh*. Cairo: Dar al-Fikr al-Arabi.

13 From 'Amr bin' Auf al-Ansari R.A. that Rasulullah (*s.a.w.*) sent Abu 'Ubaidah al-Jarrah r.a. to the Bahrain area – an area that entered the territory of Iraq – and his arrival there was to take taxes. Then after he finished his assignment, he came with the treasure from Bahrain. The Ansar hears of the arrival of Abu Ubaidah, they then perform the Fajr prayer – this is subuh – with Rasulullah (*s.a.w.*). After Rasulullah (*s.a.w.*) finished praying, then returned, then they headed to him to meet him. Rasulullah (*s.a.w.*) then smiled when he saw them continuing to say: "I think you all have heard that Abu Ubaidah arrived from Bahrain with something in his possession." They replied: "Yes, Rasulullah." He then said: "Rejoice all of you and may expect something that will please all of you. By Allah, it is not disbelief that I fear about you all, but I fear that if the wealth of this world is extended to all of you - that you all become rich, as has been extended to those who were before you, then all of you vying with each other to look for it as they also competed to pursue it, then the treasures of the world would destroy your religion as he had corrupted their religion" (Muttafaq 'alaih).

From Abu Said al-Khudri, he said: "Rasulullah (*s.a.w.*) sat on the pulpit and we sat around him, then he said: 'Indeed, one of the things that I fear for you will be what I will open for you, all of it from the beauty of the treasure the world and its ornaments - that this is the overflowing of wealth in the people of Muhammad that is very feared, because it can damage religion if it is not vigilant to control it'" (Muttafaq'alaih).

14 Chapra, M. U. (September 2007). The Islamic Vision of Development in the Light of *Maqāsid Al-Sharīah*.

15 This is in accordance with QS al-A'lā: 87: 14–15.

16 Kamil, N. M., Sulaiman, M., Aahad, O-G., and Ahmad, K. (n.d). Spirituality in the Workplace: The Role of Taqwa towards the Advancement of the Contemporary Organization. *Social Science Research Network*. 8th International Conference on Tawhidic Methodology Applied to Microenterprise Development, 2010. http://papers.ssrn.com/sol3/papers.cfm?abstract_id=1718946. Accessed on 11 April 2012.

17 Zaharah, M. A. (1958). *Usul al-Fiqh*. Cairo, Egypt: Dar al-Fikr al-Arabi.

18 To adjust to the changes that occur, the job description must be regularly reviewed. Review of work descriptions is carried out according to the needs of the organization. The compilation of work descriptions refers to the design of work systems and work processes.

19 Nancy R. Lockwood. (2006). Talent Management: Driver for Organizational Success. *HRMagazine*; Alexandria Vol. 51. Iss. 6 (Jun 2006): 1-11. https://www.proquest.com/docview/205016356

20 Adawiyah, W. R. (June 2011). Workplace Spirituality as a Moderator in the Relationship between Soft TQM and Organizational Commitment. *International Journal of Business and Social Science*. Vol. 2. No. 10: 93–100.

21 An example is what has been done by medicinal products, which include contraindications for certain people when taking the drug.

22 Coyle, D. (2009). *The Talent Code, Greatness Isn't Born, It's Grown, Here's How*. New York: Bantam Dell.

23 QS al-Baqarah 2: 186 And when My servants ask you, [O Muhammad], concerning Me – indeed I am near. I respond to the invocation of the supplicant when he calls upon Me. So let them respond to Me [by obedience] and believe in Me that they may be [rightly] guided.

In one Hadits Qudsi, Allah (*s.w.t.*) also said:

> From Abu Hurairah ra, he said: Prophet (*s.a.w.*). Saying: "Allah Ta 'ala said: 'I according to my servant's presumption to Me, and I am with him when he remembers Me. If he remembers Me in him then I remember it in Me. If he remembers Me

in a group of people who are better than their group. If he draws near to me for a while, I approach him a cubit. If he draws close to me, then I approach him as soon as possible. If he comes to me by walking, then I come to him jogging'" (narrated by Bukhari).

24 QS al-Baqarah 2: 197, QS Ali-'Imran 3: 159.
25 QS al-Baqarah 2: 40, 116, 128, 131, 133, 136, QS al-An'ām 6: 42, 43, QS al-A'rāf 7: 54, 94, QS al-Ḥaj 22: 34, QS al-Mu'min 40: 66, QS al-Rūm 30: 26.
26 QS Al-Baqarah 2: 11.
27 The work system refers to the National Institute of Standards and Technology, "2011–2012 Criteria for Performance Excellence," Baldrige Performance Excellence Program is referring to how the organization's work is completed. Work systems involve workplaces, suppliers and partners, sub-contractors, collaboration, and other components related to the supply chain path needed to produce and deliver products, organizations and supporting processes. The Work System coordinates the internal work processes and external resources needed to develop, produce, and deliver products to customers and to be successful in the market.
28 Rampersad, H. (2008). The Way to a Highly Engaged and Happy Workforce Based on the Personal Balanced. *Total Quality Management*. Vol. 19, No. 1–2, January–February 2008, 11–27.
29 TGO. (December 8, 2005). *Employee Discrimination in the Workplace*. Washington DC: The Gallup Organization.
30 National Institute of Standards and Technology. *2011–2012 Criteria for Performance Excellence, Baldrige Performance Excellence Program*.
31 Ibid.
32 Can be done through collaboration with third parties or carried out by internal organizations themselves.
33 *"I took refuge in God from kufr and debt. Then a man asked: Do you equate kufr with debt O Messenger of Allah? He replied: Yes!"* (narrated by Nasa'i and Hakim).
34 *"O my Lord! I take refuge in you from committing sin and debt. Then he is asked: Why do you ask for protection from debt, O Messenger of Allah?"* (narrated by Bukhari).
35 One of the national herbal medicine producers allocates funds specifically for customer relationships, namely the cost of going home together on each Eid al-Fitr together with its herbal agents. The costs incurred are very large, but the results obtained are the loyalty of the agents to herbal products. Automotive factories foster their customers by forming automotive clubs. Various activities are routinely carried out such as gatherings, social services, etc. The costs incurred are not small but give results, namely customer loyalty to motorized vehicles.
36 Hill, P. C. and Hood. Jr., R. W. (1999). *Measures of Religiosity*. Birmingham, AL: Religious Education Press.
37 Abu Raiya, H. (August 2008). A Psychological Measure of Islamic Religiousness: Evidence for Relevance, Reliability and Validity. PhD diss., College of Bowling Green, State University.
38 Khraim, H. (November 2010). Measuring Religiosity in Consumer Research from Islamic Perspective. *International Journal of Marketing Studies*. Vol. 2. No. 2: 166–179.
39 Amin, A. R. (November 2007). *The Celestial Management*. Jakarta: Embun Publishing. Business was created as a centre of 3W, namely business as the centre of engagement or worship, business as a gathering centre and the sharing of welfare, business as the centre of battle for the empowerment of the people.
40 Farook, S. (2007). Social Responsibility for Islamic Financial Institutions: Laying Down a Framework. *Journal of Islamic Economics, Banking and Finance*. Vol. 62: 61–82.
41 Dusuki, A. W. and Abdullah, N. I. *Maqasid* al-Shari'ah, *Maslahah*, and Corporate Social Responsibility. *The American Journal of Islamic Social Sciences*. Vol. 24. No. 1: 26–45.

42 Mohammed, M. O. and Razak, D. A. (2008). The Performance Measures of Islamic Banking Based on the *Maqasid* Framework. *Paper presented in The IIUM International Accounting Conference (INTAC IV)*, Putra Jaya.

43 Chen, C. Y., Yang, Y-F., Chen, C-W, Chen, L-T. and Chen, T-H. (4 August 2010). Linking the Balanced Scorecard (BSC) to Business Management Performance: A Preliminary Concept of Fit Theory for Navigation Science and Management. *International Journal of the Physical Sciences*. Vol. 5. No. 8: 1296–1305.

44 Ellingson, D. A. and Wambsganss, J. R. (2001). Modifying the Approach to Planning and Evaluation in Governmental Entities: A Balanced Scorecard Approach. *Journal of Public Budgeting, Accounting and Financial Management*. Vol. 13. No. 1: 103–120.

45 Libby, T., Salterio, S. E. and Webb, A. (2004). The Balanced Scorecard: The Effects of Assurance and Process Accountability on Managerial Judgment. *Accounting Review*. Vol. 79. No. 4: 1075–1094.

46 Ullrich, M. J., Tuttle, B. M. (2004). The Effects of Comprehensive Information Reporting Systems and Economic Incentives on Managers' Time Planning Decisions. *Behavioral Research in Accounting*. Vol. 16: 89–105.

47 Kaplan, R. S. and Norton, D. P. (2004). *Measuring the Strategic Readiness of Intangible Assets*. Boston: Harvard Business School Press.

48 Martinsons, M., Davidson, R. and Tse, D. (1999). The Balanced Scorecard: A Foundation for the Strategic Management of Information Systems. *Decision Support Systems*. Vol. 25: 71–88.

49 Mohammed, M. O. and Razak, D. A. (2008). The Performance Measures of Islamic Banking Based on the *Maqasid* Framework. *Paper Presented in The IIUM International Accounting Conference (INTAC IV)*, Putra Jaya.

50 Shaukat, M. (2009). *The Recent Financial Growth of Islamic Banks and Their Fulfilments of Maqāsid Al-Sharīah, Gap Analysis*. INCEIF: Kualalumpur, Malaysia.

51 Cahyono, M. N. and Judisiawan, F. (October 2011). Menilik Alat Ukur Penilaian Kinerja BUMN. *Jurnal Riset Kementerian BUMN*. Vol. 2: 1–10.

10 Performance Implementation

Implementing Strategic Planning

The sixth step of the MaP performance system is to implement the *Maslahah* performance. This stage is the stage of carrying out all performance planning. Obviously, it is expected that all the targets set in the strategic planning can be exceeded. Strategy implementation is a step to translate strategies on paper into operational activities in all work functions/individuals. This step is used to put the various types of strategic plans into action.

The annual plan is a reference direction for operational techniques that covers all relevant work functions and also all work levels. If needed, the organization can develop and elaborate a more detailed work plan that includes all suppliers and business partners. The description of the annual plan is done through various mechanisms such as:

- Coordination meetings between the heads of the organizations and middle management.
- Subsequently, middle management describes the annual plan with the management levels below, and so on.
- Related officials describe the work plans for suppliers and business partners in a specific forum.

Each individual in the organization needs information about the relationship between the performance measures that must be achieved with the parties involved. Information is needed so that each work function and individual has a sense of accountability for the success of performance measures. Examples of how to describe the relevance of performance measures can be found in Table 10.1.

In allocating staff resources to each work program in the annual plan, consideration is given to whether the program can be performed directly by the work function itself or requires coordination with other work functions or even coordination with the work function above it. Sometimes special considerations are required for certain tasks where specially qualified personnel are needed to perform the work, such as performing welding processes,

DOI: 10.4324/9781003390947-13

Table 10.1 Linkage of Performance Measures to Related Parties

	Linkages to Stakeholders							
Measure	*Shareholders*	*Customer*	*Employee*	*Distributor*	*Agent*	*Partner*	*Supplier*	*Environment*
Profit	√	√	√	√	√	√	√	
Customer satisfaction survey		√		√	√	√	√	√
Audit findings		√	√	√	√	√	√	√
GCG score			√	√	√	√	√	
Learning index			√					
Employee satisfaction survey			√					
Amount of *Zakat*	√	√	√	√	√	√	√	√
Others								

Source: Processed data.

performing the transportation process, auditing process, employee recruitment process, management and hazardous material, etc.

To implement an ad-hoc work program, a special team needs to be formed. For example, the special team for the cooperation agreement revision, the consignment inspection team, the high-risk claim investigation team, the team for bad credit collection that lasted more than three months, etc. In order to manage risks such as financial risks, health risks, safety risks, environmental risks, operational risk processes, natural disaster risks, and other risks, there are certain work functions that conduct risk assessments. Risk mitigation measures are then developed based on the results of the risk assessment. The risk mitigation measures are constantly monitored so that the negative impact of the risk can be controlled (Figure 10.1).

Figure 10.1 The Series of Strategic Planning of Implementation.

Source: Processed data.

Funding for all work programs is allocated through the mechanism of the annual budget meeting during the preparation of the annual plan. In addition, the budget submission for each work program is in the form of an activity proposal. Thus, even though the entire annual work program is described in the annual plan, the implementing work function or ad-hoc team must still submit an activity proposal to the unit responsible for the financial functions for the technical implementation of the activities.

Summary

Strategy implementation is the stage of carrying out all performance planning. It is a step to translate strategies on paper into operational activities in all work functions/individuals.

11 Performance Evaluation

Monitoring

The seventh step of the MaP performance system is performance monitoring. The organization monitors the achievement of all targets. The purpose of the performance monitoring process is to ensure that the performance and goal measures agreed upon between the performance measure owner and the supervisor can be implemented and achieved according to the agreement.

There are three sub-processes that need to be performed in performance monitoring, namely: monitoring individual and job functions performance, performing the coaching process, and monitoring organizational performance. The performance of the owner of performance measures is monitored on a regular basis. The process is done by comparing performance results to agree upon goals.

The next, the superior, acts as a coach for subordinates. The supervisor provides feedback to subordinates on changes or performance improvements that should be followed up. There is a performance dialog between the supervisor and subordinates. The superior must also be able to motivate subordinates to perform as expected (Figure 11.1).

The results of the performance of all individuals in the organization ultimately lead to the performance of the organization. In addition, the performance of the well-being of the organization is measured. This is done to ensure whether the organization has created *Maslahah* or not.

Individual/Work Functions Performance

The performance of the owner of the measures is monitored at regular intervals, such as monthly, three times, quarterly, biannually, or annually. The period of performance measurement shall be based on the agreement previously reached.

DOI: 10.4324/9781003390947-14

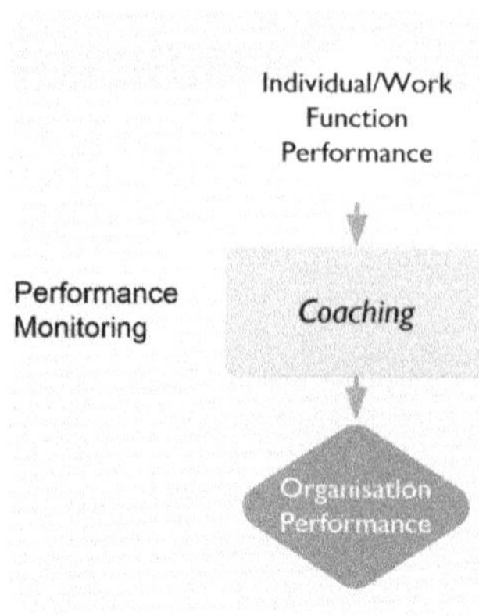

Figure 11.1 Performance Monitoring Process.

Source: Firdaus (2017: 193).

Performance monitoring is done by comparing the achieved performance with the agreed targets. There are three conditions (status) (Figure 11.2; Table 11.1):

1. Not Achieved, that is a condition where the performance does not reach the agreed target. The percentage of performance achievement ranges from 0% to 90%.
2. Achieved, that is a state where the performance has reached the agreed target. The percentage of performance achieved ranges from 90% to 100%.
3. Exceeded, that is a condition where the performance exceeds the agreed target. The percentage of performance achieved is between 100% and 120%.

Coaching Process

The organization leaders must play an active role as coaches, *Murobi*, mentors, and *guru* to the employees under their leadership. The organization leaders shall engage in a performance improvement dialogue process with workers. The performance dialogue is conducted through a coaching process.

Coaching is the process of teaching, guiding, and directing subordinates to learn new skills or methods to achieve desired goals. As a coach, supervisors must be able to guide their employees to find solutions to any problem that occurs.

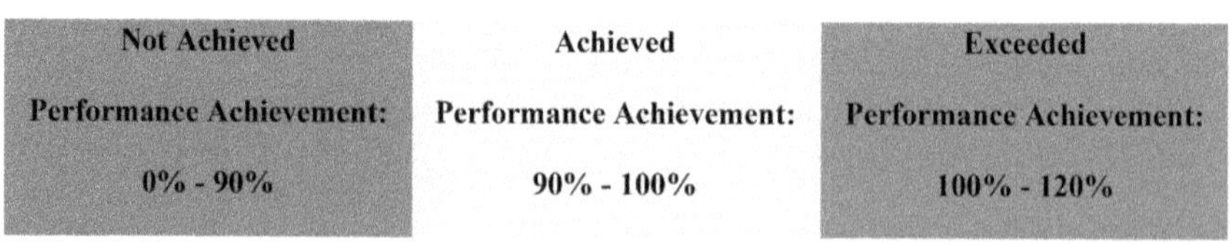

Figure 11.2 The Performance Achievement Status.

Source: Processed data.

Table 11.1 Performance Monitoring

Measure Group	*Types of Measures*	*Name of Measures*	*Weight*	*Monitoring Frequency*	*Target of the Year*	*Quarterly Target and Result*			
						Q1	*Q2*	*Q3*	*Q4*
Obligatory	*Shari'ah* compliance								
	Legality compliance								
	GCG								
	CSR								
	Disaster/Emergency Management								
	HSE								
Total score									
Individual	Worship								
	Internal process								
	Talent								
	Learning								
	Customers								
	Wealth								
Total score									
(Refer to *Table 9.2*, Joint measure)	Strategy								
	Sustainability								
	Innovation								
	Risk management								
Total score									

Source: Processed data.

Coaching is a process of dialogue between subordinates and supervisors that focuses on solving problems by teaching subordinates how to do new methods. This method is used to solve problems. In this way, the subordinates' performance reaches the expected conditions.

An owner of performance measures who does not achieve the expected goal is in dire need of coaching. Subordinates' underperformance may have one or more causes. The cause of the problem may or may not be known to the employees. To find a solution, the problems must be identified. It should be clear that coaching is a process that focuses on solutions, not problems. However, mistakes in identifying problems result in the solution offered being one-sided. The actions taken do not eliminate the root cause, so the performance of the owner of the performance measures cannot reach the expected conditions. Coaching is carried out in steps as shown in Figure 11.3.

Organizational Performance

Maslahah performance is measured in two areas, the *Maslahah* process (process-oriented) and the *Maslahah* result performance (result-oriented).

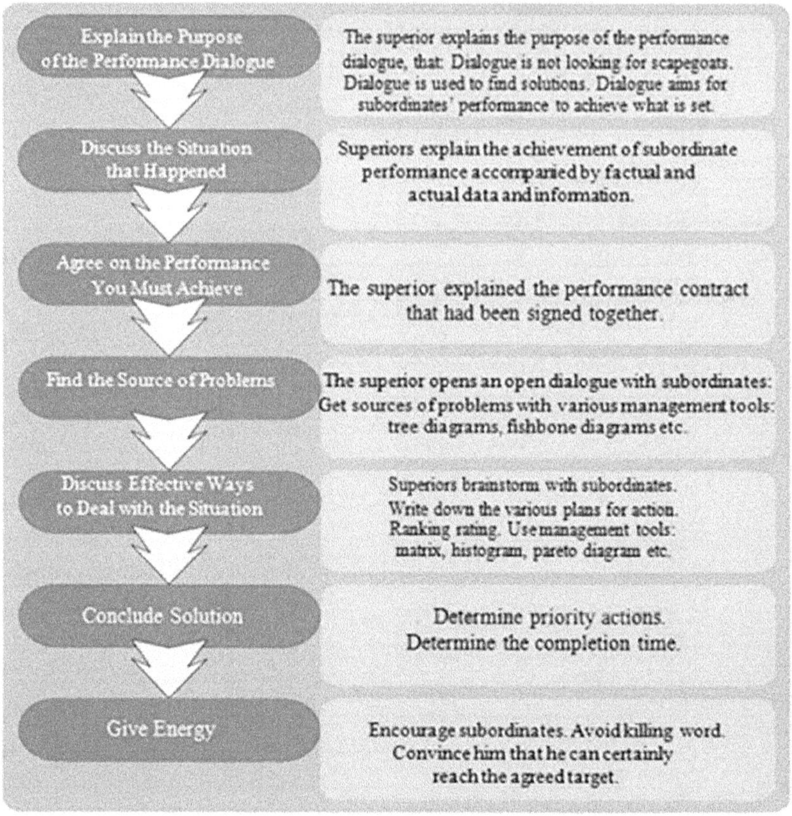

Figure 11.3 Performance Dialogue Coaching.

Source: Processed data

The *Maslahah* process is the organization's performance in implementing the MaP performance system. The *Maslahah* result is the result of the organization's performance that affects all stakeholders.

Process-oriented measurement of *Maslahah* is carried out by comparing the application of each step of MaP's performance to the eight-step standard of the MaP performance system. Process performance measurements are calculated by:

$$\mathrm{P}(p) = \sum_{i=1}^{n=20} W_{\mathrm{i}} \; x \; S_{\mathrm{i}}$$

$\mathrm{P}(p)$ = Performance of the MaP process
W_{i} = Weight of the step-i of MaP performance
i = The step-i of MaP performance

$$S_i = \begin{cases} 1, \text{ the } \textit{Maslahah} \text{ performance step is applied} \\ 0, \text{ the } \textit{Maslahah} \text{ performance is not applied} \end{cases}$$

The weight of each step of the MaP performance (W_i) is 0.05 and is obtained from 100% or 20 steps of MaP performance. The weight of each step of the MaP performance has the same value. The consideration is the balance of the fulfilment of the *Maslahah*. Twenty steps of MaP performance are the first step consists of three sub-steps. The second step consists of one sub-step, and the third step consists of one sub-step. The fourth step consists of six sub-steps. The fifth step consists of two sub-steps. The sixth step consists of one step. The seventh step consists of four sub-steps. The eighth step consists of two sub-steps.

The *Maslahah* process performance has a range between 0.000 and 1.000. An organization with a *Maslahah* process performance value of 0.000 means that the organization does not implement any MaP performance. An organization with a *Maslahah* process performance value of 1.000 means that the organization has fully implemented MaP performance.

Result-oriented measurement of *Maslahah* is carried out by measuring the results of MaP performance. Measurement is done by comparing the results of each *Maslahah* performance alignment to the established targets for each *Maslahah* that have been set. The performance measure of the *Maslahah* results is calculated by

$$P(r) = \sum_{i=1}^{n=8} W_i \, x \, \frac{A_i}{T_i}$$

$P(r)$ = Result performance of MaP
i = Orientation-i of MaP
A_i = The number of targets achieved in orientation-i of MaP
T_i = The number of targets set at the orientation-i of MaP
W_i = Weight of the orientation-i of MaP

The weight of each *Maslahah* orientation (W_i) is 0.125 and is calculated as 100% or all eight of the organization's *Maslahah* orientation including the Compliance and Sustainability groups. The weight of each *Maslahah* orientation of the organization has the same value. The consideration is the balance of *Maslahah* fulfilment. The eight orientations are worship orientation, obedience orientation, internal process orientation, sustainability orientation, talent orientation, learning orientation, customer orientation, and wealth orientation.

The *Maslahah* performa score ranges from 0.000 to 1.000. An organization with a *Maslahah* score of 0.000 indicates that the organization does not provide *Maslahah* to stakeholders. An organization with a *Maslahah* value of 1.000 indicates that the organization provides full *Maslahah* to stakeholders.

MaP performance is measured using two methods, outcome-based *Maslahah* and process-based *Maslahah*. This refers to Sen (1992), who refers to two perspectives in creating wealth, namely the extent of achievement and the freedom to achieve. The measurement of the *Maslahah*'s achievement outcomes is the extent of achievement, namely the object of achievement. Measuring the process performance of the *Maslahah* indicates the freedom and opportunities that the organization has in achieving the *Maslahah* (freedom to achieve).

Performance Monitoring Through an Online System

The performance management system is a complex strategic management tool. It is a necessity to manage the *Maslahah* performance system through an online system. No matter how good a performance management system is, if it does not incorporate an online system, the efforts made will not be effective.

Dashboard performance is a performance-reporting method often used in performance monitoring systems. Robert S. Kaplan and David P. pioneered BSC performance reporting by using the dashboard. They described organizational leaders performing the organizational performance monitoring function like a pilot in a flying airplane.

A pilot needs information about outside temperature, outside air pressure, humidity, wind direction, wind speed, cloud thickness, altitude, speed, lifting force, thrust, etc. These data are very important for pilots to perform their duties and obligations. All data can be accessed in the cockpit of the aircraft. The data is presented with different displays, shapes, colours, and alarm sounds. An organizational leader needs performance data from all the existing work functions in the organization. If he wants to monitor the marketing function, he does not have to go right into the field. If he needs financial performance data, he simply monitors the dashboard display from his room.

To facilitate the above monitoring, the performance dashboard is a necessity that must be applied. To be able to display a reliable and trustworthy dashboard, the online system must necessarily be implemented.

Summary

Maslahah performa (MaP) is measured in two areas, the *Maslahah* process (process-oriented) and the *Maslahah* result performance (result-oriented). The *Maslahah* process is the organization's performance in implementing the MaP performance system. The *Maslahah* result is the result of the organization's performance that affects all stakeholders.

12 Performance Action

Countermeasure

The eighth step of the *Maslahah* Performa (MaP) performance system is to follow up. Follow-up is done after carrying out the monitoring process. Follow-up is carried out with two sub-activities, namely: giving appreciations and making improvements.

Giving Appreciation

Should the reward system be applied in the organization when the competence level of employees in terms of worship is already so high? If the level of individual sincerity at work is immense, will the reward system damage the level of sincerity itself? Will the reward system increase work motivation and productivity, or will it damage the foundation of *Maslahah*?

It is natural that people need encouragement at work, both from themselves and from outside. However, it is important to realize that the reward system is not the main goal at work. The main goal in work is to worship Allah (*s.w.t.*), the Supreme Giver of work. Therefore, it must be understood that the reward system is essentially a down payment that Allah (*s.w.t.*) pays to the workers through the organization in which they work. The repayment of the entire payment is made by Allah (*s.w.t.*) in the hereafter.

Appreciation is a form of expression given to workers who have successfully exceeded agreed upon goals. Appreciation aims to motivate employees to do better work. Rewards given to work functions or individuals depend on the performance of the work function or individual performance.

An inspiring story is that of Agus Chaerudin. An office worker at Bank Syariah Mandiri, Kalimalang Sub-Branch Office, Bekasi City. One afternoon in Ramadan, 4 August 2011, when the office where he worked was quiet, Agus was cleaning the office as usual before leaving. Behind the trash can, Agus found Rp 100,000.00 in 10 bundles. Agus did not dare to touch the money and called the security guard. The security guard then reported the finding of the money to the bank staff. The total amount is Rp 100 million. The money did not belong to the customers but to the bank. The money was scattered due to the carelessness of a teller.

DOI: 10.4324/9781003390947-15

Agus was appointed the Ambassador of Honesty, a title that is very rare in this country. Agus also received a certificate of honesty from his employer. The man with three children received an award of Rp 1.75 million from BSM's supervisory authority in Bekasi Raya. From BSM headquarters, Agus received the charter for the Integrity Award. He was also awarded prizes by various institutions. A political party even gave him an Umroh gift for him, his wife, and his parents.

Agus explained that his honesty was the result of the learning he had received from his parents. "When I return to Garut, I always wash my parents' feet. I told them that I could not meet my parents' expectations because for years I only became office boy." Some of Agus' colleagues admitted that Agus' daily life has not changed, even though he has received several awards. Agus remains simple and humorous, innocent, polite, and diligent in performing worship.

Improvement Actions

There are three sub-items of improvement action, namely: continuous improvement, corrective action, and preventive action. Continuous improvement is an action taken in a sustainable manner to improve the effectiveness of the performance management system. Corrective actions are actions taken to eliminate the cause of nonconformity and to prevent a reoccurrence of an event. Preventive actions are actions taken to eliminate problems that have the potential to cause nonconformities.

The process of improvement and prevention is carried out by ensuring that the root causes of problems encountered in implementing the performance system have been found. If the corrective or preventive actions do not address the root cause, the results of the improvement will not eliminate the root cause of the problem. Thus, there is a high probability that the same problem occurs again.

The improvement action is in line with Al-Shāṭibi's opinion that the fulfilment of *Maslahah daruriyah* is carried out in two approaches, first from the point of view of *al-Wujud* or affirming the existence and approach of *al-'adam* or guarding things which can harm or damage.

The *al-'adam* approach in the *Maslahah* performance system can be implemented as follows:

a Establishing performance guidelines.
b Revising guidelines or instructions for the *Maslahah* performance system.
c Developing performance procedures.
d Developing a code of conduct.

The *al-Wujud* approach in the *Maslahah* performance system can be implemented through the following measures:

a Revising the long-term plan, the medium-term plan, and the annual plan.
b Reviewing the fundamentals and behaviour of the *Maslahah*.

c Learning through best practices or benchmarking in setting performance measures.
d Reviewing targets with the intention of development.
e Re-evaluating weighting systems for performance measures.
f Improving the cascading system.
g Making effective performance dialog system.
h Improving the effectiveness of coaching and counselling.
i Improving the reward system.

Summary

Performance action is carried out with giving appreciations and making improvements. Three kinds of improvement action measures, namely: continuous improvement, corrective action, and preventive action. Continuous improvement is an action taken in a sustainable manner to improve the effectiveness of the performance management system. Corrective actions are actions taken to eliminate the cause of nonconformity and to prevent a reoccurrence of an event. Preventive actions are actions taken to eliminate problems that have the potential to cause nonconformities.

Part IV

Application of *Maslahah*-Based Performance System

13 *Maslahah* Performa Building

Maslahah Performa (MaP) Building is established in several steps: (1) The organization determines the strategic objective and the strategic initiatives that must be carried out by the organization. Both are defined in the corporate strategic planning. (2) The organization establishes a strong *Maslahah* foundation. The *Maslahah* foundation is built on each *Maslahah* orientation. (3) The organization determines the *Maslahah* behaviours to be cultivated in the organization. (4) The organization determines three *Maslahah* variables associated with the strategic objective and strategic initiatives.

For example, the strategic objectives and initiatives of each *Maslahah* orientation are shown in Table 13.1. Worship Orientation has two strategic objectives, namely: "achieving a visionary organization" and "improving social function." The strategic initiatives undertaken to achieve both objectives are: *Dzikrullah* before work; forming a team to create a code of conduct, long-term objective, medium-term objective, and annual program; integrating performance management with Spiritual Quotient; developing the skills of the auditor team; and empowering the community.

Compliance has a strategic objective, namely "to realize an obedient and consistent organization." The strategic initiative is accomplished through the same activities as Worship Orientation.

Internal process orientation has three strategic objectives, namely "realizing justice," "improving economic functions," and "creating high productivity." The strategic objectives to be achieved through the implementation of strategic initiatives are Introduction of new products that are free from usury, supplier satisfaction survey, evaluation of outsourcing, and cost reduction program.

Sustainability has a strategic objective of "creating organizations that are flexible and nimble in the face of change." Strategic objectives are expected to be achieved through the implementation of strategic initiatives: Competency Development Program, Integration between Performance Management System (PMS), and Spiritual Quotient (SQ).

Talent orientation has two strategic objectives, namely increasing satisfaction of talented employees and ensuring sustainability of leadership. Both strategic objectives are to be achieved through the implementation of strategic initiatives: Integrating recruitment and selection systems with competency

DOI: 10.4324/9781003390947-17

Table 13.1 Strategic Objective and Strategic Initiatives

Orientation		*Strategic Objective*	*Strategic Initiative*
Worship	1	Realizing a visionary organization	• *Dzikrullah* before work • The team composes code of conduct, long-term, mid-term, and annual program • Performance management integration with spiritual quotation • Development of audit competencies for the audit team
	2	Improve social function	*Ummat* empowerment program
Obedience	1	Realizing an obedient and consistent organization	• Competency Development Program • *Dzikrullah* before work • The team composes code of conduct, long-term, mid-term, annual program • Performance management integration with SQ • Development of audit competencies for the audit team
Internal proces	1	Realizing justice	Launching new products that are free of usury
	2	Enhancing economic functions	• Vendor satisfaction survey • Evaluate outsourcing
	3	Creating high productivity	• Cost Cutting Program
Sustainability	1	Creating organizations that have flexibility and dexterity towards change	• Competency Development Program • Integration of PMS with SQ
Talent	1	Increase the satisfaction of talented workers	• Integrate recruitment and selection systems with competency development
	2	Ensuring leadership sustainability	• Management development program • Implementing a career system and the performance of talented workers
Learning	1	Increasing the empowerment of workers	Propose TQM
	2	Establishment of a learning work culture	Promote self-development
	3	Integration of IT infrastructure as a learning media	Design training based on worship competency and organizational competency
	4	Establishment of learner-based reward systems	• Online process • In-house training (language) • Speech contest
Customer	1	Increase customer satisfaction	• Review all customer service procedures • Satisfaction survey on working with third parties
	2	Realizing customer engagement	• Increase customer mobilization activities • Form a customer community
Wealth	1	Realizing double profit	Business Process Re-engineering on distribution network systems
	2	Realizing the purification of wealth	LAZ Cooperation
	3	Creating an efficient organization	Grand strategy that connects the vision, mission, targets, objectives, and action plans to the budget

development, developing talent pool programs, implementing career systems, and performance for talent.

The learning orientation has four strategic objectives, namely: enhancing employee ownership, creating a learning work culture, integrating the infrastructure of IT as a learning medium, and creating learning-oriented reward systems. It is expected that the strategic objectives will be achieved through the implementation of strategic initiatives: Total Quality Management (TQM) proposal, promotion of self-development, design of training based on worshippers' competencies and organizational competencies, implementation of online process, internal training program, and speech contest.

Customer orientation has two strategic objectives, namely: increasing customer satisfaction and realizing customer engagement. Both strategic objectives are to be achieved through the implementation of strategic initiatives: Review of all service procedures, customer satisfaction survey in collaboration with third parties, increased customer mobilization activities, and customer community support.

The wealth orientation has three strategic objectives, namely: achieving double profit, achieving clean wealth, and creating an organization that becomes an efficient organization. The strategic objectives are to be achieved through the implementation of strategic initiatives: Business Process Re-engineering at the systems of the distribution network in cooperation with Amil Zakat Institute (LAZ), Grand strategies that connect the vision, mission, objectives, and action plans with the budget.

The Composition of Worship Orientation

The organization sets a strong *Maslahah* foundation. The *Maslahah* foundation is built on each *Maslahah* orientation. From each *Maslahah* foundation, the organization identifies the *Maslahah* behaviour that must be cultivated in each *Maslahah* orientation.

The foundation of worship orientation comes from the aspects of *Aqidah, Shari'ah,* and *Akhlaq*. From the *Aqidah*, the identified *Maslahah* behaviours is positive thinking, optimistic, confident, goal achiever, learner, and problem solver, personalities emerge. From the aspects of *Shari'ah* identified *Maslahah* behaviour includes obedience, consistency, and integrity. From the moral aspect identified *Maslahah* behaviour includes open-mindedness, honesty, justice, carefulness, concern, and patience. The structure of the *Maslahah* foundation and the *Maslahah* behaviour of the worship orientation is explained in Figure 13.1.

The next composition of worship orientation is to determine the three *Maslahah* variables that relate to the Strategic Objective and Strategic Initiatives, namely: measure, formula, and target. The worship orientation has two strategic objectives, namely: realizing a visionary organization and improving social functions. The visionary organizations have performance measures in the form of numbers of products that are free of usury. The formula determined to calculate performance results is the number of products

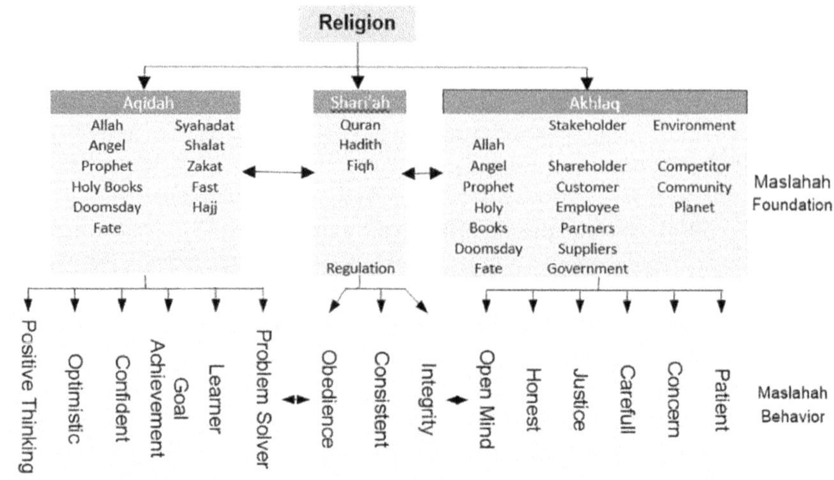

Figure 13.1 Maslahah Foundation and *Maslahah* Behaviour from Worship Orientation.

Source: Processed data.

that are free of usury divided by total products. The target set is 100% of the product to be usury free.

The strategic objective of improving social function has a performance measure of Percentage increase in CSR budget. The formula used to measure performance results is the percentage increase in the CSR budget. The target set is 25%. Explanation of the relationship between worship orientation performance variables is explained in Table 13.2.

In Obedience, there is one Strategic Objective, namely "Realizing an Obedient and consistent organization." Strategic objectives have two performance measures, namely: the availability of code of conduct and follow-up

Table 13.2 Worship Orientation Performance

Strategic Objective	*Measures*	*Formula*	*Target (5 Years)*	*Strategic Initiative*
Realizing a visionary organization manager	Number of products that are free of usury	Number of products that are free of usury divided by total products	100%	• *Dzikrullah* before work • The team composes code of conduct, long-term, mid-term, and annual program • Performance management integration with SQ • Development of audit competencies for the audit team
Improving social function	Percentage increase in CSR budget	Percentage increase in CSR budget	25%	*Ummat* empowerment program

Source: Processed data.

Table 13.3 Compliance Performance

Strategic Objective	*Measures*	*Formula*	*Target (5 Years)*	*Strategic Initiative*
Realizing an obedient and consistent organization	The availability of code of conduct	Availability: before the new fiscal year begins	100%	• Competency Development Program • *Dzikrullah* before work • The team composes code of conduct, long-term, mid-term, and annual program • Performance management integration with SQ • Development of audit competencies for the audit team
	Follow-up of audit findings	Number of follow-up findings	100%	

Source: Processed data.

of audit findings. The formula used to calculate the availability of code of conduct is time of supply before the new fiscal year begins. The target set is 100%. While the formula used to measure performance Follow up of audit findings is the number of follow-up findings. The target set is 100%. An explanation of the relationships between obedience performance variables is explained in Table 13.3.

The Composition of Internal Process Orientation

The *Maslahah* foundation of the Internal Process Orientation originates from physical and non-physical factors. From these two factors, the *Maslahah* foundation is identified: *Maqashid Shari'ah*, input process, supporting process, core process, process improvement, sustainable process, disaster and emergency management, risk management, *Shari'ah* and legal compliance, and output process.

The *Maslahah* behaviours to be cultivated by the organization are happiness, willingness to work, productivity, non-*maysir*; non-*gharar*; non-*usury* and non-*dhalim*, obedience, risk management, disaster and emergency control systems, awareness, justice, preventive systems, improvement/innovation systems, and sustainability. The structure of the *Maslahah* foundation and *Maslahah* behaviour of the Internal Process Orientation is explained in Figure 13.2.

The next composition of the internal process orientation is to determine the three *Maslahah* variables associated with the strategic objective and initiatives, namely: measure, formula, and target. The internal process orientation has three strategic objectives, namely: realization of justice, improvement of economic functions, and creation of high productivity.

The "Realizing Justice" has performance measures: Fair transactions produced, products or services produced, and efforts made to eliminate injustice. The formula used to measure the performance of "Fair transactions produced" is Profit divided by total income with a target of 40%. The formula used to measure the performance of "Products or services produced" is Bad

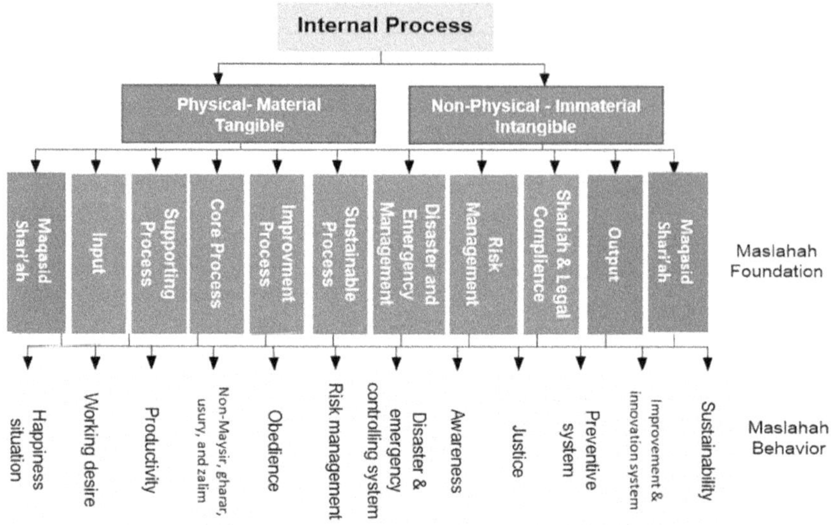

Figure 13.2 Maslahah Foundation and *Maslahah* Behaviour from Internal Process Orientation.

Source: Processed data.

debt divided by total income with a target of 5%. The formula used to measure the performance of "Efforts made to eliminate injustice" is Interest-free income divided by total income with a target of 100%.

The strategic objective "Enhancing Economic Functions" has performance measures: Time of payment to suppliers or partners, percentage of outsourcing workers who are appointed as permanent workers, and production cost efficiency. The formula used to measure the "time of payment to suppliers/partners" is less than 30 days with a target of 100%. The formula used to measure the performance of percentage of outsourcing workers who are appointed as permanent workers is outsourcing workers who are appointed as permanent divided by total outsourcing workers with a target of 30%. The formula used to measure the performance of "Production cost efficiency" is production costs divided by total costs with a target of 60%.

The strategic objective of "Creating high productivity" has a performance measure: Sales of products and services. The formula used to measure the performance of "Sales of products and services" is this year's sales divided by last year's sales with a target of 15%. The formula used to measure the performance of the "Cost of defect products and services" is Defect costs divided by fixed production costs should be 10% with a target of 100%. An explanation of the relationships between internal process orientation performance variables is explained in Table 13.4.

In the sustainability domain, there is a strategic objective of "creating organizations that have flexibility" and "dexterity to change." There is a performance measure for the strategic objective, which is the availability of

Table 13.4 Internal Process Orientation Performance

Strategic Objective	*Measures*	*Formula*	*Target (5 Years)*	*Strategic Initiative*
Realizing justice	Fair transactions produced	Profit/total income	40%	Launching new products that are free of usury
	Products or services	Bad debt/total income	5%	
	Efforts made to eliminate injustice	Interest-free income/ total income	100%	
Enhancing economic functions	Time of payment to suppliers or partners	<30 days	100%	• Vendor satisfaction survey • Evaluate outsourcing
	% of outsourcing workers who are appointed as permanent workers	Outsourcing workers who are appointed as permanent/total outsourcing workers	30%	
	Production cost efficiency	Production costs/ total costs	60%	Cost Cutting Program
Creating high productivity	Sales of products and services	This year's sales/last year's sales	15%	Creating high productivity
	Cost of defect products and services	Defect costs/fixed production costs 10%	100%	

Source: Processed data.

organizational plans (long-term, mid-term, and annual). The formula used to measure performance is the time of deployment before the new period begins. The target set is 100%. For a description of the relationships between the sustainability variables, see Table 13.5.

The Composition of Talent Orientation

The *Maslahah* foundation of talent orientation is based on aspects of work capacity and workforce capability and organization. In terms of manpower capacity and skills, the identified *Maslahah* fundamentals are *Aqidah*,

Table 13.5 Sustainability Performance

Strategic Objective	*Measures*	*Formula*	*Target (5 Years)*	*Strategic Initiative*
Creating organizations that have flexibility and dexterity towards change	The availability of organizational plans (long-term, mid-term, and annual program)	Availability: before the new period runs	100%	• Competency Development Program • Ad-hoc team • Integration of PMS with SQ

Source: Processed data.

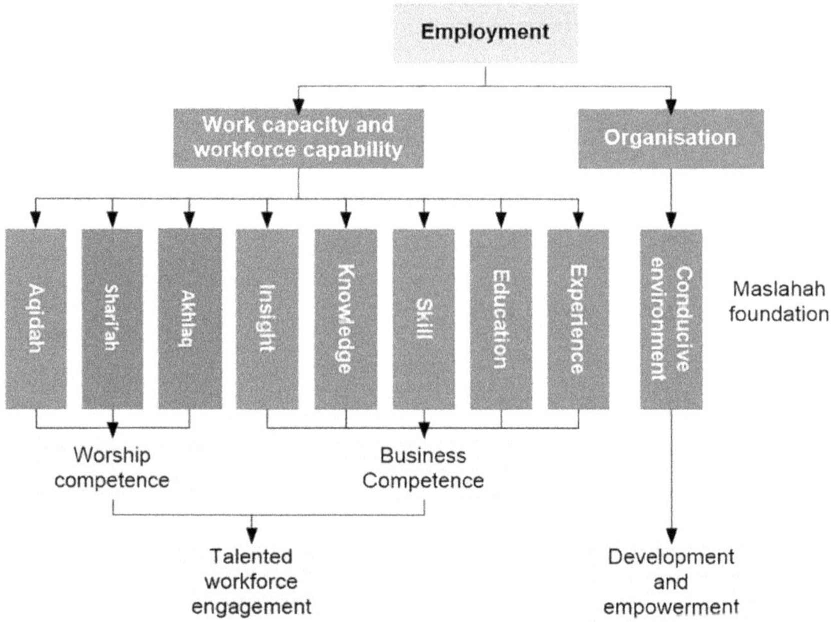

Figure 13.3 *Maslahah* Foundation and *Maslahah* Behaviour from Talent Orientation.

Source: Processed data.

Shari'ah, *Akhlaq*, insight, knowledge, skills, training, and experience. From an organizational perspective, the *Maslahah* foundation is a conducive environment. *Aqidah*, *Shari'ah*, and *Akhlaq* are part of the Godly competence for a talent. While insight, knowledge, skills, training, and experience are part of organizational competence.

Maslahah behaviour that results from the worshipful competence and the organizational competence is the talent's commitment. The *Maslahah* behaviour that results from the enabling environment is development and empowerment. The structure of the *Maslahah* foundation and the *Maslahah* behaviour of the talent orientation is explained in Figure 13.3.

The next talent orientation arrangement is to determine the three *Maslahah* variables that relate to the strategic objective and strategic initiatives, namely: measure, formula, and target (Table 13.6). Talent orientation has two strategic objectives "Increasing talent satisfaction" and "Ensuring Leadership Sustainability."

The strategic objective "Increasing talent satisfaction" has a performance measure: Talent satisfaction index. The formula used to measure the performance of the Talent Satisfaction Index is above 90% with a target of 100%. The strategic objective "Ensuring Leadership Sustainability" has a performance measure of "The number of talents who have expertise certification." The formula used to measure is the number of talents with a target of 15 persons.

Table 13.6 Talent Orientation Performance

Strategic Objective	*Measures*	*Formula*	*Target (5 Years)*	*Strategic Initiative*
Increasing the talent satisfaction	Talent satisfaction index	>90%	100%	• Integrating recruitment and selection systems with competency development
Ensuring leadership sustainability	The number of talented workers who have expertise certification of expertise	The number of talents	15%	• Management Development Program • Implementing a career system and the performance of a talented workers

Source: Processed data.

The Composition of Learning Orientation

The *Maslahah* basis of learning orientation is human capital and organizational capital. Of the human capital factors, the *Maslahah* foundation is identified as: *Aqidah*, *Shari'ah*, *Akhlaq*, insight, knowledge, skills, education, and experience. Of the organizational capital factors, the *Maslahah* foundation identified includes the working system and the working process.

The *Maslahah* behaviours that must be cultivated by the organization are worship competence, organizational competence, empowerment, and punishment and appreciation. The structure of the *Maslahah* foundation and the *Maslahah* behaviour of the learning orientation is explained in Figure 13.4.

The composition of the learning orientation is then to identify the three *Maslahah* variables associated with the Strategic Objective and Strategic Initiatives, which are measure, formula, and target. Learning orientation has four strategic objectives, namely: "Increasing the workforce engagement," "Establishment of a learning work culture," "Integration of IT infrastructure as a learning media," and "Establishment of learning-based reward systems."

The strategic objective of "increasing employees' engagement" has a performance measure: the number of improvements per work unit per year. The formula used to measure performance is number of improvements per work unit with a target of 25 improvements per work unit.

The strategic objective of "Establishment of a learning work culture" has two performance measures, namely: number of knowledges sharing events and number of man-days. The formula used to calculate the knowledge sharing performance is number of knowledges sharing events per month per work unit with a target of 15 events per work unit per month. While the formula used to measure the performance of number of man-days is number of training days times the number of employees who attended training divided by total number of employees with a target of 30 man-days.

The strategic objective of "Integration of IT infrastructure as a learning media" has a performance measure that is Employee satisfaction. The formula used to measure performance is satisfaction index above four with a minimum target of 90%.

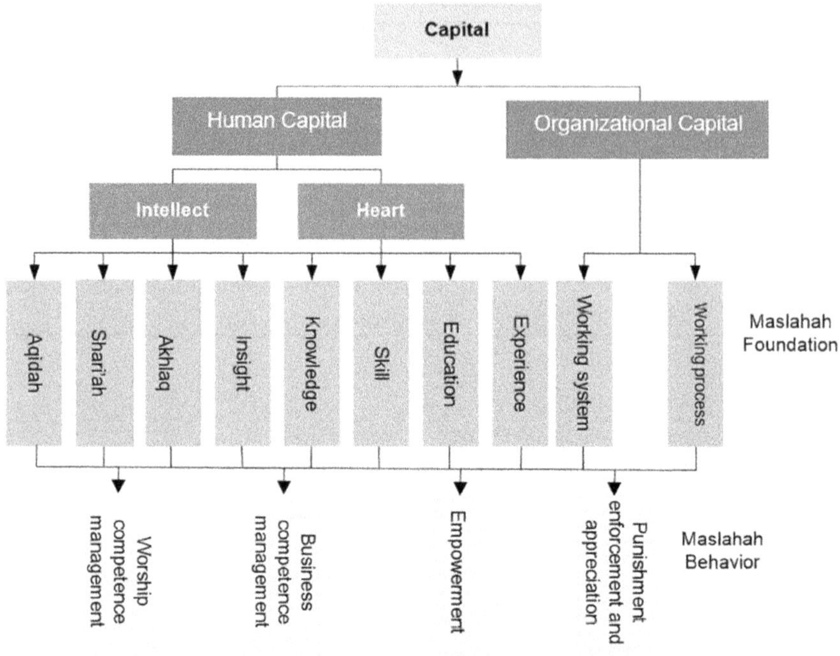

Figure 13.4 Maslahah Foundation and *Maslahah* Behaviour from Learning Orientation.

Source: Processed data.

The strategic objective of "Establishment of learning-based reward systems" has a performance measure that is Expert benefits. The formula used to measure performance is the number of workers who receive expertise allowances. The target set is 50% of the workers. Explanation of the relationship between learning orientation performance variables is explained in Table 13.7.

The Composition of Customer Orientation

The *Maslahah* foundation of customer orientation is derived from aspects of current customers and potential customers. There are two aspects identified as *Maslahah* foundation, namely: customer requirements and customer satisfaction. The *Maslahah* behaviour that must be cultivated by the organization is "Increasing customer satisfaction" and "Realizing customer engagement." The composition of *Maslahah* foundation and *Maslahah* behaviour of the customer orientation is explained in Figure 13.5.

The strategic objective of "Increasing customer satisfaction" has a performance measure that is Customer satisfaction. The formula used to calculate customer satisfaction performance is Customer Satisfaction Index above 4 with a target of 90%. The strategic objective of "Realizing customer empowerment"

Table 13.7 Learning Orientation Performance

Strategic Objective	*Measures*	*Formula*	*Target (5 Years)*	*Strategic Initiative*
Increasing the employee engagement	The number of improvements per work unit per year	Improvement/ work unit	25/work unit	• Proposing TQM
Establishment of a learning work culture	Number of knowledge sharing events	Number of knowledge sharing events/ month/work unit	15/work unit/month	• Promoting Self Development
	Number of man-days	(Number of training days × employees who attended training)/total employees	30 man-days	• Designing training based on worship competency and organ- izational competency
Integration of IT infrastructure as a learning media	Employees satisfaction	Satisfaction index reach > 4	90%	Online process
Establishment of learner-based reward systems	Expert benefits	The number of workers who receive expertise allowances.	50% of the workers	• In-house Training (language) • Speech contest

Source: Processed data.

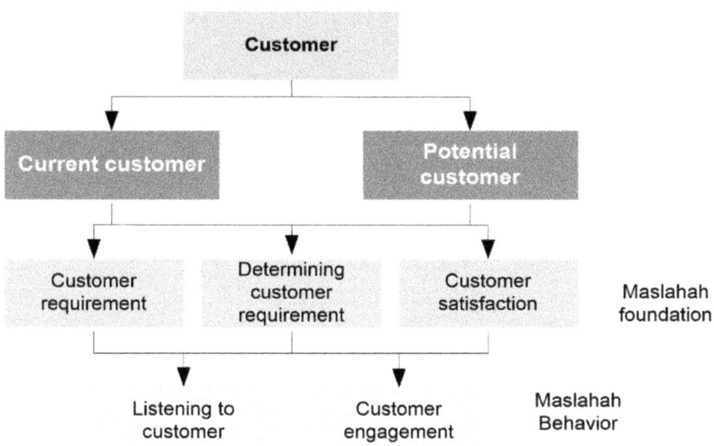

Figure 13.5 Maslahah Foundation and *Maslahah* Behaviour from Customer Orientation.

Source: Processed data

Table 13.8 Customer Orientation Performance

Strategic Objective	*Measures*	*Formula*	*Target (5 Years)*	*Strategic Initiative*
Increasing customer satisfaction	Customer satisfaction	Customer Satisfaction Index > 4	90%	• Reviewing all service procedures • Customer Satisfaction Survey in collaboration with third parties
Realizing customer empowerment	Response time to customer complaints	Response given maximum in two working days	100%	• Increasing customer mobilization activities • Forming a customer community

Source: Processed data.

has a performance measure of Response time to customer complaints. The formula used to calculate the performance is the response given in no later than two working days with a target of 100%. The relationship between customer orientation performance variables is explained in Table 13.8.

Wealth Orientation

The *Maslahah* foundation of wealth orientation lies in how to acquire and how to utilize the wealth. The *Maslahah* behaviour that must be cultivated by the organization is the creation of worship orientation, internal process orientation, talent orientation, learning orientation, and customer orientation. The structure of the *Maslahah* foundation and the *Maslahah* behaviour of the wealth orientation is explained in Figure 13.6.

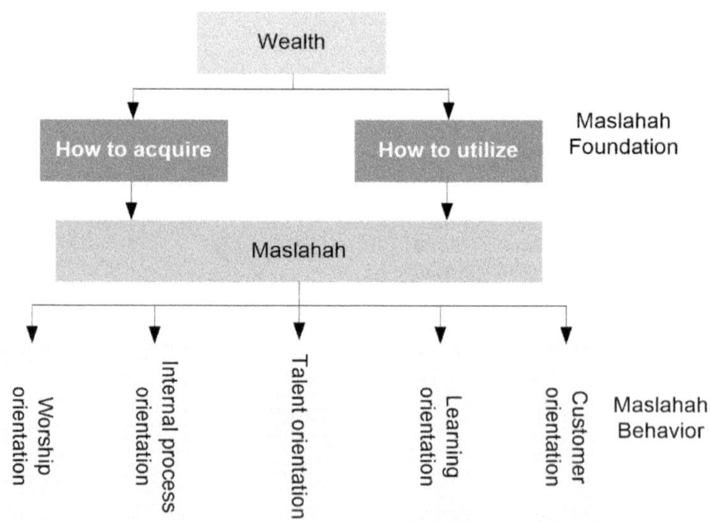

Figure 13.6 Maslahah Foundation and *Maslahah* Behaviour from Wealth Orientation.

Source: Processed data.

Table 13.9 Wealth Orientation Performance

Strategic Objective	*Measures*	*Formula*	*Target (5 Years)*	*Strategic Initiative*
Realizing double profit	Net profit	This year's net profit/last year's net profit	200%	Business Process Re-engineering on distribution network systems
Realizing the purified wealth	Amount of *Zakat* payment	This year's *Zakat* payment/*Zakat* last year	200%	Cooperation with Zakat Institution
Creating an efficient organization	Availability of work plan, budget and monitor process	Availability before the new fiscal year starts	100%	Preparing grand strategy that connects the vision, mission, targets, objectives, and action plans to the budget

Source: Processed data.

The next structure of wealth orientation is to determine the three *Maslahah* variables that are linked to the Strategic objective and Strategic Initiatives, namely: measure, formula, and target. Wealth orientation has three strategic objectives, namely: "Realizing double profit," "Realizing the purified wealth," and "Creating an efficient organization."

The strategic objective of "Realizing double profit" has a performance measure of net profit. The formula used to measure performance is this year's net profit compared to last year's net profit with a target ratio of 200%. The strategic objective of "Realizing the purified wealth" has a performance measure of "amount of *Zakat* payment." The formula used to measure the performance is this year's zakat paid compared to last year's zakat payment with a target ratio of 200%. The strategic objective of "Creating an efficient organization" has a performance measure of "Availability of work plans" and "budgets and monitoring processes." The formula used to measure the performance is the availability before the new fiscal year starts with a target of 100%. The relationship between variables on wealth orientation is explained in Table 13.9.

Summary

The key success factor of *Maslahah* Performa building is strategic objective, strategic initiatives, *Maslahah* foundation, *Maslahah* behaviours, measures, formula, and target. These aspects need to be in synergy for achieving the desirable results.

14 Case Study

PT. X has a vision: to become the leading Islamic Life Insurance Company in Indonesia in the areas of services, operations, and growth of Islamic business, with a professional, trustworthy, and beneficial approach to the community. The missions are:

- Carrying out Islamic insurance business in a professional manner by having excellent operational and service standards.
- Creating reliable human resources through sustainable human resource development programs.
- Utilizing integrated technology that is service-oriented, fast, convenient, and informative.

In the vision, the company's clearly identifiable goal is to be a role model for other companies as a Shari'ah compliance company. Another goal is to always provide *Maslahah* to the community. The proclaimed vision reflects the goals of the company's sustainability of being the pioneer. The vision also shows that the company has a goal to provide *Maslahah* to people. The mission carried out by PT. X has three structures, namely operation, human resources, and information technology.

The company received various awards from many institutions. In 2015 the company received some awards, among them: The Best Sharia Insurance, Runner Up for Life Insurance, Runner Up for Human Capital, Second Runner Up for Marketing, on the 4th Economic Review Indonesia Insurance Award 2015; Score "B" (Good) for Good Corporate Governance Insurance Company on Indonesia's 1st Economic Review Good Corporate Governance Award 2015; and Best Risk Management for Islamic Full Fledge Life Insurance on the 11th Islamic Finance Award 2015.

In 2016, the company received: Best Life Insurance under category of Equity between IDR 150 and 350 billion on Media Insurance Award 2016; Top Life Insurance under category of Asset between IDR 1–3 Trillion on Business News Top Insurance 2016; "Very Good" predicate on the Performance of Unit Link, Unit Link Shares Category during 2011–2015,

DOI: 10.4324/9781003390947-18

and Unit Link Stocks Category during 2013–2015 on the 1st Infobank Unit Link Award 2016.

In 2017, the company received: "Five Star" Predicate for Unit Link Performance in 2012–2016 on the 2nd Infobank Unit Link Award; Best Financial Performance for Life Insurance Company with Asset Category IDR 400 billion to 1.5 trillion on Indonesia's Economic News Insurance Consumer Choice Award; Best Sharia Life Insurance on Media Insurance Award; "Very Good" Predicate for Financial Performance in 2016 on the 6th Infobank Sharia Awards 2017. In 2018, this company was awarded The Runner Up of Digital Sharia Life Insurance Brand on the 7th Infobank Digital Brand Awards.

Performance of Worship Orientation

PT.X builds *Maslahah* foundation of worship orientation by applying three basic aspects of religion in a holistic manner, namely *Aqeedah, Shari'ah*, and *Akhlaq* in all its organizational activities. Management guides employees, work units, and organizations to maintain patient behaviour in daily life towards members, employees, supervisors, subordinates, partners, suppliers, shareholders, and the surrounding community. The concern of PT.X is demonstrated by the commitment of PT.X in various social activities such as giving donation to orphans and poor people, procuring Wakaf al-Quran, helping communities affected by disasters and calamities. Workers are required to work diligently. This is reflected in the consistent implementation of the Quality Policy of ISO 9001: 2015.

PT.X applies fair and honest conduct in product development and maintain *Shari'ah* Compliance. Coordination between the actuarial department and *Shari'ah* Compliance has resulted in product drafts to be further discussed further with the *Shari'ah* Supervisory Board (DPS).

The compliance and consistency of PT.X is evidenced by the existence of the Internal Audit Department, the Islamic Compliance Department, and the Legal Compliance Department. The internal quality audit team of ISO 9001: 2015 routinely conducts internal quality audits at least once a year. While audits from external parties, the ISO 9001: 2015 certification is conducted once a year.

PT.X shows achievements in problem solving, learning process, goal achievement, confidence, optimism, and positive thinking with various improvement and innovation programs. Various strategies such as business process reengineering of agency system have been carried out. PT.X has imposed a full agency system. Agents are encouraged to have high entrepreneurship. They are given an opportunity to manage their team. The worship orientation performance is carried out by compiling four main variables of *Maslahah* Performa (MaP), namely: strategic objectives, measures, targets, and strategic initiatives (Figure 14.1).

Strategic objectives, "realizing the management of an organization that holds fast to the mandate," have two measures of performance. First is the involvement of *Shari'ah* Compliance in product development. This measure

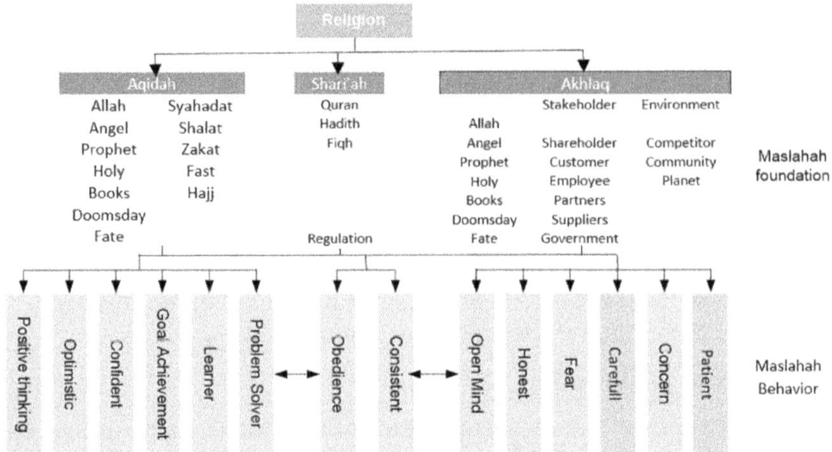

Figure 14.1 Worship Orientation Planning of PT. X.

Source: Processed data.

of performance has a target of 100% of the *Shari'ah* Compliance Division attending a meeting on product development. The results of the 2018 performance showed that the *Shari'ah* Compliant Division always attends (100%) meetings on product development. The second measure of performance is the availability of the financial statements that has a target of 100% of the public accountant's record "Unqualified Opinion."

The strategic objective "improve social function" has a measure of performance in the form of social activities. The target is the average number of social activities that occur one time per month. The performance in 2018 was 108%, where in September 2018 PT.X conducted 13 activities.

For the strategic objective "to realize a consistently obedient organization," there are performance measures in the form of internal audit findings. The target for this measure is that 100% of audit findings are followed up. The 2018 performance results have shown that all parts have followed up and the audit findings are "closed." The full results of the 2018 Worship Orientation measure are described in Tables 14.1 and 14.2.

Worship orientation is implemented through strategic initiatives in four main programs to strengthen faith, namely recitations of the Holy Quran, devotion to parents, daily charity, and *qiyamullayl*. Recitation of the Holy Quran is carried out with a target of two pages per day for each employee from the lowest to the highest level. This program is monitored through reports from employees to their respective supervisors each week and month. The program is also supported by Holy Quran recitation activities divided by department.

The program to serve the parents is fully communicated to the employees, be it the type of activities, the number of activities, the duration of the

Table 14.1 The Worship Orientation Performance of PT.X

Strategic Objective	*Measures*	*Formula*	*Target*	*Strategic Initiative*	*Results*	*Performance*
Realizing the management of an organization that holds to the mandate	The involvement of *Shari'ah Compliance* in product development	Product Development Discussion	100%	Four main programs to strengthen faith: a Recite the Holy Quran two pages per day for each staff from the lowest to the highest level. This program is also supported by Quran recitation activities divided by departments. b Program of service to parents. c Daily charity programs at all levels of the workforce. d *Tahajud* prayer is performed at home, at least one time per week, which applies to all workers. Two additional programs: a *Sunnah* fasting every Monday and Thursday for all workers, except for those who are unable to do so. b Discussion of selected hadiths after the congregational *Dhuhur* prayer.	100%	100%
	Availability of the financial statements	Records of public accountants "unqualified opinion"	100%		100%	100%
Improving social function	Corporate foundation social activities	Number of social activities	12 times		13 times	108%

Source: Processed data.

Table 14.2 Compliance Performance of PT.X

Strategic Objective	*Measure*	*Formula*	*Target*	*Strategic Initiative*	*Results*	*Performance*
Realizing a consistently obedient organization	Internal Audit Findings	Status of followed up internal audit findings	100% Closed	Four main programs to strengthen faith: a Recite the Holy Quran two pages per day for each staff from the lowest to the highest level. This program is also supported by Quran recitation activities divided by departments. b Program of service to parents. c Daily charity programs at all levels of the workforce. d *Tahajud* prayer is performed at home, at least one time per week, which applies to all workers. Two additional programs: a *Sunnah* fasting every Monday and Thursday for all workers, except for those who are unable to do so. b Discussion of selected hadiths after the congregational *Dhuhur* prayer.	100% Closed	100% Closed

Source: Processed data.

activities, the target activities, etc. The Human Resources Department controls the daily charity program for all levels of employees, with the person in charge of each work unit reporting the amount of charity collected each day. The targets for collecting alms are different for each level of employees. Actually, this activity can only be done by monthly deductions from employees' salaries, but the intention is that each employee really feels the value of charity.

Each employee at home performing *qiyamullayl* or *tahajud* prayer with a target of at least one time per week that applies to all employees. Every day, the company sends reminder on prayer times sent to the cell phones of all employees.

To support the main program of enforcing the Sunnah fasting every Monday and Thursday for all employees except those unable to do so, as well as for guests, two additional programs have also been implemented. This activity is also supported by the recitation of selected hadiths, which are performed after each *dhuhur* prayer.

Performance of Internal Process Orientation

PT.X has succeeded in building the *Maslahah* foundation of internal process orientation, as shown in Figure 14.2.

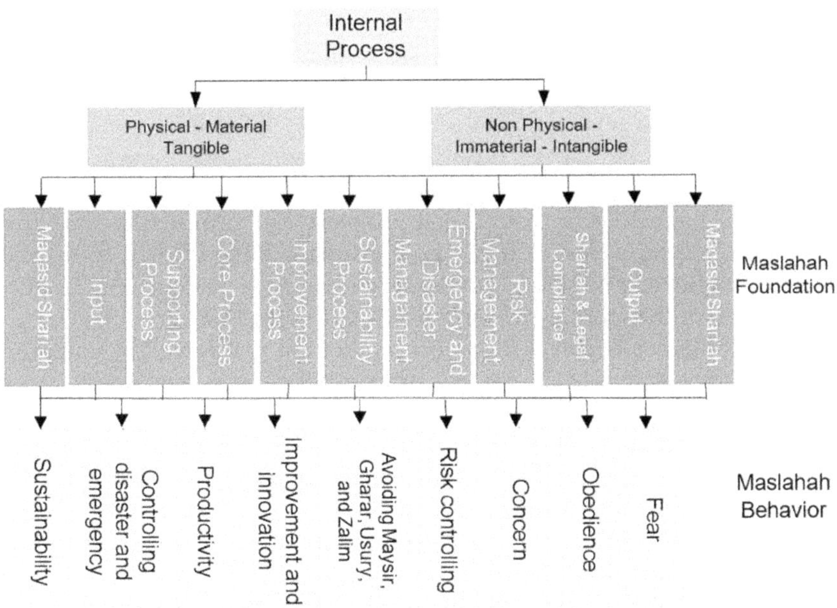

Figure 14.2 Planning of the Internal Process Orientation at PT.X.

Source: Processed data.

The input process, the process of creating value, and the output process are determined in accordance with the *Maqasid al-shari'ah* with the existence of the *Shari'ah* Supervisory Board (DPS). DPS routinely holds regular discussion sessions on the implementation of *Shari'ah* in the company. Stakeholder inputs are collected through customer satisfaction surveys, although PT.X has not routinely conducted these activities. Information about stakeholder input is also obtained through call centre media, email, SMS, WhatsApp, and agents. Workforce inputs are obtained through good communication between the union and the company. Other stakeholder input is obtained through various social activities that have been routinely conducted in the form of recitations, free health activities, sports, motorcycle clubs for employees, and direct community socialization regarding *Shari'ah* insurance.

Marketing, actuarial, underwriting, health, service, and claims are core processes to create customer value. The improvement process was carried out by implementing the ISO 9001: 2015 Quality Management System. PT.X has obtained the ISO 9001: 2000 certification in 2003, ISO 9001: 2008 certification in 2009, and ISO 9001: 2015 certification in 2019. PT.X carries out the CSR process. The *Shari'ah* compliance process ensures the obedience to *Shari'ah*. The legal process ensures compliance. The Internal Audit Department routinely controls the internal audit process. The Corporate Strategy Department carries out the sustainability process. The IT department ensures the protection of participant data to prevent emergencies and disasters. The Risk Management Department carries out the risk management process.

The completeness of the above process ensures the preservation and maintenance of organizational justice for stakeholders, compliance with both *Shari'ah* and regulations, organizational sensitivity reflected in the organization's concern for the lives of the surrounding community, control of risks that can be accepted by the organization, prevention of *Maysir*, *Gharar*, usury and *Dhalim*, increasing organizational productivity, minimizing risks from disasters and emergencies. In this way, the sustainability of the organization can be maintained. The whole process described above can be seen in detail in the design of the working system of PT.X (Figure 14.3).

The performance of internal process orientation is achieved by compiling four main variables of MaP, namely strategic objectives, measures, targets, and initiatives.

The Strategic objective of "enhancing economic function" has a performance measure in the form of several representative offices per year. This measure has a target of 40 offices. The performance in 2018 showed that the representative offices that have been inaugurated are 30 offices. This means that the achievement has reached 75% of the target.

The Strategic objective of "realizing justice" has a performance measure in the form of a claim payment process. The target for this measure is a payment period of nine days (for low-risk case). This period is calculated from the time the claim (completed with all required documents attached) is received by the

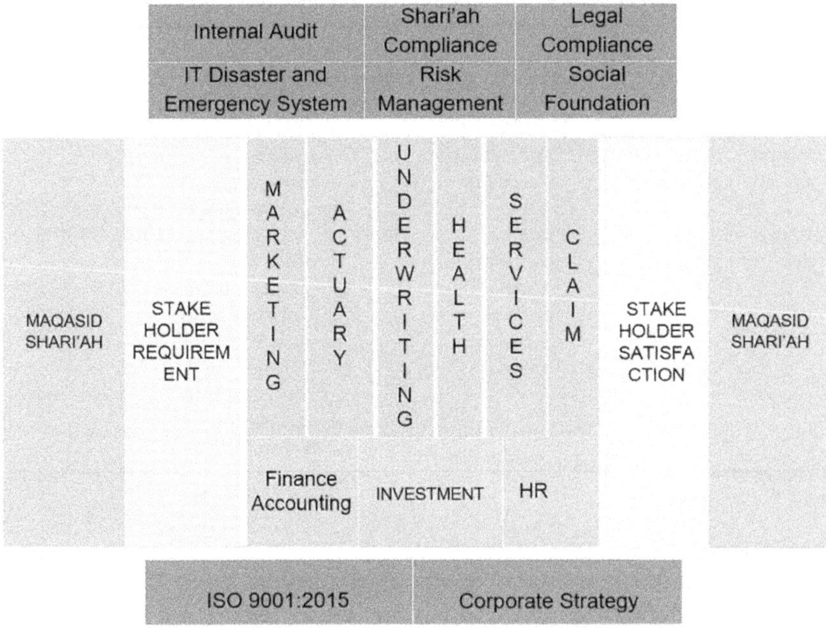

Figure 14.3 Work System Design of PT.X.

Source: Processed data.

Service Department until the claim is paid. The 2018 results show that 100% of low-risk claims are paid in an average of 7.5 days. This means that the target of paying 100% of low-risk claims within 9 days is being met (Table 14.3).

Part of the internal process orientation that needs to be managed by PT X is sustainability. The strategic objective of "Creating an organization that is always ready to face changes" has two performance measures, namely Management Meeting and Management Review Meeting (ISO 9001: 2015). For Management Meeting, the target is 100% implementation of the results followed up. For the "Management Review Meeting," the target is the same also that the results of the Management Review Meeting are implemented 100% (Table 14.3).

The strategic initiative is to completely change the agency's system. This system is business process engineering. Previously, the agency system was carried out with an incomplete system where the agents were freelancers. They are under the direct control of the marketing staff. The full agency provides the agents with the greatest possible opportunities to develop as they see fit. They are encouraged to be entrepreneurs by building their own marketing structure. As a result, marketers can open a representative office with full responsibility. PT.X will facilitate the opening of a representative office. Representatives who have organizational spirit and high expectations from the Islamic organization can realize this dream with the support of PT.X.

Table 14.3 The Internal Process Orientation Performance of PT.X

Strategic Objective	*Measure*	*Formula*	*Target*	*Strategic Initiative*	*Results*	*Performance*
Enhancing economic functions	Number of representative offices	Number of representative offices per year	40	a Full agency system initiation. b Conversion of the marketing office to a service office.	30	75%
Realizing justice	Claim payment process	Time of payment process for low-risk claims is nine days	100%	c Collaboration with PT. POS for contributions and claims payment.	100%	100%

Source: Processed data.

The opening of a representative office managed by agent will give benefit for company. Marketing office, which previously served as a marketing and service office, being available only for service offices. This improves the economic function not only for the agents but also for PT.X. Another efficiency created by PT.X is that one service office can serve multiple representatives. This will have a positive impact on the company's operating costs.

Another strategic initiative is to collaborate with other institutions such as PT. POS and banks for contributions and claims payment. Payment can be made via auto debit, Internet banking, cash deposit, and virtual accounts. As with risk-free products, participants may submit claims through the mail. Benefits may be paid on the same day.

Performance of Talent Orientation

PT.X built *Maslahah* foundation of talent orientation as shown in Figure 14.4. done by creating a supportive environment for all talented employees. There are two strategic objectives, namely creating high productivity and increasing talent satisfaction. The strategic objective of "creating high productivity" has a performance measure in the form of comparison of gross premiums to operating costs. The target for this measure is 100. In 2018 company achieved a ratio of operating costs to gross premiums of about 1566. Then, performance is achieved at 157%. The graph of the ratio of gross premiums to operating costs (Figure 14.5) shows an upward trend. This shows that the productivity of PT.X during 2001–2011 had a good performance.

The Strategic objective of increasing talent satisfaction has a performance measure in the form of a job satisfaction index. The target for this measure is 90% of talent is satisfied. This target was not met. In 2018 company have

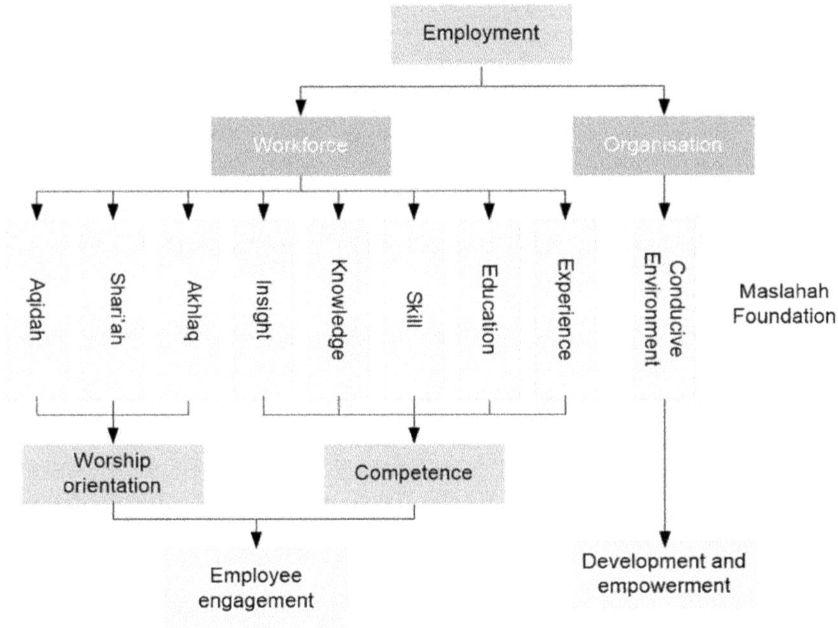

Figure 14.4 Talent Orientation Planning of PT.X.

Source: Processed data.

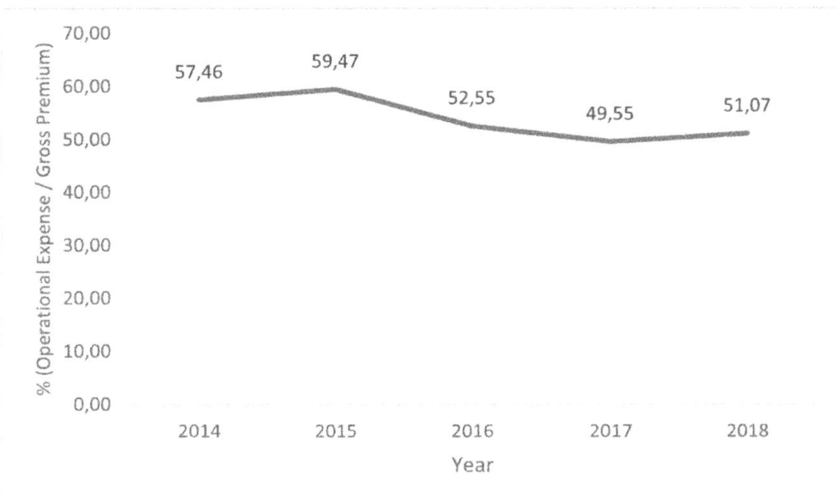

Figure 14.5 The Graph of Operational Expense on Gross Premium Ratio.

Source: Processed data.

Table 14.4 The Sustainability Performance of PT.X

Strategic Objective	*Measures*	*Formula*	*Target*	*Strategic Initiative*	*Results*	*Performance*
Creating organizations that are always ready to face change	Management Meeting	Follow-up of Management Meetings	100%	Implementation of the ISO 9001: 2015	100%	100%
	Management Review Meeting (ISO 9001: 2015)	Follow-up of Management Review Meetings (ISO 9001: 2015)	100%	Quality Management System	100%	100%

Source: Processed data.

not conducted survey. Talent satisfaction survey was not routinely conducted. Talent satisfaction survey was conducted in 2016, but no survey was conducted after that. Another issue is the lack of a career development system integrated with the workforce development system, which means the talent pool is not properly managed. All these calculations of targets, measurements, and performance assessments are shown in Tables 14.4–14.6 and 14.8.

Several strategic initiatives have been carried out by the company. Talent orientation is done by creating a supportive environment for all talented employees. Brotherhood and kinship are created through example and leadership. Work motivation is also created by meeting the basic needs of talented employees. The physical health needs of gifted employees are met by enacting reimbursement rules for prophetic medical treatments (*Thibbun nabawi*) such as cupping, acupressure, *Habatussauda*, honey, and medical check-up. Maintaining physical health is also met through the formation of sports groups

Table 14.5 The Talent Orientation Performance of PT.X

Strategic Objective	*Measure*	*Formula*	*Target*	*Strategic Initiative*	*Results*	*Performance*
Creating high productivity	Comparison of gross premiums to operating costs	Gross/ Opex Premium Ratio	1,000	• Reimbursement of expense for *Thibbun nabawi* • Use of the education and training budget according to the planning • Sports club • Study group. • Rotation and empowerment of talented workers	1,566	157%
Increasing the satisfaction of talented workers	Talent Satisfaction Index	Survey Index	90% satisfied		Not yet done	–

Source: Processed data.

Table 14.6 Training Cost of PT.X

Years	*Cost of General and Administrative*	*Allocated Budget*	*Training and Dev Expense Realization*
2014	IDR 20.309.806.268	IDR 1.015.490.313	IDR 771.313.447
2015	IDR 16.785.582.759	IDR 839.279.138	IDR 473.790.521
2016	IDR 17.246.174.653	IDR 862.308.733	IDR 351.189.324
2017	IDR 16.522.183.120	IDR 826.109.156	IDR 276.389.746
2018	IDR 17.892.025.727	IDR 894.601.286	IDR 569.160.655

such as badminton, futsal, fitness, bicycle, and motorcycle clubs. Meeting the spiritual needs of talented workers is done by giving talented workers time off every ten last days of Ramadan. For talented workers who cannot yet recite the Holy Quran, the company also offers the opportunity to learn the Holy Quran in addition to other study groups.

In terms of organizational development and self-development, the company rotates talented employees on a regular basis. In this way, each talented employee is able to perform various tasks well and with confidence. Of course, in implementing its policy, the company fulfils everything that talented employees are entitled to, such as housing allowance, holyday allowance, etc.

The Human Resources (HR) carries out the planning of the talented manpower during the preparation of the annual plan. Skill improvement needs are met through a planned recruitment and selection system. Qualifications related to education, experience, skills, knowledge, insight, *Aqeedah*, *Shari'ah*, and *Akhlaq* are determined according to the position. The policy of HR emphasizes that it is not easy to find talented workers who truly meet the set qualifications. Therefore, potential talented workers who do not understand *Shari'ah* that matches the qualifications still have the opportunity to be accepted as talented workers at PT.X, but the HR department will then offer additional training to the person in question. As for the system of education and training, this activity is supported by the agreed budget at the time of preparation of the annual plan.

Engaging the talented workforce is done by giving them the opportunity to provide feedback to the company. The company conducts daily meetings between supervisors and subordinates before work in each unit. The meeting starts with reciting the Holy Quran together and ends with a congregational prayer. In the afternoon, before going home from work, all gifted employees read the prayer together. Management meetings are also routinely held once a week. At this meeting, management provided the greatest opportunity for the talented employees to give their feedback. After a more in-depth review, suggestions from the talented workforce were followed up and implemented. Development and empowerment of talented employees is done through a system of training and development, job rotation, promotion, and through assignments. The HR manages internal and external training with the budget compiled in the annual plan.

Performance of Learning Orientation

PT.X implement a learning orientation is derived from human capital and organizational capital. Human capital consists of experience, education, skills, knowledge, insight, *Aqidah*, *Shari'ah*, and *Akhlaq* can be developed through a highly selective recruitment and selection system. The workforce is not only competent in managing the company, but also has the competence to apply the religion in daily life. The age of information technology makes it easier for the HR department to obtain information about the background, experience, and activities of potential employees.

Organizational capital is developed through the design of the work system and work processes, as shown in Figure 14.6. The management is committed to the learning process. This commitment is implemented by allocating budgets for training and development. The budget is regulated and controlled to meet the principle of equity for all levels of employee positions.

Technological advances are also utilized by PT.X in cultivating individual and learning organizations. Intranet and Internet networks are the means for PT.X to communicate not only to employees but also to all stakeholders in the organization. The website becomes a means to create openness. Various information about the company, latest information, product developments, social activities, and other information are presented on the website. Social

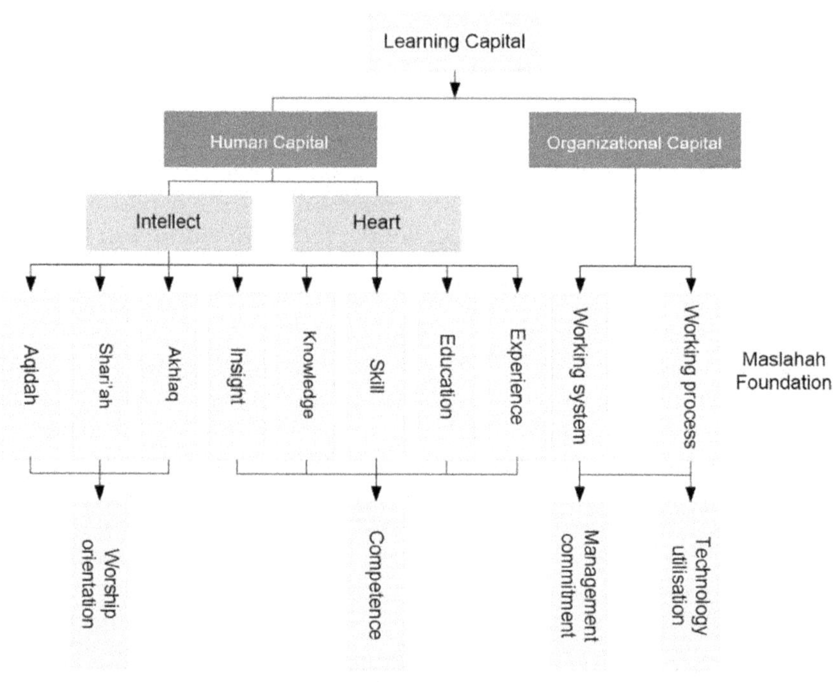

Figure 14.6 Learning Orientation Planning of PT.X.

Source: Processed data.

media networks are also maximized by PT.X to a learning medium. Media accounts are a means to educate about the company.

The learning orientation is created by allocating specific funds for training. The budget is determined when the annual plan is developed. The requirements to meet the worship orientation are also met through Islamic mentoring programs including series of overnight Islamic studies program. The company also conducts regular Islamic discussion every Friday from 8:00 to 9:30 AM. The activity of contemplating the identity of the *Caliph* of Allah (*s.w.t.*) on Earth has been followed by all employees. This activity is routinely conducted at least once a year. Motivation of the workforce is also encouraged through a reward system in the form of *Umrah* package gifts for workers, i.e., employees and representatives who have excellent performance.

Specifically for agents, PT.X facilitates agents' contact with other *Shari'ah* and conventional community organizations. PT.X regularly sends representatives of agents to participate in the MDRT (Million Dollar Round Table). This event is an award for outstanding agents. This moment is proof of the agent's accomplishments in the public eye.

There are two strategic objectives, namely establishment of learner's work culture and establishment of learner-based reward system. The strategic objective of "establishing a learning work culture" has a performance measure in the form of training hour which describes the average number of training hours/employee/year. The target is 20 training hours per employee per year. The performance shows that, on average, an employee from PT.X has attended 35 hours of training per year. This means that a performance of 175% has been achieved. The percentage of training hours looks very good, but if we take a closer look at the analysis of the financial data, namely the ratio between the realized training budget and the allocated training budget, it shows that from 2001 to 2011, the cost of training was not fully used, also the percentage of realization of the cost of training for the allocation of training and education costs is getting lower every year, –29.58% in 2001 to –91.29% in 2011 (Figure 14.7). This proves that the budget for education and training was not used optimally for the fulfilment of the learning orientation.

The strategic objective to establish learning-based reward system has a performance measure in the form of *Umrah* gifts for employees and agents. The performance measure has two objectives. First, the target agent receiving an *Umrah* prize depends on the achievement of marketing target at each agent level. Second, the allocated award is for one employee per representative office. The results show that 24 agents and 2 employees received *Umrah* awards. This means that the *Umrah* awards for employees reached 200%. The full learning orientation performance results are shown in Table 14.7.

Performance of Customer Orientation

PT.X focuses on customer orientation through two types of customers: prospective customers and existing customers. Services for both types of customers are provided by the services division, customer relation management (CRM),

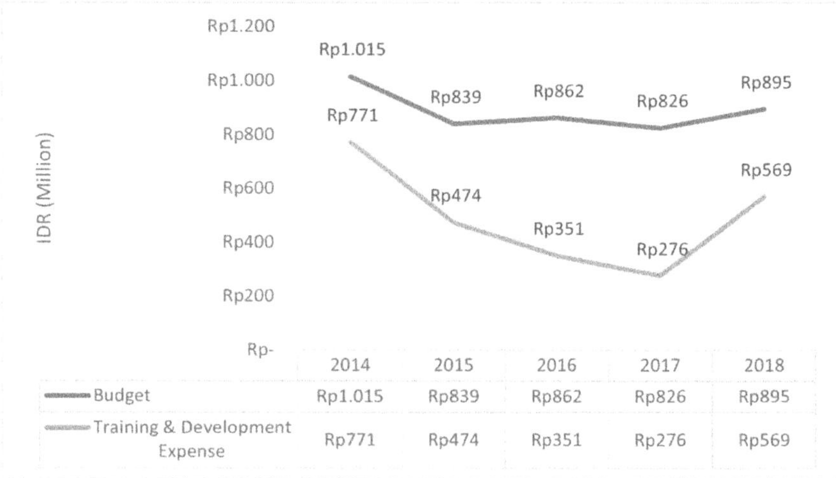

Figure 14.7 The Graph of Training, Allocation, and HR Cost Realization.

Source: Processed data.

and Policy Owner Services (POS). Existing customers are divided into regular customers and priority customers. PT.X obtains information about customer through customer feedback, customer complaints, customer information, *Shari'ah* provisions, *Ulama* fatwas, input DPS, core competencies (core competence), analysis of organizational strengths and weaknesses, opportunities and

Table 14.7 The Learning Orientation Performance of PT.X

Strategic Objective	*Measures*	*Formula*	*Target*	*Strategic Initiatives*	*Results*	*Performance*
The establishment of learner's work culture	Training hour	The duration of man hour training per employees per year	20 man-days	a *Malam Bina Ketaqwaan* (series of overnight Islamic studies program). b *Reward Umrah* for employees and agents c The best agent contests d Active participation in MDRT activity for agents e *Dhuha* lectures every Friday morning f Employee's Islamic discussion	35 man-days	175%
The establishment of learner-based reward system	*Umrah* award for employees and agents	The number of *Umrah* award per representative office per year	Depending on marketing target		24	–
		The number of *Umrah* award per year	One person per year		2	200%

Source: Processed data.

Table 14.8 The Customer Orientation Performance of PT.X

Strategic Objective	*Measures*	*Formula*	*Target*	*Strategic Initiatives*	*Result*	*Performance*
Increasing customer satisfaction	Customer Satisfaction Index	Survey index	90% satisfied.	• Cooperation with PT. POS to pay members' share and claim. • Training for agents and services • Call centre	Have not been conducted	–
Increasing the number of customers	Market share	Gross premium of PT.X compared to the entire industrial gross premium	2.00%		0.40%	20%

Source: Processed data.

challenges from the industrial environment, regulatory requirements, input from suppliers and partners, customer satisfaction surveys, previous organizational performance, opportunity for improvement (OFI) ISO 9001: 2015, operational audit results, quality audit results ISO 9001: 2015, and management review meetings (ISO 9001: 2015).

The Quality Policy, Quality Manual, Quality Procedure (SOP, Standard Operating Procedure), or in the Work Instruction are identified as customer requirements are written by PT.X. These provisions are then communicated by management to all employees to create a culture of customer satisfaction. The media used to communicate customer requirements are: website, email, fax, telephone, bulletin, meeting, training, and accompaniment.

To achieve customer satisfaction, PT.X conducts activities to listen to and to engage with customers. The process of listening is supported by opening call centres that can serve customers 24 hours a day. Complaints, information, and feedback from customers are received through call centres, email, fax, and telephone. All media are well used by customers. Customer involvement makes PT.X receives important information that can be used to renew and improve services to participants. Email, fax, phone, and CS staff is managed by the CRM department. The service for existing customers is made effective by PT. POS, which provides all forms of customer mutation and other services.

Collaboration with PT. POS is dedicated to non-risk claims service Payments which can be made directly across the entire PT network. This has been very beneficial for participants located far from office services and representative offices. PT. POS which is located in each regency or municipality facilitates the processing of non-risk claims. Participants submit a claim to PT.X via PT. POS by completing all documents as required. If the document is complete, the claim will be paid by PT. POS the next day (two business days). The whole process described above is shown in detail in Figure 14.8.

Table 14.9

Year	*2014*	*2015*	*2016*	*2017*	*2018*
Gross Premium (IDR Million)	199.570	181.671	207.325	203.285	216.560
Gross Premium of all Life Insurance (IDR Million)	112.880.000	111.230.000	167.170.000	194.420.000	198.740.000
Share of Premium (%)	0.18	0.16	0.12	0.10	0.11

The identified strategic objectives for creating customer orientation are to increase customer satisfaction and to increase the number of customers. The measure for the strategic objective of increasing customer satisfaction is the index of customer satisfaction. The measure for the strategic objective of increasing the number of customers is market share. In this case, market share shows the gross premium amount (premium) of PT.X compared to the gross premium of the industry. The performance data of the market share can be seen in (Figure 14.9).

The data shows that from 2002 to 2011, the market share of PT.X shows a downward trend. Even in a three-year comparison, the latter market share is even smaller than that of 2002. In 2008, there was an increase in market share. At that time, the growth of PT.X is 0.65%, and this is the highest market share in the last ten years.

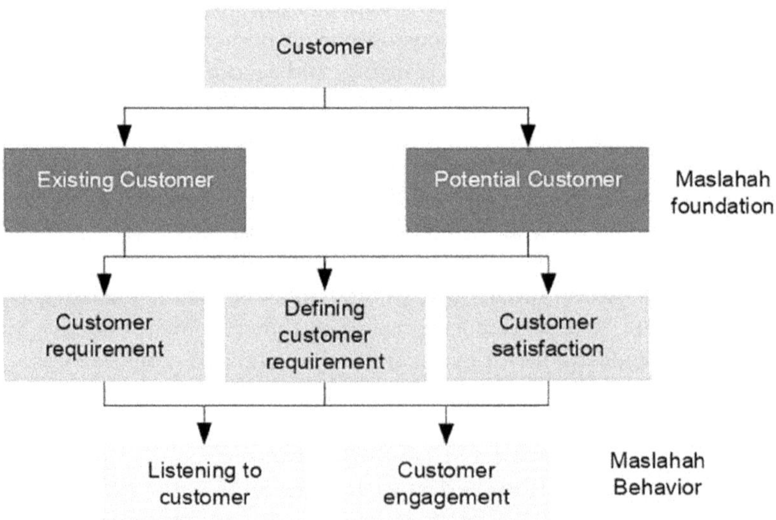

Figure 14.8 The Customer Orientation Planning of PT.X.

Source: Processed data.

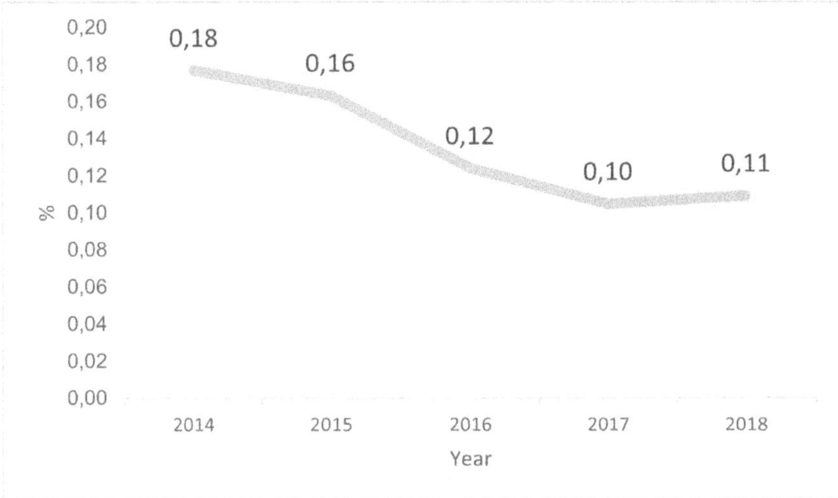

Figure 14.9 The Graph of Premium Share.

Source: Processed data.

Performance of Wealth Orientation

The management of PT.X is aware that the way of getting wealth must be in accordance with the requirements of *Aqidah* and guidelines of *Shari'ah*, i.e., halal and good, as this will affect the blessing of the acquired wealth. Therefore, PT.X in obtaining wealth always fulfils the worship orientation, internal process orientation, talent orientation, learning orientation, and customer orientation. To obtain wealth, the management of PT.X teaches the workers to always pray to the Almighty, praying that all workers work according to the mandate given to them. The management also always reminds all workers that God must test them if their business is not immediately successful. So, praying and striving according to the guidance of the *Shari'ah* and the demand for *Aqidah* to gain wealth that has already been promised by God. This is explained in Figure 14.10.

The way you spend your wealth must also be in accordance with the requirements of *Aqidah* and guidance of *Shari'ah,* that is, it must be *Halal* and *Thayyib.* The administration of PT.X is fully aware that PT.X is a virtuous fund manager collected from the participants. These funds are deposited funds that are issued as charity to other participants who receive the risk. Therefore, the process of spending assets through asset allocation based on asset orientation, customer orientation, learning orientation, energy orientation, internal process orientation, and worship orientation must be carried out in full trust. Trust from participants to PT.X as a fund manager must be carried out with full accountability.

Allocation of assets to fulfil a need of wealth orientation aims to reproduce wealth. Investment through various instruments of *Shari'ah* must be done

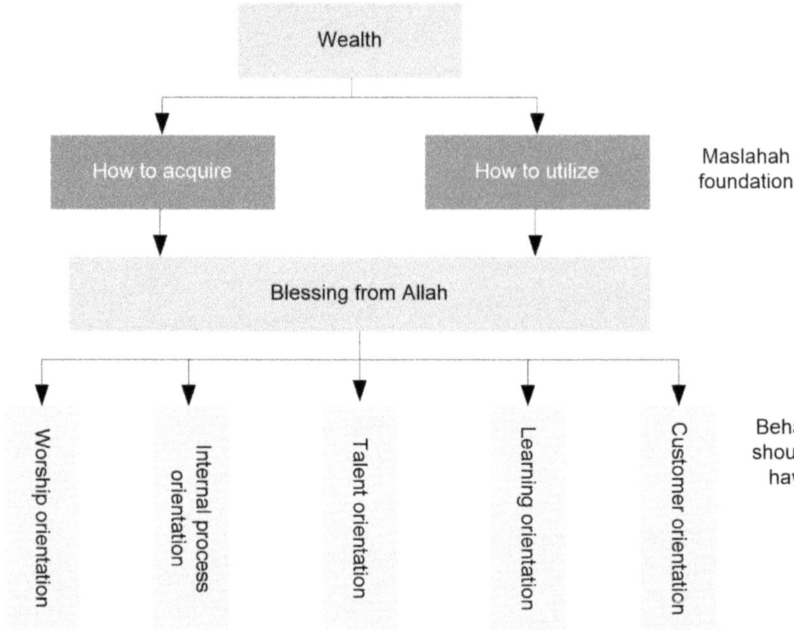

Figure 14.10 The Wealth Orientation Planning of PT.X.

Source: Processed data.

carefully and accurately. Fulfilling the needs of customer orientation aims to increase customer satisfaction and increase market share. Fulfilling the needs of learning orientation is for training, socializing, mentoring, and developing employees. Fulfilling the needs of work orientation is for current salary costs, vacation allowance, bonuses, work and family insurance, car allowances, housing allowances, medical expenses, and medical examinations. PT.X has even reimbursed fees for treatments with alternative prophetic medicine (*Tibun nabawi*) such as cupping, herbs, vacation allowance which is paid one week before Ramadan.

The fulfilment of internal process orientation needs is carried out for cost services, reinsurance costs for risk provisioning, and representative office infrastructure costs. Fulfilment of worship orientation needs related to worship of Allah (*s.w.t.*) is done through Zakat, Infaq, Shadaqoh, Waqf (al-Quran), Hajj (employees and representatives), and Qurban. In terms of stakeholders, the company's foundations are always present in various social activities, such as mass circumcisions, free medical treatments, blood donations, donations for orphans, and compensation for victims of disasters. In relation to the environment, PT.X always maintains the environment by complying with the regulations of the regional and central governments. The entire process described above is shown in detail in Figure 14.12.

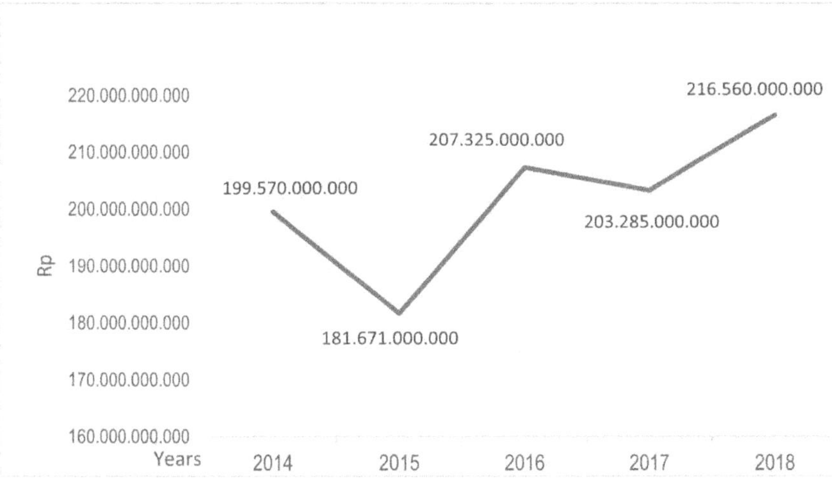

Figure 14.11 The Gross Contribution (Billion Rp).

Source: Processed data.

The target strategy for manifesting T Gross Contribution aims to reach the trillion units in gross premium acquisition. This occurs as a company has achieved a great leap, since the establishment of PT.X to 2011, the acquisition of premiums is still in billion units. Performance results show that by 2011, a new gross premium of IDR 360.37 billion was achieved (Figure 14.11). More efforts are needed by all components of PT.X to move into the trillion range. Strategic objective to achieve asset purity with the management of corporate zakat payments, participant zakat, and employee zakat (Figure 14.12).

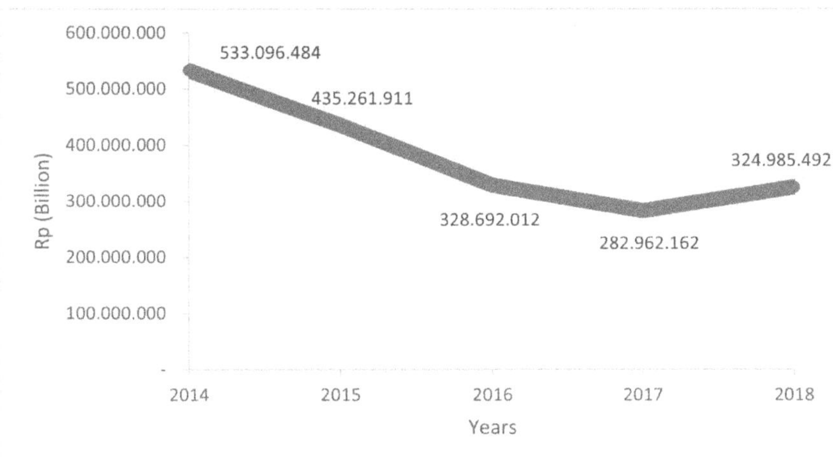

Figure 14.12 The Payment of Zakat (Million Rp).

Source: Processed data.

Table 14.10 The Wealth Orientation Performance of PT.X

Strategic Objective	*Measures*	*Formula*	*Target*	*Strategic Initiatives*	*Result*	*Performance*
Realizing "T" *Gross Contribution*	Gross premium	The amount of gross premium	1 B	• Full agent system • The opening of representative office (RO) significantly in all regions in Indonesia	0.36 B	36%
Realizing wealth purity	Zakat payment	The amount of Zakat payment	No target		–	–

Source: Processed data.

The results of measuring wealth orientation performance are fully described in Table 14.10.

Performance Results of MaP

This can be explained as follows (Table 14.11): worship orientation has a target of 3. The target was achieved at the level of 2. Compliance has a target of 1 and was met. Internal process orientation has a target of 2, the target achieved as much as 1. Sustainability has a target of 2, the target achieved is 1. Talent orientation has a target of 2, the targets achieved is 1. Learning orientation has a target of 3, the target achieved is 3. Customer orientation has a target 2, the target achieved is 1. Wealth orientation has a target of 2, the target achieved is 1.

Then the data is analysed with the following formula:

$$P(r) = \sum_{i=1}^{n=8} W_{\mathrm{i}} \ x \ \frac{A_{\mathrm{i}}}{T_{\mathrm{i}}}$$

P(r) = *P* worship orientation + *P* obedience + *P* internal process orientation + *P* sustainability + *P* talent orientation + *P* learning orientation + *P* customer orientation + *P* wealth.

Table 14.11 The Total of *Maslahah* Performa Result of PT. X

No	Maslahah *Orientation*	*Score*	*Number of Target*	*Target of Achievement*	*Achievement*
1	Worship Orientation	0.125	3	2	0.083
2	Compliance	0.125	1	1	0.125
3	Internal Process Orientation	0.125	2	1	0.062
4	Sustainability	0.125	2	1	0.062
5	Talent Orientation	0.125	2	1	0.062
6	Learning Orientation	0.125	3	3	0.125
7	Customer Orientation	0.125	2	1	0.062
8	Wealth Orientation	0.125	2	1	0.062
Total Score		1.000	Total Performance Result		0.643

Source: Processed data.

Table 14.12 The Total of *Maslahah* Performa Process of PT.X

No	*Performance Steps*	*Score*	*Number of Steps*	*Application*	*Score*
1	Arranging strategic planning	0.050	3	3	0.150
2	Identifying *Maslahah* foundation	0.050	1	0	0.000
3	Determining *Maslahah* behaviour	0.050	1	0	0.000
4	Deciding measures	0.050	6	3	0.150
5	Dealing with performance contract	0.050	2	0	0.000
6	Applying performance	0.050	1	1	0.050
7	Monitoring	0.050	4	1	0.050
8	Follow up	0.050	2	2	0.100
Total					0.500

Source: Processed data.

MaP has a range between 0.000 and 1.000. Performance of 0.000 shows that the organization does not benefit stakeholders. Performance of 1.000 shows that the organization provides full benefits to stakeholders. Performance results of benefit PT.X of 0.643 shows that PT.X has provided benefits to all stakeholders.

Process Performance of MaP

PT.X has a process performance of (Table 14.12). This can be explained as follows: steps were taken to determine the basis of the achievement. Steps to determine the behaviour of the achievement have been taken. The step to determine the strategic objectives has been performed. The step of determining the performance measure was performed. The step of setting target was not consistently performed. Step setting for the strategic initiatives was performed. The step of taking performance measurements has been done. The steps to conduct a performance evaluation were not performed. The step of taking corrective and improvement actions was not performed.

PT.X did not perform the steps to set target because MaP's performance system is one that prioritizes sustainable business. The target set must be annual-term (five years). Therefore, PT.X sets annual-term of five-year target. The target was cascaded to the annual target through milestones. The performance of the performance process of PT.X of 0.500 is achieved by the following calculation:

The performance achievement of PT.X is 0.500, obtained by this calculation:

$$P(r) = \sum_{i=1}^{n=8} W_{\mathrm{i}} \ x \ Si$$

$$P(p) = P \text{ step } 1 + P \text{ step } 2 + P \text{ step } 3 + P \text{ step } 4$$
$$+ P \text{ step } 5 + P \text{ step } 6 + P \text{ step } 7 + P \text{ step } 8$$

Performance index has a range of 0.000–1.000. A performance of 0.000 indicates that the organization is not realizing the benefits of its performance. Organizations that are not established with the purpose of goodness even tend to be destructive and contradict the aim of *Shari'ah*. 1000 performances show that the organization has fully implemented a system of performance achievement. The performance of PT.X of 0.500 shows that PT.X has implemented a welfare performance system, even if it is not yet complete.

Summary

In this chapter the company's clearly identifiable goal is set to be a role model for other companies as a *Shari'ah* compliance company, to be followed. PT.X has a process performance of 0.500. This value shows that PT.X has implemented a *Maslahah* performance system, although it is not yet perfect. PT.X has a performance score of 0.643, indicating that PT.X has provided benefits to all stakeholders.

15 Conclusion

The application of the concept of spirituality in the theory of organization, leadership, and motivation has grown rapidly. This has been triggered by the inadequacy of the concept of capitalist economics in answering various problems of economics caused by a lack of ethics and *Akhlaq*. Business ethics developed by the capitalist economy is unable to curb ethical violations by organizational practitioners.

Islam teaches that the purpose of establishing an organization is to achieve salvation in the hereafter and success of life in the world. This goal can be achieved by aligning the organizational management with human beings' duties as Allah's *Caliphs* on earth. Therefore, organizations must be managed with the promotion of ethics and *Akhlaq*, social responsibility, and faith.

The indicator of achieving *Falah* is the fulfilment of basic human needs that are balanced or fulfilled *Dharuriyah*. Basic needs include religion (*al-din*), soul (*al-nafs*), offspring (*al-nasl*), reason (*al-'aql*), and wealth (*al-mal*). This is in line with the objectives of *Shari'ah* (*Maqasid al-shari'ah*) which is preserving those five basic needs.

In the organizational context, the basic needs of the organization include six orientations, namely: (1) worship orientation as a way of looking at the awakening and maintenance of religion in the organization; (2) internal process orientation as a way of looking at the care and maintenance of the soul of the organization; (3) talent orientation as a way of looking at raising and nurturing the next generation; (4) learning orientation as a view of awakening and nurturing the intellect; (5) customer orientation as a view of cultivating and maintaining relationships with customers; and (6) wealth orientation as a way of cultivating and maintaining wealth.

Maslahah is a qualitative concept. It requires the right methodology to measure the application of *Maslahah* within the organization. The quantification score is required to manage performance in meeting the basic needs of the organization. The system in question is an organizational performance management system based on *Maqasid al-shari'ah* or also called *Maslahah* Performa (MaP).

The MaP performance system is carried out using the PDCA cycle, which has been adapted to the needs of the performance management system. The PDCA cycle has been adapted into eight steps of the MaP performance system. The first

DOI: 10.4324/9781003390947-19

step is to develop a strategic plan, a strategic goal, and a strategic initiative. The second step is to identify the fundamentals needed to achieve the MaP orientation. The third step is to determine the behaviour required for each *Maslahah* orientation. The fourth step is to determine the action. The fifth step is to agree on a performance contract. The sixth step is to implement the performance system. The seventh step is to monitor performance. The eighth step is following up or countermeasure.

Measuring business in achieving *Maslahah* is done by comparing the standard steps of the MaP performance system on its application. The measurement of the results of the *Maslahah* is done by comparing what has been achieved with the goal of each *Maslahah* orientation to the set goal. The MaP performance system is a spiritual leadership management system. This system supports the concept of man as spiritual/homo *spiritualis* or homo *ethicus*. Of course, the existence of MaP's performance system needs to be explored more deeply. The development required standardization of the assessments used to evaluate MaP's performance. The development is done through the creation of a MaP performance measurement tool that establishes interval ratings of performance and criteria for both performance of the performance process and performance of the services. For a broader purpose of standardizing MaP performance, a certification process is needed for all institutions.

Bibliography

Abbasi, Abdus Sattar, Ur Rehman, Kashif and Bibi, Amna. (August, 2010). Islamic Management Model. *African Journal of Business Management*. Vol. 4, No. 9: 1873–1882.

Abu Bakar, Mahyuddin Haji. (March 2011). Towards Achieving the Quality of Life in the Management of Zakat Distribution to the Rightful Recipients (The Poor and Needy). *International Journal of Business and Social Science*. Vol. 2, No. 4: 237–245.

Abu Raiya, Hisham. (August 2008). A Psychological Measure of Islamic Religiousness: Evidence for Relevance, Reliability and Validity. PhD dissertation, College of Bowling Green, State University.

Abu Zaharah, Muhammad. (1958). *Usul al-Fiqh*. Cairo: Dar al-Fikr al-Arabi.

Adawiyah, Wiwiek Rabiatul. (June 2011). Workplace Spirituality as a Moderator in the Relationship between Soft TQM and Organizational Commitment. *International Journal of Business and Social Science*. Vol. 2, No. 10: 93–100.

Ahmad, Ridzwan. (2008). Metode Pentarjihan dan Maslahah dan Mafsadah Dalam Hukum Islam Semasa. *Shariah Journal* Vol. 16, No. 1: 107–143.

Ahmad, Sayyid Fayyaz. (1995). The Ethical Responsibility of Business: Islamic Principles and Implications. *Journal of Objective Studies*. Vol. 3, No. 1: 74–90.

Al Imran, Ahmad bin Muhammad. (2009). *Tahifatu al Muslim Fil Aqīdah wal Sīrah*. Riyadh: Dar Ibnu Atsir.

Al-Allaf, Mashhad. (2003). *Mirror of Realization: God is a Percept, the Universe is a Concept*. USA: Islamic Information Center.

Al-Ghazali, Abu Hamid. (1982). *Al-Arba`in fi Usul al-Din*. Bayrut: Dar al-Afaq al-Jadidah.

Al-Mubarikfuri, Safi ur Rehman. Ar-Raheeq Al-Makhtum. (September 2002). *The Sealed Nectar, Biography of the Noble Prophet*. Saudi Arabia: Darussalam Publications.

Al-Qudsy, Sharifah Hayaati, Ismail, Syed and Ab Rahman, Asmak. (2011). Effective Governance in the Era of Caliphate Umar Ibn Al-Khattab (634–644). *European Journal of Social Sciences*. Vol. 18, No. 4: 612–624.

Al-Sanani, Muhammad bin Ismail. (September 2002). *Bulugh Al-Maram, Attainment of the Objevtive According to Evidence of the Ordinances*. Riyadh, Saudi Arabia: Darussalam Publications.

Al-Shātibi, Abu Ishāq. (n.d). *Al-Muwafaqatu fi Usul al-Shariah*. Bairut, Libanon: Darul al-Kutub al-'Ilmiyah.

Alamsyah, Halim. (13 April 2012). Perkembangan dan Prospek Perbankan Sharia Indonesia: Tantangan Dalam Menyongsong MEA 2015. *Paper presented at Scientific Speaking ilmiah Ikatan Ahli Ekonomi Islam (IAEI)*, Milad ke-8 IAEI.

Alawneh, Shafiq Falah. (1998). Human Motivation: An Islamic Perspective. *The American Journal of Islamic Social Science*. Vol. 15, No. 4: 14–39.

Alukal, George and Manos, Anthony. (2006). *Lean Kaizen: A Simplified Approach to Process Improvements*. Milwaukee: American Society for Quality, Quality Press.
Amin, A. Riawan. (2007). *The Celestial Management*. Jakarta: Senayan Abadi Publishing.
Amiri, S. R. Kavousy, E. and Azimi, S. Y. (2010). The Role of Cultural Strategic Planning in Increasing Organizational Productivity, Development and Perfection. *European Journal of Social Sciences*. Vol. 15, No. 2.: 235–240.
An-Nabahani, Taqiuddin. (2002). *The System of Islam*. London: Al-Khilafah Publications.
Ariff, Mohamed. (2007). Economics and Ethics. *Reading in the Concept and Methodology of Islamic Economics*. Kualalumpur, Malaysia: Cert Publication.
Ash-Shadr, Muhammad Baqir. (2008). *Buku Induk Ekonomi Islam Iqtishaduna*. Jakarta: Zahra Publishing House.
Asshiddiqie, Jimly. *Pesan Konstitusional Keadilan Sosial*, http://www.jimly.com_makalah_namafile_75_PESAN_KEADILAN_SOSIAL (Accessed on 25 January 2012).
Awang, Rohila Norhamizah and Mokhtar, Mohd Zulkifli. (April 2012). Comparative Analysis of Current Values and Historical Cost in Business Zakat Assessment: An Evidence from Malaysia. *International Journal of Business and Social Science*. Vol. 3, No. 7: 286.
Azmi, Sabahuddin. *An Islamic Approach to Business Ethics*. (n.d). Dubai: College of Islamic Banking, World Al-Lootah University.
Bakar, A. Amir R. and Hashim, R. (2011). Knowledge Management Innovation: Perspectives from the Islamic Development Bank. *Journal of Organizational Knowledge Management*. Vol. 2011: 1–8.
Barskey, N. P. and Marchant, G. (February 2000). *Measuring and Managers Intellectual Capital. Strategic Finance*. BBC Indonesia. http://www.bbc.co.uk/indonesia/dunia/2012/02/120228_samsunginheritance.shtml (Accessed on 3 June 2012).
Bedoui, M. Houssem Eddine (January 2012). Shari'a-Based Ethical Performance Measurement Framework. *Chair for ethics and Financial Norms, Working Paper in Islamic Economics and Finance*. No. 1020: 1–12.
Beekun, Rafik I. (1996). *Islamic Business Ethics*. Washington [D.C.]: International Institute of Islamic Thought.
____________. (2006). *Strategic Planning and Implementation for Islamic Organizations*. Washington [D.C.]: International Institute of Islamic Thought
Beekun, Rafik I. and Badawi, Jamal A. (2005). Balancing Ethical Responsibility among Multiple Organizational Stakeholders: The Islamic Perspective. *Journal of Business Ethics*. Vol. 60: 131–145.
Bramhandkar, Alka, Erickson, Scott and Applebee, Ian. (2007). Intellectual Capital and Organizational Performance: An Empirical Study of the Pharmaceutical Industry. *Electronic Journal of Knowledge Management*. Vol. 5. No. 4: 357–362.
Bris, Arturo. (May 2010). The Lehman Brothers Case, a Corporate Governance Failure, Not a Failure of Financial Markets. *IMD International*. Lausanne, Switzerland: 1–7. https://www.yumpu.com/en/document/view/21863924/the-lehman-brothers-case-imd
Bruce, Skaggs C. and Youndt, M. (2004). Strategic Positioning, Human Capital, and Performance in Services Organizations: A Customer Interaction Approach. *Strategic Management Journal*. Vol. 25: 85–99.
Buang, Ahmad Hidayat. (2008). Appreciation of Syari'ah Principles in Property Management in Contemporary Malaysia Society. *Shariah Journal*. Vol. 16: 555–566.
Bukh, P. N. Larsen, H. T. and Mouritsen, J. (2001). Constructing Intellectual Capital Statements. *Scandinavian Journal of Management*. Vol. 17: 87–108.

Bullock, S. and Pimlott, N. (2008). How to Help Young People Explore and Develop Their Spirituality, Working Towards a Faith and Culturally Sensitive Youth Sector. *Glimpses, National Youth Agency*. Leicester. 1–10. https://www.yumpu.com/en/document/view/4889872/how-to-help-young-people-explore-and-develop-their-spirituality

Cahyono, Moh Nurhadi and Fadjar, Judisiawan. (October 2011). Menilik Alat Ukur Penilaian Kinerja BUMN. *Journal Riset Kementerian BUMN*. Vol. 2: 1–10.

Catherine, Morrison and Siegel, Donald. (February 1998). Knowledge Capital and Cost Structure in the US. Food and Fiber Industries. *American Journal of Agricultural Economics*. Vol. 80, No. 1: 30–45.

Cathy, Enz. A. (April 2009). *Hospitality Strategic Management: Concepts and Cases*. Hoboken, N.J: John Willey and Son Inc.

Chaleff, Ira. (May 1998). Spiritual Leadership. *Executive Excellence*. Vol. 15. No. 5: 9.

Chapra, Umer M. (September 2007a). *The Islamic Vision of Development in the Light of* Maqāsid Al-Sharī'ah. Jeddah: Islamic Research and Training Institute Islamic Development Bank.

Chapra, Umer M. (2007b). *Islam and Economic Development*. New Delhi: Adam Publishers & Distributors.

Chen, Chen Yuan, Yang, Yi-Feng, Chen, Cheng-Wu, Chen, Lien-Tung and Chen, Tsung-Hao. (4 August 2010). Linking the Balanced Scorecard (BSC) to Business Management Performance: A preliminary Concept of Fit Theory for Navigation Science and Management. *International Journal of the Physical Sciences*. Vol. 5, No. 8: 1296–1305.

Choudhury, Masudul Alam. (1986). *Contributions to Islamic Economic Theory, a Study in Social Economics*. New York: St. Martin's Press.

____________. (2007). *The Universal Paradigm and the Islamic World System, Economy – Society – Ethics – and Sciences*. Singapore: World Scientific Publishing Co. Pte. Ltd.

Chowdury, Subir. (2005). *21st Century Organization*. Jakarta: Index Publishers.

Çizakça, Murat. (2007). Democracy, Economic Development and Maqasid Al-Shari'ah. *Review of Islamic Economics*. Vol. 11, No 1: 101–118.

Cizek, Gregory J. (2003). Performance Standards: Selected Response Item Formats. *Encyclopedia of Psychological Assessment*. SAGE Publications. http://www.sage-ereference.com/psychassessment/Article_n148.html (Accessed on 4 May 2010).

Cokins, Gary. (2004). *Performance Management, Finding the Missing Pieces (to Close the Intelligence Gap)*. New Jersey: John Wiley & Sons. Inc.

Cooper, Donald R. and Schindler, Pamela S. (1998). *Business Research Methods*. Singapore: McGraw-Hill.

Coyle, Daninel. (May 2009). *The Talent Code, Greatness Isn't Born, It's Grown, Here's How*. New York: Bantam Dell.

Cunningham, Gary M. and Harris, Jean E. (2006). Enron and Arthur Andersen: The Case of the Crooked E and the Fallen A. *Global Perspectives on Accounting Education*. Vol. 3: 27–48.

Curry, Timothy and Shibut, L. (2000). The Cost of the Savings and Loan Crisis: Truth and Consequences. *FDIC Banking Review*. Vol. 13, No. 2: 26–35.

Qing-ling, Du, Cao Shu-min Ba Lian-liang Cheng Jun-mo. (2008). Application of PDCA Cycle in the Performance Management System. *Paper presented at 4th International Conference on Wireless Communications, Networking and Mobile Computing WiCOM '08*: Dalian, China, 12–17 October 2008. https://doi.org/10.1109/WiCom.2008.1682

Dahan, Mohd Hayati, Ahmad, Noryati and Mohamad Basir, Faziatul Amillia. (12–13 March 2012). Factors Inhibiting Islamic Will Adoption: Focus on Muslim Community. *Paper Presented at 3rd International Conference on Business and Economic Research (3rd ICBER 2012)*. Bandung, Indonesia.

Dusuki, Asyraf Wajdi and Abdullah, Nurdianawati Irwani. (2007). Maqasid al-Shari'ah, Maslahah, and Corporate Social Responsibility. *The American Journal of Islamic Social Sciences*. Vol. 24, No. 1: 26–45.

Dworkin, Ronald. (2000). *Sovereign Virtue, the Theory and Practice of Equality*. Cambridge, USA: Harvard University Press.

El-Ghazali, Abdel Hamid. (1994). *Man Is the Basis of the Islamic Strategy for Economic Development*. Islamic Economics Translation Series. No 1. Jeddah, Saudi Arabia: Islamic Research and Training Institute.

Ellingson, D. A. and Wambsganss, J. R. (2001). Modifying the Approach to Planning and Evaluation in Governmental Entities: A Balanced Scorecard Approach. *Journal of Public Budgeting, Accounting and Financial Management*. Vol. 13, No. 1: 103–120.

Fahd bin Abdil Azizil Su 'ud and Ash-Sharifain, Khadim al-Haramain. (1971). *Al-Quran and the Translation*. Jeddah, Saudi Arab: Darussalam Publications.

Fairchild, Alea M. (2002). Knowledge Management Metrics via a Balanced Scorecard Methodology. *Proceedings of the 35th Hawaii International Conference on System Sciences*, Hawaii.

Farook, Sayd. (2007). Social Responsibility for Islamic Financial Institutions: Laying Down a Framework. *Journal of Islamic Economics, Banking and Finance*. Vol. 62: 61–82.

Fatah, Dede Abdul. (January 2012). *Pasar & Keadilan dalam Perspektif Ekonomi Islam*. Jakarta: Gaung Persada Press.

Firdaus, Achmad. (15 September 2012a). Maslahah Scorecard, Sistem Manajemen Kinerja Berbasis Maqasid Shariah. *Call for Paper 2012 Islamic Banking & Finance Conference*. Islamic Economy Revivalism: Between Theory and Practice, Faculty of Economics and Business Syarif Hidayatullah UIN, Jakarta.

____________. (2–22 November 2012b). Pengukuran Kinerja PT. Asuransi Takaful Keluarga dengan Menggunakan Sistem Pengukuran Kinerja Maslahah Scorecard (MaSC). *Call for Paper The 1st Islamic Economics and Finance Research Forum (ISEFRF), New Era of Indonesian Islamic Economics and Finance*. The Indonesian Association of Islamic Economist, Bank Indonesia and Universitas Islam Negeri Sultan Syarif Kasim, Pekanbaru.

____________. (2017). *Maslahah Performa (MaP) Sistem Manajemen Kinerja Berbasis Maslahah*. Yogyakarta, Indonesia: Penerbit K-Media.

____________. (January 2018). Mengembangkan Siklus Penerapan Sistem Manajemen Kinerja Berbasis Kemaslahataan. *Al-Uqud: Journal of Islamic Economics*. UNESA. Vol. 2 No. 1.: 94–120.

Firdaus, Achmad and Yusuf, Mukhlis A. (2014). Maslahah Performa, Maslahah Based Organization. The 4th ISRA International Colloquium for Islamic Finance (IICIF 2014), The Role of Islamic Finance in Socio-Economic Development: Ideals and Realities. ISRA-Bank Negara Malaysia, 3–4 September 2014. Kualalumpur, Malaysia.

Friedman, Hershey H. and Linda W. Friedman. (2008). Can "Homo Spiritualis" Replace Homo Economicus in the Business Curriculum? *e-Journal of Business Education & Scholarship of Teaching*. Vol. 2, No. 2: 1–11.

Froilan, William S. (2008). Performance Modeling. *Encyclopedia of Counseling*. SAGE Publications. http://www.sageereference.com/counseling/Article_n567.html (Accessed on 4 May 2010).

Fry, Louis W. (2003). Toward a Theory of Spiritual Leadership. *The Leadership Quarterly*. Vol. 14: 693–727.

Fry, Louis W. and Matherly Laura L. (2006). *Spiritual Leadership and Organizational Performance: An Exploratory Study*. Tarleton State University – Central Texas.

Fry, Louis W. and Matherly, Laura L. (2006). *Spiritual Leadership as an Integrating Paradigm for Positive Leadership Development*. Tarleton State University – Central Texas, University of Dallas Irving, Texas. Paper presented at the 2006 Gallup Leadership Summit, Washington D. C., October, 2006.

Fry, Louis W. and Matherly, Laura L. (29 March 2006). *Performance Excellence through Spiritual Leadership*. http://www.iispiritualleadership.com/ (Accessed on 27 April 2012).

Fry, Louis W. Matherly, Laura L. and Whittington, Lee J. (2007). Spiritual Leadership as an Integrating Paradigm for Servant Leadership. *Integrating Spirituality and Organizational Leadership*. 70–82. https://www.researchgate.net/publication/228665610_Spiritual_leadership_as_an_integrating_paradigm_for_servant_leadership

Fry, Louis W. and Slocum, John W. Jr. (2008). Maximizing the Triple Bottom Line through Spiritual Leadership. *Organizational Dynamics*. Vol. 37, No. 1: 86–96.

Fry, Louis W. and Whittington, Lee J. (n.d). Spiritual Leadership as a Paradigm for Organization Transformation and Development. Tarleton State University – Central Texas, University of Dallas Irving, Texas. 1–45.

Gardiner, Chris. (2002). Balanced Scorecard Ethics. *Business & Professional Ethics Journal*. Vol. 21, No. ¾.: 129–150.

Gash, Alexander and John Wanna. (2006). Performance Measurement. *Encyclopedia of Governance*. Vol. 2: 672–674. California: SAGE Publications.

Ghazanfar, Mohammad S. and Islahi, Abdul Azim. (1997). Economic Thought of Al-Ghazali (450–505 A.H./1058–1111 A.D.). *Islamic Economics Research Series,* King Abdulaziz University.

Guillory, William A. (1997). *The Living Organization Spirituality in the Workplace*. Salt Lake City, UT: Innovations International.

Gumbus, A. and Lyons, B. (Nov. 2002). The Balanced Scorecard at Philips Electronics. *Strategic Finance*. Vol. 84, No. 5: 4.

Haberberg, Adrian and Rieple, Alison. (2007). *Strategic Management, Theory and Application*. New York: Oxford University Press.

Habibie, Bacharuddin Jusuf. (1997). "Pembangunan Sumber Daya Manusia Berorientasi NilaiTambah," *Wawasan dan Visi Pembangunan Abad 21*, Editor M. Dawam Rahardjo. Jakarta: PT. Intermasa.

Hasan, Zulkifli. (28–29 June 2008). Corporate Governance of Islamic Financial Institutions. *Paper presented at Conference on Malaysian Study of Islam*. University of Wales, Lampeter, United Kingdom.

Hassan, Abul, Chachi, Abdelkader and Abdul Latiff, Salma. (2008). Islamic Marketing Ethics and Its Impact on Customer Satisfaction in the Islamic Banking Industry. *JKAU: Islamic Econ*. Vol. 21, No. 1: 27–46.

Hawa, S. (2004). *Tarbeitena alruhiya*. Cairo: Dar-Alsalam.

Heidrick and Struggles. (2012). Strategic Talent Management, *The Emergence of a New Discipline*.

Lockwood, N.R. (2006). Talent Management: Driver for Organizational Success. *HRMagazine; Alexandria*. Vol. 51. Iss. 6 (Jun 2006): 1–11. https://www.proquest.com/docview/205016356

Hill, Peter C. and Hood. Jr., Ralph W. (1999). *Measures of Religiosity*. Birmingham, AL: Religious Education Press.

Hj. Don, Abdul Ghafar and Awang, Jaffary. (2009). Knowledge Management and Its Impact on Islamic Da'wah: A Historical Perspective. *Journal of Islamic and Arabic Education*. Vol. 1, No. 2: 61–68.

Hoque, Zahirul and James, Wendy. (2000). Linking Balanced Scorecard Measures to Size and Market Factors: Impact on Organizational Performance. *Journal of Management Accounting Research*. Vol. 12: 1–17.

Howard, Barbara B. and White, Stephen R. (November 2009). Spiritual Intelligence and Transformational Leadership: A New Theoretical Framework. *Journal of Curriculum and Instruction (JoCI)*. Vol. 3, No. 2: 54–67. https://doi.org/10.3776/joci.2009.v3n2p54-67

Hunger, David and Wheelen, Thomas L. (2006). *Essentials of Strategic Management*. 4th Ed. Prentice Hall. http://www.ti.or.id/media/documents/2011/12/01/f/i/file_2.pdf (Accessed on 10 November 2012).

Ibn 'Ashur, M. al-Tahir. (1998). *Maqasid al-Shari'ah al-Islamiyyah*. Kuala Lumpur: al-Basa'ir.

International Organization for Standardization. (2015). *Quality Management Principles*. Geneva, Switzerland.

Ismail, Abdul Ghafar and Arshad, Noraziah Che. (2010). Financial Ratio and Maqasid Shariah in Evaluating the Performance of Microfinance Institutions. *Paper dipresentasikan pada The 2nd International Workshop in Islamic Economics Theory: Islamic Micro-finance Towards Global Poverty Alleviation and Sustainable Development*, Bangi, 8–9 December 2010.

Jacobson, G. H. McCoin, N. S. Lescallette, R. Russ, S. and Slovis, C. M. (2009). Kaizen: A Method of Process Improvement in the Emergency Department. *The Society for Academic Emergency Medicine*. Vol. 16, No. 12: 1341–1349. https://doi.org/10.1111/j.1553-2712.2009.00580.x

Jacobson, Göran, and Roos, Johan. (1997). Measuring your Company's Intellectual Performance. *International Journal of Strategic Management, Special Issue on Intellectual Capital*. Vol. 30, No. 3: 413–426.

James, S. Coleman. (1988). Social Capital in the Creation of Human Capital. *The American Journal of Sociology*. Vol. 94, Supplement: Organizations and Institutions: Sociological and Economic Approaches to the Analysis of Social Structure: S95–S120.

Janfeshan, Kamran, Belal, P. Seid, M. V. and Farideh, K. (2001). Spirituality in the Work Place and Its Impact on the efficiency of Management. *Paper presented at 2nd International Conference on Business and Economic Research (2nd ICBER 2011)*. 14th to 15th March 2011. Langkawi, Kedah, Malaysia.

Jauhar, Ahmad Al-Mursi Husain. *Maqosidu al-Shari 'ati fi Al-islam*. (2009). Translated by Khikmawati. Jakarta, Indonesia: Penerbit AMZAH.

Johannsen, Hano and Page, Terry, G. (1999). Performance Measurement. *Encyclopaedia of Management Dictionary of Management* 7. New Delhi: Crest Publishing House.

Jones, Catherine Cartwright. (2002). *The Functions of Childbirth and Postpartum Henna Traditions*. Kent, Ohio: Kent State University.

Kahf, Monzer. (8–10 August 2006). Maqasid al Shari'ah in the Prohibition of Riba and Their Implications for Modern Islamic Finance. *Paper presented IIUM International Conference on Maqasid al Shari'ah*. Kualalumpur, Malaysia.

Kahf, Monzer. (2007). Islamic Economics System – A Review. Syed Omar Syed Agil and Aidit Ghazali (ed). *Reading in the Concept and Methodology of Islamic Economics*. Kualalumpur, Malaysia: Cert Publication.

Kamil, Naail Mohammed, Al-Kahtani, Ali Hussain and Sulaiman, Mohamed. The Components of Spirituality in the Business Organizational Context: The Case of Malaysia. *Asian Journal of Business and Management Sciences*. Vol. 1, No. 2: 166–180.

Kamil, Naail Mohammed, Mohamed Sulaiman, Aahad Osman-Gani and Khaliq Ahmad. (2010). Spirituality in the Workplace: The Role of Taqwa towards the Advancement of the Contemporary Organization. *Social Science Research Network*. 8th International Conference on Tawhidic Methodology Applied to Microenterprise Development, 2010. http://papers.ssrn.com/sol3/papers.cfm?abstract_id=1718946 (Accessed on 11 April 2012).

Kaplan, R. S. (2009). Conceptual Foundations of the Balanced Scorecard. *Handbook of Management Accounting Research*. Vol. 3. (Elsevier, 2009): 1–36.

Kaplan, R. S. and Norton, D. P. (January–February 1992). The Balanced Scorecard – Measures that Drive Performance. *Harvard Business Review*. Vol. 70, No. 1: 71–79.

____________. (1996a). *The Balanced Scorecard: Translating Strategy into Action*. Boston: Harvard Business School Press.

____________. (1996b). *The Balanced Scorecard: Translating Vision into Action*. Boston: Harvard Business School Press.

____________. (January–February 1996c). *Using the Balanced Scorecard as a Strategic Management System*. Boston: Harvard Business Review.

____________. (2001). *The Strategy Focused Organization, How Balanced Scorecard Companies Thrive in the New Business Environment*. Boston: Harvard Business School Publishing Corporation.

____________. (2004a). *Measuring the Strategic Readiness of Intangible Assets*. Boston: Harvard Business School Press.

____________. (2004b). *Strategy Maps, Converting Intangible Assets into Tangible Outcomes*. Boston: Harvard Business School Publishing Corporation.

Khan, Muhammad Akram. (1994). *Introduction to Islamic Economics*. Islamabad, Pakistan: International Institute of Islamic Thought and Institute of Policy Studies.

Khan, Muhammad Muhsin. (September 1996). *Summarized Sahih Al-Bukhari*. Jeddah, Saudi Arabia: Darussalam Publications.

Khraim, Hamza. (November 2010). Measuring Religiosity in Consumer Research from Islamic Perspective. *International Journal of Marketing Studies*. Vol. 2, No. 2: 166–179.

Kotler, Philip and Armstrong, Gary. (2012). *Principles of Marketing*. 14th ed. New Jersey, US: Pearson Education. Inc.

Lajnah Pentashihan Mushaf al-Quran Badan Litbang dan Diklat Kementrian Agama. (2010a). *Tafsir Tematik, Hukum, Keadilan, dan Hak Azasi Manusia*, Seri 5. Jakarta: Kemenag RI.

Lajnah Pentashihan Mushaf al-Quran Badan Litbang dan Diklat Kementrian Agama RI. (2010b). *Tafsir al-Quran Tematik, Kitab Spiritualitas dan Akhlak*. Jakarta, Indonesia: Kemenag RI.

Laluddin, Hayatullah, Kusrin, Zuliza Mohd., and Samuri, Mohd. Al-Adib. (2012). Maslahah and Its Potential Role in Formation of Islamic Perspective on Sociology. *International Business Management*. Vol. 6, No. 2: 256–263.

Li, Yuhao. (October 2010). The Case Analysis of the Scandal of Enron. *International Journal of Business and Management*. Vol. 5, No. 10: 37–41.

Libby, T, Salterio, S. E. and Webb, A. (2004). The Balanced Scorecard: The Effects of Assurance and Process Accountability on Managerial Judgment. *Accounting Review*. Vol. 79, No. 4: 1075–1094.

Lumpkin, Dess. (2003). *Strategic Management, Creating Competitive Advantage*. New York: McGraw-Hill.

Lungu, Carmen Claudia. (Summer 2008). The Role of Human Resources from Hotel Industry for Improving Organizational Performance. *The Business Review Cambridge*. Vol. 9, No. 2.

Maiga, Adam S. and Jacobs, Fred A. (Fall 2003). Balanced Scorecard, Activity Based Costing and Company Performance: An Empirical Analysis. *Journal of Managerial Issues*. Vol. 15, No. 3: 283–301.

Mannan, Muhammad Abdul. (1970). *Islamic Economic: Theory and Practice*. Islamabad: Houder and Stoughton.

____________. (1984). *The Making of Islamic Economic Society, Islamic Dimension in Economics Analysis*. Cairo, Egypt: International Association of Islamic Banks.

Markum, Enoch M. (2009). Pengentasan Kemiskinan dan Pendekatan Psikologi Sosial. *Psikobuana*. Vol. I, No. 1: 1–12.

Martinsons, Maris, Davidson, Robert and Tse, Dennis. (1999). The Balanced Scorecard: A Foundation for the Strategic Management of Information Systems. *Decision Support Systems*. Vol. 25: 71–88.

Masud, Muhammad Khalid (1977). *Islamic Legal Philosophy, a Study of Abu Ishaq al-Syathibi's Life and Thought*. Islamabad, Pakistan: Islamic Research Institute.

Mawdudi, Abul A'la. (1960). *Islamic Law and Constitution*. Lahore: Islamic Publication.

McGhee, Peter and Grant, Patricia. (2008). Spirituality and Ethical Behaviour in the Workplace: Wishful Thinking or Authentic Reality. *EJBO Electronic Journal of Business Ethics and Organization Studies*. Vol. 13, No. 2: 61–69.

McKinsey & Company. (April 2001). *The War for Talent. Organization and Leadership Practice*. New York: McKinsey & Company.

Mohammed, Mustafa Omar and Razak, Dzuljastri Abdul. (2008). The Performance Measures of Islamic Banking Based on the Maqasid Framework. *Paper presented at the IIUM International Accounting Conference (INTAC IV)*. Putra Jaya, 2008.

Moullin, Max. (2004). Eight Essentials of Performance Measurement. *International Journal of Health Care Quality Assurance*. Vol. 17, No. 3: 110–112.

Mubyarto. (1987). *Ekonomi Pancasila: Gagasan dan Kemungkinan*. Jakarta: LP3ES.

____________. (1997). "Paradigma Pembangunan yang Bertumpu pada Kekuatan Ekonomi Rakyat," *Wawasan dan Visi Pembangunan Abad 21*, Editor M. Dawam Rahardjo. Jakarta: PT. Intermasa.

____________. (1 May 2011). "Ekonomi Indonesia Terjajah Kembali," *Swara 33 eBulletin Mubins*, 2011: 9–13.

Muhsin, Muhammad Khan and Al-Hilal, Muhammad Taqi-ud-Din. (September 1996). *Interpretation of the Meanings of the Noble Quran*. Jeddah, Saudi Arabia: Darussalam Publications.

Naqwi, Syed Nawab Haider. (1985). *Ethics and Economics: An Islamic Synthesis*, Terjemahan Bahasa Indonesia. Bandung: Penerbit Mizan.

Nash, Laura. (1990). *Good Intention Aside; a Manager's Guide to Resolving Ethical Problem*. Boston: Harvard Business School Press.

Nasution, Mustafa Edwin. (2009). Islamic Spirit and Morale in Economics. *Journal of International Development and Cooperation*. Vol. 15, No 1–2: 113–124.

Nata, Abuddin. (2008). *Kajian Tematik al-Quran tentang Fiqih Ibadah*. Bandung: Penerbit Angkasa.

National Institute of Standards and Technology. (2012). Criteria for Performance Excellence, Baldrige Performance Excellence Program. Gaithersburg, US.

Neely, Andy. (2004). *Business Performance Measurement, Theory and Practice*. Cambridge: Cambridge University Press.

Nofal, Nabil. (1993). Al-Ghazali, (A.D. 1058–1111; A.H. 450–505). *Prospects: The Quarterly Review of Comparative Education*. Vol. 23, No. 3/4: 519–542.

Nor, Mohd Roslan Mohd, Abdullah, A. T. Ali, A. K. and Zakaria, M. F. (29 February 2012). Historical Development of Islamic Institutions: A Case of Malaysian Government. *African Journal of Business Management*. Vol. 6, No. 8: 2766–2772.

Nyazee, Imran Ahsan Khan. (2003). *Islamic Jurisprudence*. Selangor, Malaysia: The Other Press 607 Mutiara Majestic.

Pearce, John A. and Robinson Jr., Richard. (2007). *Strategic Management, Formulation, Implementation and Control*. 10th Ed. New York, McGraw-Hill.

Petrisor, Ioan. (1998). Managerial Ethics – Strategic Issues. *The Scientific Journal Facta Universitatis Series: Economics and Organization*. Vol. 1, No. 6: 43–47.

Pfeffer, Jeffrey. (October 2001). Business and the Spirit: Management Practices that Sustain Values. *Research Paper* No. 1713. Graduate School of Business, Stanford University.

Porter, Michael E. (1998). *Competitive Advantage, Creating and Sustaining Superior Performance*. New York: The Free Press.

Qardhawi, Yusuf. (2004). *Daurul Qiyam Wa al-Akhlak Fil Iqtishadil Islami, Terjemahan Bahasa Indonesia*. Jakarta: Robbani Press.

Qing-ling, Du, Cao Shu-min, Ba Lian-liang, Cheng Jun-mo. (2008). Application of PDCA Cycle in the Performance Management System. *Paper presented at 4th International Conference on Wireless Communications, Networking and Mobile Computing WiCOM '08*: Dalian, China, 12–17 October 2008. https://doi.org/10.1109/WiCom.2008.1682

Rane, Halim. (2009). Maqasid, Contextualisation and Social Science towards a Contemporary Methodology of Interpreting the Quran. *Islamic Perspective*. Vol. 1, No. 2: 55–85.

Rahardjo, Dawam M. (1999). *Intelektual, Intelegensia dan Perilaku Politik Bangsa, Risalah Cendekiawan Muslim*. Bandung: Penerbit Mizan.

Rampersad, Hubert K. (June 2006). *The Personal Balanced Scorecard; the Way to Individual Happiness, Personal Integrity and Organizational Effectiveness*. Greenwich, CT: Information Age Publishing Inc.

Rampersad, Hubert. (2008). The Way to a Highly Engaged and Happy Workforce Based on the Personal Balanced. *Total Quality Management*. Vol. 19, No. 1–2, January–February 2008, 11–27.

Rawls, John. (1999). A *Theory of Justice*. Cambridge, Massachusetts: Harvard University Press.

Ricardo, David. (2004). *The Principles of Political Economy and Taxation*. New York: Dover Publications Inc: 52.

Richard, Pierre J., Devinney, Timothy M., Yip, George S. and Johnson, Gerry. (2009). Measuring Organizational Performance: Towards Methodological Best Practice. *Journal of Management*. Vol. 35, No. 3: 718–804. https://doi.org/0.1177/10149206308330560

Rokhman, Wahibur. (2010). The Effect of Islamic Work Ethics on Work Outcomes. *EJBO Electronic Journal of Business Ethics and Organization Studies*. Vol. 15, No. 1: 21–27.

Saeed, Muhammad Mohtsham, Shah, Syed Zulfiqar and Qureshi, Tahir Masood. (4 October 2010). Organizing and Executing a Strategy for Firms Operating in and from the Islamic World. *African Journal of Business Management*. Vol. 4, No. 13: 2899–2902.

Salem, Hanine. (July 2003). *Organizational Performance Management and Measurement*. Economic and Social Council, United Nations. Beirut: Economic and Social Commission for Western Asia, UN.

Sani, M.D. (2012). A Conceptual Model of Measuring Performance Efficiency of Islamic Banks: Objectives of Islamic Law (*Maqasid al-shariah*) Approach. http://ssrn.com/abstract=2070397 (Accessed on 5 August 2012).

Sarif, Suhaili and Kamri, Nor'Azzah. (2009). A Theoretical Discussion of Zakat for Income Generation and Its Fiqh Issues. *Shariah Journal*. Vol. 17, No. 3: 457–500.

Sekaran, Uma. (2000). *Research Methods for Business: A Skill Building Approach*. New York: John Wiley & Sons.

Sen, Amartya A. Kumar. (June 1999). The Possibility of Social Choice. *American Economic Review*. Vol. 89, No. 3: 349–378.

Serrat, Olivier. (December 2008). *Picking Investments in Knowledge Management.* Asian Development Bank, Mandaluyong City, Philippines.

Shaharuddin, Amir. (October 2010). Maslahah-Mafsadah Approach in Assessing the Shari'ah Compliance of Islamic Banking Products. *International Journal of Business and Social Science.* Vol. 1, No. 1: 129–136.

Sharma, Subhash. *Towards Holistic Performance Scorecard: A New Strategic Imperative.* Indian Business Academy Bangalore & Greater Noida.

Shaukat, Mughees. (2009). *The Recent Financial Growth of Islamic Banks and Their Fulfillments of Maqāsid Al-Sharīah, Gap Analysis.* Kualalumpur, Malaysia: INCEIF.

Sheep, M. L. (2003). Nurturing the Whole Person: A Model of Spirituality at Work and Performance. *Journal of Business Ethics.* Vol. 66: 357–375. https://doi.org/10.1007/s10551-006-0014-5

____________. (1996) *Role of the State in the Economy, an Islamic Perspective.* Leicester, UK: The Islamic Foundation.

Skerlavaj, M. Stemberger, M. I. Skrinjar, R. and Dimovski, V. (2007). Organizational Learning Culture, the Missing Link between Business Process Change and Organizational Performance. *International Journal of Production Economics.* Vol. 106: 346–367.

Smith, Craig N. and Quirk, Michelle. (2004). From Grace to Disgrace: The Rise & Fall of Arthur Andersen. *Journal of Business Ethics Education.* Vol. I, No. 1: 91–130.

Sokovic, M. Pavletic, D. and Kern Pipan, K. (November 2010). Quality Improvement Methodologies – PDCA Cycle, RADAR Matrix, DMAIC and DFSS. *Journal of Achievement in Materials and Manufacturing Engineering* Vol. 43, No. 1: 476–483.

Strohhecker, Jürgen. (July 2007). Does a Balanced Scorecard Management Cockpit Increase Strategy Implementation Performance? Paper presented: 25th International Conference of the System Dynamics Society. 29 July - 2 August 2007, Boston, Massachusetts. Frankfurt School of Finance and Management.

Sulaiman, Ruslinda. (2011). Realizing Maqasid Al-Shariah in Islamic Financial Planning. *The 4E Journal.* Vol. 11, No. 1: 13–17.

Sulistyono, Adi. (17 November 2007). Pembangunan Hukum Ekonomi Untuk Mendukung Pencapaian Visi Indonesia 2030. Pidato Pengukuhan Guru Besar Hukum Ekonomi Pada Fakultas Hukum Universitas Sebelas Maret Surakarta. Surakarta. UNS.

Swasono, Sri-Edi. (1987). Pandangan Islam dalam Sistem Ekonomi Indonesia. *Paper Presented at the Scientific Speech of the Third State Graduation*, Universitas Muhammadiyah, Medan, Indonesia, 14 March 1987.

____________. (13 July 1988). Demokrasi Ekonomi: Komitmen dan Pembangunan Indonesia. *Paper Presented at the Inauguration of Professor of the Faculty of Economics*, Universitas Indonesia, Jakarta.

Swasono, Sri-Edi. (2 August 2002). Prospek dan Perkembangan Perekonomian Rakyat: Antara Kedaulatan Rakyat dan Kedaulatan Pasar, *Kedaulatan Rakyat Daily*, Friday, 2 August 2002.

____________. (2003). *Ekspose Ekonomika, Mewaspadai Globalisme dan Pasar Bebas.* Yogyakarta: Pusat Studi Ekonomi Pancasila (Pustep) UGM.

____________. (2004). *Kebersamaan dan Asas Kekeluargaan, Mutualism & Brotherhood, Kerkayatan, Nasionalisme, dan Kemandirian.* Jakarta: UNJ Press.

____________. (1–3 Agustus 2008). Konomi Islam dalam Pancasila. *Paper Presented at International Seminar on Implementation of Islamic Economic*, Annual Meeting of Indonesian Economics Experts Association, Unibersitas Airlangga, Surabaya.

____________. (2010a). *Kembali ke Pasal 33 UUD 1945 Menolak Neoliberalisme.* Jakarta: Penerbit Yayasan Hatta.

____________. (2010b). *Testimoni Sri Edi Swasono, Permohonan Judicial Review UU No. 30 Tahun 2009 oleh DPP SP-PLN Tentang Ketenagalistrikan berkaitan dengan Pasal 33 ayat (2) UUD 1945*. Constitutional Court, Jakarta, 29 April 2010.

____________. (May 2011). Jangan Menjual Indonesiaku. *Swara 33 eBulletin Mubins*, Edisi 1 2011: 5–6.

____________. (2012). Demokrasi Volkssouvereiniteit / Kedaulatan Rakyat. *Paper Presented at Deklarasi Gerakan Pemantapan Pancasila*, Jakarta, 5 July 2012.

Swasono, Sri-Edi and Ridjal, Fauzie. (1992). *Mohammad Hatta, Demokrasi Kita, Bebas Aktif, Ekonomi Masa Depan*. Jakarta: UI Press.

TGO. (December 8, 2005). *Employee Discrimination in the Workplace*. Washington DC: The Gallup Organization.

Thompson, A. and Strickland, A. J. (2002). *Strategic Management: Concepts and Cases*. Boston: McGraw Hill.

Ul-Islam, Sheikh and Wahhab, Muhammad bin Abdul. (September 1996). *The Book of Monotheism*. Jeddah, Saudi Arabia: Darussalam Publications.

Ullrich, M. J. and Tuttle, B. M. (2004). The Effects of Comprehensive Information Reporting Systems and Economic Incentives on Managers Time Planning Decisions. *Behavioral Research in Accounting*. Vol. 16: 89–105.

Vogel, Frank E. and Samuel L. Hayes, III. (1998). *Islamic Law and Finance, Religion, Risk, and Return*. The Hague, the Netherlands: Kluwer Law International.

Wade, Michael and Hulland, John. (2004). Review: The Resource-Based View and Information System Research: Review, Extension, and Suggestions for Future Research. *MIS Quarterly*. Vol. 28, No. 1: 107–142.

Watson, Gregory H. and DeYong, Camille F. (2010). Design for Six Sigma: Caveat Emptor. *International Journal of Lean Six Sigma*. Vol. 1, No. 1: 66–84.

Weber, M. (1958). *The Protestant Ethnic and the Spirit of Capitalism*. New York: Charles Scribner's Sons.

Yeniyurt, S. (2003). A Literature Review and Integrative Performance Measurement Framework for Multinational Companies. *Marketing Intelligence and Planning*. Vol. 21, No. 3: 134–142.

Zaharah, Muhammad Abū. (1958). *Usul al-Fiqh*. Cairo, Egypt: Dar al-Fikr al-Arabi.

Zaman, Hasanuz. (1991). *Economics Functions of an Islamic State*. Karachi, Pakistan: The Islamic Foundation.

Zarqa, Anas. (2007) Islamic Economics: An Approach to Human Welfare. *Reading in the Concept and Methodology of Islamic Economics*. Kualalumpur, Malaysia: Cert Publication.

Zeno bin Jamil, Shaikh Muhammad. (September 1996). *The Pillars of Islam & Iman & What Every Muslim Must Know about His Religion*. Jeddah, Saudi Arabia: Darussalam Publications.

Zidan, Ahmad. (1997). *Al-Ghazali's Ihya' Ulum al-Din, revitalization of The Sciences of Religion*. Cairo Egypt: Islamic Inc. for Publishing and Distribution.

Zohar, Danah dan Ian Marshal. (2004). *Spiritual Capital, Wealth We Can Live by Using Our Rational, Emotional, and Spiritual Intelligence to Transform Ourselves and Corporate Culture*. San Francisco: Berrett-Koehler Publishers.

Glossary

BSC Balanced Scorecard is a strategic management system tool that enables organizations to translate vision – mission and strategy into a series of measurable actions. BSC has four perspectives on performance measurement, namely learning and growth, internal business processes, customers, and finance.

Doctrine The way or method chosen and followed by the community in its economic life and in solving every practical problem that is followed.

Economic transformation Upholding economic democracy, carrying out joint ventures, implementing kinship principles, rejecting individual principles, upholding the implementation of Article 33 of the 1945 Constitution in economic activities.

Falah Luck, success, safety, glory, happiness, both material and non-material, and dimension of time in the life of the world and the afterlife.

Foundation of *Maslahah* The basic conditions that must be owned by the business in order to realize the fulfilment of *Maslahah*.

Homo economicus Humans' nature always put the economic side in their activities.

Homo ethicus Humans' nature that emphasizes ethics in carrying out its activities.

'Izz Strength, glory, and honour in the life of the world. In the afterlife, *'izz* has the meaning of eternal glory without humiliation.

Mafsadah Damage, the opposite of *Maslahah*.

Maqasid al-shari'ah The goal of *shari'ah* is to protect religion (*Hifzu 'ala al-din*), soul *Hifzu 'alaal-nafs*), intellect (*Hifzu 'alaal-'aql*), descendant (*Hifzu 'alaal-nasl*), and wealth (*Hifzu 'ala al-mal*),

Maṣhalih Plural form of *Maslahah*.

Maslahah A condition that resulted from the balanced fulfilment of needs, the balance in question is a balance of both material and non-material, short-term (world) and long-term goals (hereafter).

Maslahah daruriyah Fulfilment of five basic (primary) human needs in the world and the hereafter, which include religion, soul, lineage, wealth, and intellect.

Maslahah hajiyah Supporting (secondary) needs, namely the needs for which existence is needed to eliminate difficulties or make maintenance of five primary or basic needs even better.

***Maslahah* performa** The *Maslahah* business performance system, namely the performance system based on *Maqasid al-shari'ah* by fulfilling six business-oriented orientations consisting of worship orientation, internal process orientation, workforce orientation, customer orientation, learning orientation, and wealth orientation.

Maslahah tahsinat/tahsiniyah Complementary (tertiary) needs, that is, the needs that are right there because of the demands of politeness and customs. The need for divinity is intended so that humans can do their best towards improvement in order to preserve the five primary needs (*Maslahah daruriyah*).

Milestone Steppingstone, the target stage to achieve a large target.

Operational Sustainability (OST) Operational efficiency, operating percentage, and expenditure. OST > 100% shows that the company can cover all operating costs.

PDCA Management cycle consisting of Plan – Do – Check – Action.

Populist economy Economic development that is centred on the people. The populist's economic system places the people as the goal of economic development in addition to placing the people as means and actors of development.

Profit Margin (PM) Net amount of rupiah earned after deducting various costs.

Return on Assets (ROA) The measure of net operating income is the ratio of net income to total assets.

Return on Equity (ROE) The measure of net operating income is the ratio of net income to net assets.

Rububiyah Recognition of the deeds of Allah (*s.w.t.*), the Almighty and the Arrangement of the universe. This means believing in *Rububiyah* Allah (*s.w.t.*) is a form of acknowledgment of a servant that only Allah (*s.w.t.*) is the Almighty, Who Gives *Rizq*, the Almighty and Regulates, the Most Giving and Retaining, the Most Elevating and the Dropping, the Glorifying, and the Humiliating, Who Turns and the deadly one. *Rububiyah* means to believe in God as the subject of what He did.

Index

Note: *Italicized* and **bold** page numbers refer to figures and tables. Page numbers followed by "n" refer to notes.

For Product Safety Concerns and Information please contact our EU
representative GPSR@taylorandfrancis.com
Taylor & Francis Verlag GmbH, Kaufingerstraße 24, 80331 München, Germany

www.ingramcontent.com/pod-product-compliance
Ingram Content Group UK Ltd.
Pitfield, Milton Keynes, MK11 3LW, UK
UKHW020142200926
475702UK00005B/868
* 9 7 8 1 0 3 2 4 8 8 2 2 6 *